Transforming Childcare and Listening to Families

POLITICS AND SOCIETY IN WALES SERIES
Series editors: Paul Chaney and Andrew Thompson

The Politics and Society in Wales series examines issues of politics and government, and particularly the effects of devolution on policy-making and implementation, and the way in which Wales is governed as the National Assembly gains in maturity. It will also increase our knowledge and understanding of Welsh society and analyse the most important aspects of social and economic change in Wales. Where necessary, studies in the series will incorporate strong comparative elements which will allow a more fully informed appraisal of the conditions of Wales.

Transforming Childcare and Listening to Families

POLICY IN WALES AND BEYOND

By

WENDY BALL

*Published on behalf
of the University of Wales*

UNIVERSITY OF WALES PRESS
CARDIFF
2013

British Library Cataloguing-in-Publication Data.
A catalogue record for this book is available from the British Library.

ISBN 978–0–7083–2551–3
e–ISBN 978–0–7083–2552–0

The right of Wendy Ball to be identified as author of this work has been asserted by her in accordance with the Copyright, Designs and Patents Act 1988.

Printed by MPG Group, Bodmin, Cornwall

Contents

Tables

Series Editors' Foreword

This is the tenth volume in the Politics and Society series. With a focus on childcare policy it explores an enduring issue, one that reflects wider social attitudes and practices and is a key indicator of the changing nature of gender relations in society. In the discussion, Wendy Ball heeds earlier calls for 'gendered social policy analysis to be transformed from a uni- or even bifocal into a multi-focal lens' (Lister, 2000: 33). She presents an examination of the implications of constitutional reform and whether devolution in Wales has enabled the emergence of a distinctive social policy agenda on childcare – as well as the impact that Welsh policy may have on the well-being of mothers, fathers and children. The result is a thoughtful analysis of recent public policy responses to asymmetric gendered behaviour whereby women have entered the labour market to a much greater extent than men have increased their childcare role.

Theoretically informed analysis is used to locate post-devolution developments within the context of the changing childcare policy landscape in the United Kingdom (UK). The volume is based on rich research data derived from interviews with mothers and fathers in three urban neighbourhoods with contrasting socio-economic profiles. This enabled the construction and analysis of childcare 'life histories'. These personal accounts were then compared with emergent themes from UK, Welsh and local authority policy documents and complemented by interviews with regional and local policy officers.

This comprehensive methodology has delivered an account which considers tensions in the policy shift witnessed over post-war decades from the male breadwinner model towards the adult wage-earner model. Attention is given to how this may conflict with the wishes of many mothers to give priority to the care of their children. Such a focus also underpins the strong case presented by the author for an 'ethic of childcare' which leads to a model combining universalism with choice and support. In this way, the discussion underlines the need for recognition of diversity amongst parents and cognizance of the impact material inequalities have on their childcare arrangements.

Transforming Childcare and Listening to Families is an important and timely contribution to contemporary policy debates. It finds evidence of a different policy style and vision in Wales and that this may provide opportunities to safeguard the rights and well-being of mothers, fathers and children. Yet the author also shows how childcare policy is a long way from fully promoting gender equality, supporting parents and meeting the interests of all children. Not least it has been constrained by a limited understanding of the connections between gender and childcare. Instead it has placed an emphasis on supporting role equity in paid work and an assumption that improved access to childcare will enable mothers to enter paid work. The discussion outlines how this has been accompanied by a general failure to understand the value of unpaid care. The author cogently observes how, *inter alia*, this is a function of gender-neutral policy language that downplays or ignores the discourses and social conditions of motherhood and fatherhood and fails to fully appreciate their implications for policy.

The first title in the series, *New Governance – New Democracy?*, concluded that 'the creation of the National Assembly for Wales has altered the democratic landscape in Wales . . . [it] promises innovation in governance and there are high expectations that devolution will bring about significant improvements in Welsh life' (Chaney et al., 2001: 43). Notwithstanding significant developments witnessed over intervening years, one of the emerging messages of this book is that greater policy divergence between Wales and Westminster may be necessary if a fully effective policy response is to be developed that recognizes diverse needs, matches the initial high expectations associated with devolution and delivers on the post-1999 social policy discourse of equality and social justice.

Paul Chaney and Andrew Thompson
Series Editors

Preface

Childcare is a topic that attracts considerable public, political and media interest in relation to debates about work–life balance, parenting and welfare reform. Since the launch of the National Childcare Strategy (DfEE, 1998)[1] academic and policy interest in childcare has grown considerably. The starting point for the research presented in this book was to explore how changes in childcare policy and provision impacted the daily lives of mothers with young children. Were mothers aware of developments in childcare policy and service delivery? Did they feel that policy made any difference in terms of their family life and childcare organization? Were their preferences and needs for support being met? What did mothers really think and were policies and services responsive to their views? How were these matters shaped by access to informal support for childcare and families' material circumstances? This research revealed that there remains a significant gap between what mothers say they need in terms of support for childcare, how they want to organize their family lives and what is currently being offered. Extending the research to incorporate the experiences of a small sample of fathers, the capacity of policy, and provision to enable diverse and non-traditional caring roles for both men and women was also addressed.

This book explores these connections between childcare, gender relations and social policy in post-devolution Wales. Childcare provided the focus for assessing whether devolution has enabled a distinctive social policy agenda to emerge in Wales. How could such a policy make a difference to the well-being of mothers, fathers and children? In voicing these questions, the changing childcare policy landscape in the UK is discussed and the making of childcare policy in Wales following devolution is traced. New Labour and recent UK Coalition government social policy agendas are assessed in relation to questions about their potential to progress gender equality, offer parental choice, extend support to parents and meet the interests of children. Childcare thus provides the spotlight for looking at the degree to which a distinctive social policy agenda in Wales has transpired. The book presents new research material that indicates there *is* evidence of a different style and vision in Wales that may provide opportunities to safeguard the rights and well-being of mothers, fathers and children in Wales within the changing UK policy landscape. In the current climate of economic austerity and reshaping of political interests under the UK Coalition government, it is important to identify Welsh policy priorities for families, with recognition of related matters. Such matters include the impact of high levels of family poverty and the distribution of material resources available in different communities across Wales.

The *Introduction* opens with one mother's narrative in order to illustrate the interaction between private dilemmas in organizing childcare and the public matter of childcare policy. Following analysis of policies and legislation made at UK level (*Chapter 1*) and in Wales following devolution (*Chapter 2*), the book turns to the interviews with mothers (*Chapter 3*), presenting their perspectives on caring for their children and how they are shaped by material and emotional concerns. These accounts highlight tensions between policy agendas, gender politics and parental preferences. This is followed by attention to the relationship of families to local childcare and early years services (*Chapter 4*), revealing the socio-spatial inequalities in service provision across local neighbourhoods and the significance of informal care as a key support for families. In the next chapter (*Chapter 5*) the perspectives of mothers and fathers are reviewed in relation to interview data with policy officers to highlight common ground and key differences of view between these stakeholders in policy. It is argued that childcare policy in Wales has been limited by a narrow understanding of the connections between parental preference, gender and childcare. The interconnections between informal care provided through networks of social support, mainly provided by women, and formal childcare provision deserve to be recognized in policy. In the *Conclusion* the features of a more reflexive and sensitive childcare policy agenda are suggested, an agenda capable of responding to parental needs in their diversity. A case study of the experiences of the small group of fathers included in the research is offered to illuminate the failure of policy so far to address the connections between childcare and gender in ways that will encourage a real sharing of childcare between women and men. It is concluded that stakeholders with an interest in the well-being of mothers, fathers and children should engage in a progressive alliance, to shape an ethic of childcare policy, in light of concerns that families with children living in poor and modest material circumstances are likely to face significant hardship as UK Coalition government politics and policies take shape.

Acknowledgements

Many people have kindly given up their time to participate in this research. I would like to thank all the mothers and fathers who were interviewed for their generosity in sharing their personal experiences with me. I am also indebted to the regional and local policy officers and the practitioners in the city's early years and childcare services for their participation despite heavy workloads.

The research was undertaken for my doctorate while I was a PhD student in sociology at the University of Wales Swansea and I am very grateful to Nickie Charles and Charlotte Davies for their support and encouragement in their role as supervisors. Thanks are also due to the University of Wales Swansea for the award of a postgraduate bursary during the period 2002–5.

My appreciation is due to Nickie Charles again for encouraging me to submit a book proposal to University of Wales Press, and to Ralph Fevre, who was then editor of the Politics and Society in Wales series, for supporting this. I am also grateful to Valerie Walkerdine, who read my PhD thesis and provided guidance in turning it into something of potential interest to a wider audience. Thanks also to the current series editors, Paul Chaney and Andrew Thompson, and the editorial team at University of Wales Press for their excellent support during the writing process. The book has also benefited from the consideration of an anonymous reviewer and I offer my appreciation of the helpful reader's report and encouragement that the messages of the research should reach policy-makers as well as an academic audience.

Finally, and most importantly, my love and thanks go to my family: my husband, Darryl, and children, Nicholas and Christopher. This book is in loving memory of my father, Fred Ball (1923–99), and my mother, Mavis Ball (1928–2003), who are both sadly missed by all of us.

Some parts of some of the chapters in the book draw on material that has previously appeared in my chapter on 'Devolution, gender and childcare: a distinctive agenda for Wales?' in N. Charles and C. A. Davies (eds.), *Gender and Social Justice in Wales*, Cardiff: University of Wales Press, 83–104.

Glossary

CIS	Children's Information Service
CWG	Childcare Working Group
CYPP	Children and Young People Partnership
DfEE	Department for Education and Employment
DfES	Department for Education and Skills
DTI	Department of Trade and Industry
EOC	Equal Opportunities Commission
EU	European Union
EYDCP	Early Years Development and Childcare Partnership
IFSS	Integrated Family Support Service
MEWN	Minority Ethnic Women's Network
NAfW	National Assembly for Wales
NCSTF	National Childcare Strategy Task Force
UK	United Kingdom
UNCRC	United Nations Convention on the Rights of the Child
WAG	Welsh Assembly Government
WLGA	Welsh Local Government Association

Introduction

This book presents research that sought to get to the heart of mothers' everyday caring practices and link this to the public matter of childcare and family policies. It is surprising that childcare has historically 'not generally [been] understood to be a glamorous or exciting topic' (Vincent and Ball, 2001: 633), for it has the capacity to illuminate matters of gender, care, class and politics across many dimensions. Nevertheless, following the launch of the National Childcare Strategy (DfEE, 1998) by the former New Labour government, public and academic interest in childcare became more pronounced (Ball and Vincent, 2005; Daycare Trust, 2003; Duncan et al., 2004; Lewis, 2003). This research offers an insight into the changing childcare policy landscape in the UK with particular focus on post-devolution Wales and the prospects for regional policy engagement with an 'ethics of care' (F. Williams, 2001).

The book seeks to illuminate the capacity of social policy to embrace a 'childcare ethic' in relation to the achievements and legacy of New Labour and the prospects for the future following the global economic crisis of 2008–9 and the formation of the UK Coalition government in 2010. The government is now making policies in a climate that is austere and arguably unfriendly to ordinary families. These interests shape the central research questions that explore the links between motherhood, family lives and childcare policy in Wales and the interaction between private choices, family, gender and public matters. The central focus of the study was on mothers and motherhood as a social institution. However, the research also incorporated perspectives from a smaller sample of fathers, and whose views illuminate one of the book's central arguments: that current policy has failed to encourage a progressive reshaping of gender, paid work and childcare within families. The narrative of one mother will be offered next in order to provide the reader with a sense of the book's central message: that public policy is failing to grasp what matters to ordinary families.

SHEILA'S STORY: A MOTHER'S REFLECTIONS ON CARE, WORK AND FAMILY

A feature of the sensitive mother then is that her domestic life is centred around her children and not around her housework. (Walkerdine and Lucey, 1989: 20)

I want to go back part-time. I will be asking to go back part-time in September. I feel I am missing out. Taking Monday, for example, I was home at quarter past six and she was fed and she goes to bed at seven so I see her for three quarters of an hour, so I feel guilty over that. It is guilt mainly. (Sheila)

The book begins with a case study of one of the mothers, Sheila, who was interviewed in this research. As the book unfolds, the connections between personal accounts from mothers and the processes that shape the conduct of mothering will be reviewed as a basis for assessing childcare policy. Sheila shared her reflections on what she enjoyed about childcare, what she found difficult and what she would like to change. She was employed as a full-time professional in the field of education and her husband was also in full-time paid work. They had one daughter aged three years. Sheila explained that she did not use any formal childcare as she had considerable informal support from her mother and mother-in-law. She also described a shared division of domestic responsibilities with her husband:

We share things equally. A lot of the time he works from home. So he takes [daughter] to my mother's or my mother-in-law's on a morning and I pick [daughter] up. And generally we share the ironing, the housework, the cleaning.

Nevertheless, Sheila made a distinction between household tasks that she would share with her husband and certain aspects of the care of their daughter, for example the bedtime and bathtime routines, for which she wished to take responsibility. In this sense she appeared to support progressive discourses around gender equality and the sharing of domestic labour, yet she also held strong views regarding how she wished to perform the maternal role. Sheila was striving to be a 'sensitive mother' as described by Valerie Walkerdine and Helen Lucey, a cultural construct that they argue has played a pivotal role in the regulation of women:

The path to democracy begins in the kitchen of the sensitive mother. Here, there is supposed to be a nurturant presence which facilitates the development of her child towards natural language and reason. These develop because the sensitive mother is finely tuned to her child's struggle for meaning, extends and elaborates her utterances, transforms her own domestic work into play for her child's cognitive development. (1989: 101)

The maternal role according to this construct is defined in terms of meeting children's needs and has developed to meet particular understandings of healthy child development promoted by professionals within the systems of education, health and social welfare. Walkerdine and Lucey focus specifically on relationships between mothers and their young daughters during post-war Britain in the context of educational expansion. The sensitive mother appreciates that she has an educational role and will aid the development of her child by ensuring day-to-day domestic tasks are turned into opportunities for learning. In addition, the sensitive mother never disciplines her child in an overt way because this is seen to undermine the child's sense of autonomy. The expectations that mothers experience in seeking to meet their child's needs may lead to feelings of guilt and failure should they fall short of these idealized child-rearing practices. In Sheila's experience, there was a considerable overlap between her professional work within the early years education system and her understanding of how mothering should be performed.

Sheila had the benefit of favourable family-friendly employment conditions and actively used this to maximize the time spent with her daughter. Nevertheless, she was making plans to change her situation so that the balance between paid work and childcare shifted more towards care of her daughter. She had been working full-time until her pregnancy and converted to a part-time contract after the birth until her daughter was two years old. However, she was then persuaded to go back on a full-time contract:

> I made a kind of deal with the [line manager] that I would work full-time (because he wanted me to go full-time) if he allowed my daughter to come in the [education setting] with me for half a day. Which he agreed on. So for a year she came with me half day so I could still see her. *I didn't want to work all day without seeing her.* [my emphasis]

After this year, Sheila's daughter began school nursery for half days. Sheila had support from family to cover the other half of the day while she was still working. Despite this support, Sheila was unhappy that she was now working full-time and no longer seeing her daughter during the day. At the time of interview this new arrangement had been going on for two months and Sheila had decided it was unsatisfactory and she regretted the agreement to go full-time:

> My mother was always at home for me and everyone else in the family was at home with their children so I always felt that I should be. But [in education] if you give up your job for children, you won't get back in, well not at the same

level. So, I thought when [daughter] is in full-time school, I would want to get a job and then I wouldn't have the [school] holidays, so I thought if I can keep the job going at least it would pay off later. That was the aim. But it has been a struggle until then.

This account indicates that making formal childcare more available and accessible as enshrined in the public policies to be described in Chapters 1 and 2 will not necessarily meet the *emotional* or *moral* preferences of mothers. Sheila had no need to pay for childcare as she had regular informal support from her family. She also commented on the flexible approach of her employer in agreeing time off for family illness and special occasions.

This support at home and at work placed Sheila in a strong position compared with other mothers who took part in this research. However, she believed she was missing out and felt guilty that she spent a full day without seeing her daughter. She also believed that she was no longer able to commit to her paid work with the same intensity as prior to becoming a mother. She went on to talk about how going part-time again would be of benefit:

I rush in. That doesn't seem to bother her but it bothers me. I think I am missing out on, and she is missing out on, me going as a volunteer into her class. There are parents who do cooking sessions and I know from my [work in education], they are not the same as everybody else. They do know and feel at that age. Then my job side. There are times when I really need to spend an hour after [work] but I can't. Or not that I can't, but I won't. Because my parents would be quite happy to look after [daughter] for another hour. So, if I worked part-time I could give that extra hour and still have more time with [daughter].

Sheila was planning to request that she move to part-time hours in her paid work in education so that she could act as an unpaid volunteer in her daughter's primary school. She explained her decision in relation to her inside knowledge as an educator that it was beneficial for children, within the social relations of the school, if their mother was actively involved in their schooling in this way. Sheila wished to maximize opportunities to perform a pedagogical role in relation to her child; a role that is central to the construct of the 'sensitive mother'.

The account revealed how many mothers may feel caught between those agendas that encourage them to return to paid work and to maintain a career and those that cast them in the role of educator and primary carer for their child, that is, as a 'sensitive mother'. The decision of this mother appeared to be in tension with the emphasis of childcare policy in the UK as mainly supporting a route into paid work for both parents. *Emotions* about childcare and work are more pronounced in Sheila's account than *practical* considerations because availability of informal childcare really is not a barrier. Diverse policy agendas (work, equality, education, motherhood) all link together to construct feelings of guilt. Sheila is caught between competing discourses and is trying to find a way of reconciling them.

Mothers' feelings about 'being there' for their children in order to secure emotional and educational benefits on their behalf may cut across their wish for independence and equality in the public sphere. The impact of the ideal of 'sensitive mothering' as described by Walkerdine and Lucey is strong and is also class-based: 'The women oppressed by their labours in the middle-class households act out of a set of scientific ideas which tell them that they are right, that this is the proper thing to do' (1989: 8). This sense of morality, that Sheila would be doing the 'right thing' by reducing her working hours, was communicated during the interview. Sheila also had a choice in that her financial resources and working arrangements would enable this. Some of the mothers whose stories are presented in this book were not free to act from such a position of choice. Moreover, this vision of child rearing as pedagogy involves a celebration of white, middle-class understandings of the maternal role, meaning that the child-caring practices of mothers from other social backgrounds can be deemed to be deficient. This may lead to practices of 'mother-blaming' (Turney, 2000: *passim*) for women who hold less privileged positions within the social structure.

In view of the wider political and cultural changes relating to the role of women in the UK since Walkerdine and Lucey (1989) conducted their study, the research sought to explore whether the expectations that underpin the role of the 'sensitive mother' have shifted. In Sheila's case, it appeared that the role resonated with her own expectations. Yet contemporary mothers like Sheila perform this role within a different social and political context from the generation of mothers considered by Walkerdine and Lucey (1989). Sheila also reported feelings of guilt with regard to the performance of both her professional role and her capacity to engage actively in her child's schooling. The pressures on mothers and the impact of expert models of child-rearing have intensified according to Sharon Hays (1996), who has explored contemporary expectations of mothers through the concept of 'intensive mothering':

> The ideology of intensive mothering is a gendered model that advises mothers to expend a tremendous amount of time, energy, and money in raising their children. (1996: x)

Childcare involves more than the routine practical care of children. It also embraces educational support (David et al., 1997; Reay, 1998, 2000; Standing, 1999) and 'emotion work' (Duncombe and Marsden, 1999), and mothers are the central players in doing this. The mothers in Hays's study were all aware of what was expected in the performance of 'intensive mothering' based on a child-centred model and informed by the advice of experts. Whilst mothers in different situations may have interpreted this model in particular ways, Hays notes that they all used it as a reference point:

> No matter how different the circumstances and beliefs of the mothers in my study, my interviews suggest that almost all mothers recognize and respond to this ideology – either by accepting it or, if they reject it in whole or in part, by feeling the need to justify that rejection. (1996: 72)

As Susan E. Bell has observed, this model acts as a 'normative standard against which all mothering practices and arrangements in US society are evaluated' (2004: 46). Although Hays developed this model on the basis of interviews with mothers in the United States of America, 'intensive mothering' is recognized as an international ideology (Cheal, 2002). David Cheal has observed that the ideology 'is found in any society where the dominant culture stresses collective progress based on individual effort and achievement' (2002: 105). The ideologies of 'sensitive mothering' and 'intensive mothering' refer to broad belief systems surrounding motherhood that have evolved over a long historical period within particular societies. The pressures on mothers have intensified with wider social and cultural change and the growth of consumerism. It seems that 'intensive mothering' has evolved from earlier models of mothering and is the compromise 'sensitive mothers' may have to make in order to balance paid work, the pursuit of personal achievement and economic well-being with their caring duties. Intensive mothering is, therefore, an accommodation of 'sensitive mothering' to wider social transformation and changing gender roles. The terms 'sensitive mothering' and 'intensive mothering' will both be used in this study to signify that both traditional models of mother-care persist and yet there has been a transition and some reshaping of how this is conducted in specific circumstances.

This research emerged from an interest in developing an ethnographic study of childcare from the perspective of mothers that could provide a basis from which to assess emerging childcare strategies in the UK, with particular reference to Wales. Sheila's account provides one example of the dilemmas that may emerge for a mother in reconciling different expectations. Later in the book, mothers' personal accounts will be compared with the perspectives of policy officers involved in campaigns for improving work–life balance as well as gender equality in paid work and care. When interviewed, it was clear that some of the policy officers' assumptions about what mothers wanted from policy were contradicted by the research material provided by the mothers. These competing perspectives illuminated wider debates about the balance between work and childcare and views on motherhood; and revealed that mothers and policy officers may not share the same understandings. This gulf in interpretations sets the foundation for the focus of the book. In the next section I will describe why this interplay between personal accounts of mothers and public childcare policy was viewed to be worth opening up to critical scrutiny.

SETTING THE SCENE: PERSONAL INFLUENCES

The study originated from my personal experience as a mother of young children, experiencing the tensions between the goals of gender equality in public life, the promises of childcare policy and the real, day-to-day practical and emotional problems of reconciling work and care during the early years of parenthood. With the transition to motherhood I became aware that I was being judged by others in new ways. The practicalities of having to care for a new baby were demanding but what was most difficult was to find that others now judged me in relation to my competence as a mother. The division between public and private life was eroded and the choices made about the balance between paid work and childcare, and how this was shared between my husband and me was questioned by others.

I was surprised to find that, despite our decision to share childcare, I was still treated as the parent with main responsibility for our son in any contact with health, childcare and education professionals. On one occasion, for example, a health visitor requested that my husband leave the baby room at our health centre while she discussed the business of weaning with me. Yet I had just informed her that I would soon be returning to work and my husband would be the main carer for our son. This personal experience reminded me daily that childcare and gender are intimately linked whatever 'private' choices may be agreed over the division of labour. I felt the impact of domestic ideologies that are reproduced in policy, by professionals who work with mothers and children and by mothers themselves. In addition, with the exhaustion that comes from looking after a baby, I found myself feeling resentful that I had not had the opportunity to extend my maternity leave or to work part-time because I was the main earner. At this point I would have described myself as a 'reluctant breadwinner' (Charles and James, 2003: 246), feeling that I had been forced to return to a full-time job before I was ready. It seemed that I was beginning to accept those ideologies that I had previously questioned and that I was starting to act according to the rules of 'sensitive motherhood' (Walkerdine and Lucey, 1989) in order to fit in to traditional ways of organizing childcare. I also started to feel that unless I played according to those rules my son would lose out. In order to explore these dilemmas I sought refuge in literature on motherhood, in studies that appeared to help me relate my 'personal trouble' to the 'public issue' (see Mills, 1959: 14–15) of motherhood, childcare and policy.

There were two studies that were compelling and both were sources of inspiration for this research. The first of these is *Democracy in the Kitchen: Regulating Mothers and Socialising Daughters* (Walkerdine and Lucey, 1989), which is the source of the idea of the 'sensitive mother' introduced earlier. Having been impressed with the study when it was first published, I read it again after the birth of my eldest son in 1995. The theorization of 'sensitive mothering' now resonated at a deeper level and helped me to interpret some of my own exasperation. I was aware that the pressures I was experiencing as a mother were linked to ideas that limit women's independence and yet simultaneously I found I was compelled to play the 'sensitive mother' role at least some of the time.

The second source of inspiration was the study *Mothers and Their Children: A Feminist Sociology of Childrearing* (Ribbens, 1994), an ethnographic account of women with young children in which Ribbens explores their perspectives on child-rearing. I was moved by the idea of developing an ethnographic study in relation to childcare that, like Ribbens's work, would place mothers' experiences centre-stage. At the same time my study aimed to be distinct in that I wanted to find a way of mediating between how mothers 'do childcare' and the shifting policy landscape following the National Childcare Strategy (Daycare Trust/NCSR, 2007; DfEE, 1998).

In making my personal childcare arrangements during the period in which childcare was being placed high on the political agenda, I was exasperated that policy did not seem to do justice to the daily challenges of balancing work, study and the needs of children. Nor did policy appear to engage fully with the gendered relations of childcare and the capacity of discourses of motherhood to inhibit efforts to move away from traditional family and care practices. In addition, the emergent policy debates relating to the offer of 'family-friendly' employment rights did not seem to offer sufficient resolution to the day-to-day prejudices and practical difficulties that working mothers may face, which were also having a personal impact. This research emerged from my interest in how mothers in different circumstances interpret and negotiate these issues. I envisaged that their accounts could provide the basis for a critique of policy. I had not initially planned to interview fathers because my intention was to look at childcare from a mothering standpoint. However, as the research unfolded, I realized that the research should recognize fathers and fatherhood in order to consider more thoroughly the links between childcare, gender and parenthood. Owing to time constraints, this remained a minor theme deserving of further research in future.

RESEARCHING FAMILIES, CHILDCARE AND POLICY

The study was based in Wales and with a focus on the city to which I had moved with my family in 2002. The choice of locality was not incidental but central to the goal of developing an ethnographic study of childcare, building from my personal circumstances as a mother of young children. The personal decision to move our family from England to Wales three years on from devolution had been reached, in part, in relation to knowledge that Welsh educational policy was moving in a way that was distinctive and potentially progressive. The research aimed to incorporate this interest and to explore the trajectory of policy in Wales in the context of devolution. The methodology was based on local area studies and interviews with mothers and a smaller sample of fathers as the starting point. The local area studies focused on three neighbourhoods of the city with contrasting socio-economic profiles. A map of local childcare services was developed through visits to relevant agencies such as primary schools and day nurseries. Qualitative interviews with mothers and fathers were arranged in each area and involved the recording of childcare 'life histories'. These personal accounts were then compared with themes emerging from policy analysis. The policy analysis included a review of national (UK), regional (Wales) and local (city) policy documents alongside the conduct of interviews with regional and local policy officers.

The sources of data and stages of the research process are outlined in Table 0.1 and then discussed in fuller detail.

Stage one: mapping provision in three localities

An ethnographic study of family childcare practices was to be conducted through focused work in specific neighbourhoods in the tradition of community studies (Davies and Jones, 2003; Rosser and Harris, 1965) and with family and kinship networks at the heart of the analysis (Charles and Davies, 2005; Devine and Heath, 1999). The intention was to gather personal

Table 0.1: Key stages in the research and sources of data

Stage one	Identification of three localities within city with contrasting socio-economic profiles. Development of a map of local early years, childcare and parenting support services through contact with local practitioners.
Stage two	Qualitative interviews with a sample of mothers and fathers living in each locality.
Stage three	Analysis of policy texts at national, regional and local levels of government.
Stage four	Interviews with a sample of regional and local policy officers located in the childcare and parenting policy arenas. Interview themes based on issues arising from interviews with mothers and fathers and from the policy analysis.

accounts from mothers and fathers in the context of detailed knowledge of the communities in which they lived. This would develop a picture of the local childcare service and other services for parents and children. Early years and childcare services vary considerably between local areas leading to an interest in the geographies of childcare (England, 1996; Holloway, 1998; Vincent et al., 2004a). The National Childcare Strategy in the UK has supported the continuation of local childcare markets (Dickens et al., 2005; Vincent and Ball, 2001) through a mixed economy of provision (Lewis, 2003). This has led to questions regarding whether the reliance on the private for-profit sector alongside limited public provision in the most deprived areas will deliver childcare for all (Land, 2002a; McDowell et al., 2005) and whether these childcare markets can be sustained during a period of economic crisis (Caluori, 2009). The research design would enable an insight into how informal and formal childcare arrangements vary across geographical areas. This involved a focus on one city and three areas within this city. Following Simon Duncan and Darren Smith's claim that there is a 'geography of family formations' (2002: 31), which may vary across local neighbourhoods, this study began from meetings with families and local practitioners at the neighbourhood level and worked upwards.

The research was thus conducted in three areas of the city with contrasting socio-economic and ethnic profiles. The areas will be referred to by pseudonyms as *Crossland, Tinbury* and *Shaw*. These areas contrast across a range of criteria such as type of housing and local amenities, and their populations vary by occupational status, educational attainment, age profile, household composition and ethnic origin. Both Crossland and Tinbury had been designated as Communities First areas and each was a base for Sure Start initiatives.[1] In addition, Tinbury was placed as one of the highest out of the top 100 most deprived wards in Wales and had a very high score on the child poverty index. Crossland was selected because it is an ethnically and religiously diverse area with a relatively high proportion of Muslim families. The Minority Ethnic Women's Network (MEWN) had conducted research in Wales that indicated the childcare needs of Muslim families were not being met (MEWN, 1998). It was therefore important to ensure the study examined the capacity of policy to reflect the needs and preferences of minority ethnic families. All three areas were places where I was involved in local networks and facilities in relation to my children. The study was to explore how far childcare policy was capable of responding to diversity amongst families and this guided the selection of locations. Further details of the profile of each area are provided in Appendix 1.

Meetings were arranged with local practitioners in the field of early years education, childcare and parenting support in order to develop a map of local provision in each area and to facilitate contacts with parents. These 'childcare maps' were intended to explore how childcare policy was changing the shape of local provision and to determine the degree of local support for parents and children across a range of service areas.

Stage two: interviews with mothers and fathers

The main focus of the research was on mothers' accounts of their childcare practices and these mothers were contacted through early years and childcare settings in the three areas. The research also included a smaller number of interviews with fathers. A leaflet was circulated outlining the research, and inviting mothers and fathers to participate who were involved in the regular care of at least one child under the age of eleven years.[2] All those who volunteered were interviewed.

As Fiona Devine and Sue Heath observe, 'qualitative methods have remained the predominant approach within sociological research on the family' (1999: 43). Whilst the method of participant observation has been particularly associated with ethnography, it would have been difficult to use this method to study the private world of families (Ribbens, 1994). Many studies concerned with capturing private accounts have been based on biographical methods (Roberts, 2002) such as life history interviews (Geiger, 1986; Ribbens, 1994) and diaries (Bell, 1998). Whilst these were attractive as sources of information on daily childcare practices they were also time-consuming methods and would rely on the capacity of parents to give considerable time to the research. It seemed unlikely that many mothers or fathers of young children would have this time to spare. A compromise was reached by conducting 'childcare life histories' through qualitative interviews conducted in the family home or a setting such as a school or nursery. These individual interviews were conducted with twenty-five mothers and six fathers. There were also two group interviews: one with four mothers using a local nursery in Tinbury and the other with eight fathers contacted through a Sure Start project.[3]

The interviews began with an exploration of the mother's or father's family circumstances and their perspectives on caring for their child(ren). How did they distribute caring responsibilities within the family and what were the factors that shaped the roles that were adopted? What use, if any, was made of early years and childcare provision and did they feel they had any choice in patterns of use? How did families combine paid employment, study and leisure with childcare and what were the reasons that underpinned particular ways of organizing childcare? Finally, the interview would conclude with an exploration of the parent's perspectives on childcare policy and local services for parents and children. Within this framework there was flexibility in the questions that were explored according to the circumstances of each parent.[4]

Stage three: analysis of policy texts

The analysis of policy texts involved selection of various documents produced at different levels of governance including the national (UK), regional (Wales) and local (city) levels. The analysis was based on a search of websites for documents pertaining to the policy arenas of childcare, support for parents, gender equality and social justice.[5] Overall, texts were read with three aims: first, to critically evaluate the content of childcare and parenting policy produced by the UK government, the Welsh Government and key partnerships within the city;[6] second, to assess claims that policy will progress gender equality and work–life balance, offer parental choice, extend support to parents and meet the interests of children; and, finally, to identify issues that could be explored further in interviews with policy officers.

Stage four: interviews with policy officers in local and regional childcare policy arenas

Policy officers working across a range of social policy arenas at both regional (Wales) level and at the local (city) level were invited to take part in the study. Fourteen individuals were interviewed.[7] Members of regional and local government and other bodies with an interest in childcare, parenting support and equality matters were included. The local Early Years Development and Childcare Partnership (EYDCP) and Sure Start Partnership were both used as routes of access to invite relevant professionals to take part in the research.

The intention was to explore policy officers' responses to the personal accounts that had been collated from mothers and fathers, so policy officers were interviewed in the final stages of the research following fieldwork with parents. The interview themes were personalized according to the role and institutional affiliation of each participant. All participants were invited to reflect on childcare policy in relation to UK and Welsh government agendas and with regard to the benefits and challenges involved in delivering those agendas.[8]

These different sources of information enabled the study to locate mothers' and fathers' experiences and perspectives in relation to the claims of policy texts, and to explore policy in practice and examine policy loopholes with service professionals and policy officers. The structure of the book reflects this intention to illuminate the interplay of public policies, professional viewpoints and mothers' and fathers' personal accounts of childcare in their diversity.

SUMMARY OF CHAPTERS

This *Introduction* has made a case for opening up the interaction between personal matters and public interests in understanding childcare and setting this in the context of family lives in their diversity. The book's chapters move next to a consideration of the policy context. In *Chapter 1*, the policy landscape in the UK is examined with regard to family, parenting and childcare policy at national level. The analysis begins with the election of New Labour in 1997 and the launch of the National Childcare Strategy (DfEE, 1998) and moves through to more recent shifts in policy priorities within the UK Coalition government (HM Government, 2010). The chapter provides some critical observation about the emphases and direction of policy at the UK level with regard to gender relations and parent support. This provides a framework for comparison in *Chapter 2* with the direction of Welsh policy following devolution and the creation of the NAfW in 1999. This chapter makes use of policy documents and interview material with regional and local policy officers to explore the making of childcare policy in Wales. The chapter will pursue the question of how much scope there is for doing things differently in Wales with reference to the making of childcare policy and the Welsh Government's commitment to the key political values of equality, social justice and inclusion, and children's rights.

These chapters help to point to some of the emphases in policy and I will proceed in Chapters 3 and 4, through interview material, to illustrate how those emphases may not always connect with parental preferences, needs and circumstances with implications for family well-being and access to support.

In *Chapter 3* the interviews with mothers are presented to illuminate their daily caring practices, the social relations of care and their shaping through material and emotional concerns. This will add more depth to the personal dilemmas illustrated by the case study of one mother in the Introduction. The mothers' accounts provide an insight into the varied social conditions of motherhood in contemporary Wales and the implications of this for the conduct of childcare and gender relations. As Dorothy Smith points out, 'Notions of good mothering practices take no account of the actual material and social conditions of mothering work' (1988: 168). This analysis approaches the mothers' accounts as a means to understanding mothering as an institution, social practice and source of identity illuminating its 'taken for granted' nature.

In *Chapter 4*, the study continues to focus on the interviews with mothers and also draws in the perspectives of the fathers with reference to their use of local childcare and early years services. The degree to which services meet the needs of parents and the tension between targeted services and the case for universal childcare (Ben-Galim, 2011a; Land, 2002a) are discussed. The three selected neighbourhoods in this city are described with regard to service provision. How different families use formal childcare services is examined and material is presented to illustrate that patterns of use can be more fully understood in relation to the availability of local networks of social support and informal care and in the context of the range of services used by and needed by families with young children. The socio-spatial inequalities of provision that have resulted from the creation of a childcare market are also illustrated forcefully.

The remaining two chapters seek to bring together the insights gained from the policy analysis and the interview material in order to consider ways forward in public policy. *Chapter Five* provides an opportunity to review the material from the parent interviews and the neighbourhood case studies and illuminate their implications for UK and Welsh policy agendas. This chapter will consider the key gaps and disconnections that were revealed by this research as a basis for moving towards a more sensitive and reflexive childcare policy agenda. The key points of difference between parents' needs and experiences and childcare policy will be highlighted. Interview material from the policy officers will reveal how they interpreted parental perspectives, indicating that there are differences of view between officers depending on whether they are located at regional or local level. In the *Conclusion*, the material presented in the earlier chapters is revisited in relation to questions about how this can shape future childcare policy in ways that are responsive to parental needs in their diversity. Some final thoughts are offered on how childcare policy can both attend to calls for gender equity and yet chime with what mothers and fathers would like. The chapter provides some new material from the fathers' accounts, revealing the different connections between childcare and work for men in diverse family contexts. This material also makes a case for revisiting the connections between childcare and gender relations at home and work.

The prospects for developing an 'ethics of childcare' in policy terms are considered and related to the matter of the scope for a fresh style and vision in Wales and future regional policy divergence within the UK. These questions take on fresh significance in the context of wider UK political agendas moving from New Labour to UK Coalition government priorities for the welfare state and their impact on ordinary families. Given that the current UK economic and political climate appears to be distinctly unfriendly to families, it is hoped that this book will highlight the need for an alternative.

1

Shaping Childcare Policy in the United Kingdom

INTRODUCTION

This chapter will introduce the social policy context in the UK through an examination of childcare, family and parenting policy at national level since the election of New Labour in 1997. The assessment of policy is shaped by a specific approach to policy analysis that is outlined in the first section. In the second section the focus will be on the New Labour project for childcare. This will offer an overview of the National Childcare Strategy (DfEE, 1998) and link it to a range of other policy agendas including the promotion of gender equality, work–life balance, welfare-to-work and the emergence of child-focused policies. Childcare and parenting policies will be evaluated with regard to their implications for gender relations and for supporting parents. The assessment of the New Labour agenda is intended to reveal the policy infrastructure and legacy that had been shaped prior to the transition to a new UK government in 2010. In the section that follows, the emphases in social policy that have been emerging since the formation of the UK Coalition government in May 2010 will be identified and the implications of economic austerity, welfare reform and the notion of the 'big society' for service provision and family well-being will be addressed. The chapter will conclude with some critical observation about the highlights and direction of policy at the national UK level in relation to the matter of 'who benefits?' This will provide a framework for comparison with the direction of Welsh policy in the next chapter.

APPROACHES TO POLICY ANALYSIS

How is childcare understood and presented in policy texts? This research explored public policies relating to childcare, gender equality, work–life balance and parenting support. A policy text can be viewed as an 'attempt at persuasion' (Sparks, 1992: 112) that represents a particular construction of social reality, and specific presentations may be deployed in order to increase a policy's appeal to its audience. It is, therefore, important for analysis to go deeper than a surface reading of the text. 'Frame analysis' of policy texts was used in this research as a means of illuminating 'master narratives' relating to childcare and parenting and the relationship of these narratives to wider public agendas and power relations.

Policy documents and interview transcripts were, therefore, analysed in relation to the concepts of framing and the discursive opportunity structure (Ball and Charles, 2006; Ferree, 2003; Naples, 2002). Framing is broadly defined as 'signifying work or meaning construction' (Benford and Snow, 2000: 614) whilst a frame may be viewed as an 'interpretive package' (Ferree, 2003: 308) that draws from ideologies and discourses. The positioning of lone mothers in relation to the 'welfare to work' agenda, for example, is a means of framing that celebrates the citizen's moral duty to engage in paid work. In order to link framing processes with power relations it is necessary to locate 'the construction and interpretation of frames within the broader discursive and institutional context' (Naples, 2002: 244). The idea of the 'discursive opportunity structure' (Ferree, 2003: 309) has been proposed in order to achieve this goal and can be defined as 'institutionally anchored patterns of interpretation' (Ferree, 2003: 309). The interpretations underpinning 'welfare to work' policies, to return to this example, reveal an agenda that is anchored within the systems of governance. Interest groups campaigning on behalf of parents will be more likely to be heard by government if their demands are framed in ways that echo favoured patterns of interpretation. Put simply, they must use the 'right language' and accepted rules of engagement to make their case. On the basis of this framework, the analysis focused on policy texts produced by national, regional and local public institutions in order to uncover their 'patterns of interpretation' in relation to childcare and parenting, how those patterns link to broader discourses (for example, those relating to welfare reform) and the implications with regard to the pursuit of gender equality and social justice.

In view of the study's focus on gender relations and motherhood, the approach also followed Catherine Marshall's model of feminist critical policy analysis in which research 'asks an often neglected question of every policy or political action: how is it affected by gender roles?' (1997: 2). In identifying 'patterns of interpretation' in childcare policy texts, the issue of how this positioned mothers, fathers and gender roles was central to this analysis. Similarly, in discussions with policy officers, the intention was to identify master narratives, to consider their implications for gender roles and to illuminate potentially beneficial or harmful consequences.

Policy texts are part of a wider web of discursive and social relations and play a key part in the organization of social action (Smith, 1990a). One of the dominant textual discourses important for this research is that surrounding 'mothering' and policy texts may reinforce, reshape or challenge ideologies and discourses that shape mothering practices. Childcare manuals, advertising and magazines aimed at mothers can be significant in influencing the conduct of mothering. Childcare policies, however, may support or challenge this, for example, by recognizing the role of fathers as well as mothers in care. In this sense, policy texts can be located within the framework of the 'institutional' networks of ruling and social relations and can be analysed as part of the method of institutional ethnography (Smith, 1988). The focus of this method is on how individual practices are socially ordered through the variety of 'institutions organizing and regulating society' (Smith, 1988: 3) and which impact on forms of consciousness. In this way, Smith claims, we are influenced by networks of ruling as we go about our business and texts play a part in this process. However, these texts do not necessarily present a consistent message. On the contrary, the messages can be in conflict, which was illustrated in the Introduction to this book in relation to Sheila's anxieties over keeping her professional life open and giving time to her paid work whilst also being true to her understanding of what it would take to perform the role of the 'sensitive mother'. This chapter seeks to identify the variety of master narratives surrounding childcare policy in the UK and in doing so will reveal the patterns of interpretation that may serve to organize the social practices of mothers and fathers. In the next section the analysis of policy will begin with New Labour.

NEW LABOUR'S CHILDCARE POLICY

Since the New Labour government was first elected in 1997 a trend towards a more *explicit* approach to family and childcare policy (Driver and Martell, 2002; Lewis, 2003; Maclean, 2002) has been identified. Jane Lewis refers to the 'historical reluctance of UK governments to develop an explicit policy on childcare' (2003: 219); a reluctance that rested on the view that childcare was a 'family concern' (Scott, 1998: 519) and that 'mother-care' was best for children. In this context, New Labour social policies reflected a turning point in how childcare was framed in relation to gender, parenting and the needs of children: a shift in the construction of 'political motherhood' (Windebank, 1999); that is, understandings of mothering implicit in state policies and institutional frameworks. This shift has been evident in other advanced industrial societies beyond the UK, so much so that Rianne Mahon (2005) has claimed that recognition of the need for post-maternalist childcare policies has emerged as an international phenomenon albeit with variation in national responses. With the trend towards increased labour market participation of mothers, she argues, it 'can no longer be assumed that care will be provided as an unpaid "labour of love" by women within the realm of the family household' (Mahon, 2005: 343). How did New

Labour shape its agenda for childcare in this context of changing labour market and household relations?

In May 1998 the UK government announced the National Childcare Strategy (DfEE, 1998) in the inter-departmental Green Paper *Meeting the Childcare Challenge: A Framework and Consultation Document* and in October the Green Paper *Supporting Families* (Home Office, 1998) was also issued for consultation. Both papers reflected some of the wider priorities of New Labour in relation to combating poverty, promoting social inclusion and investing in children (Millar, 2003). Taken together these proposals introduced a wide variety of initiatives that may impact on parents' childcare decisions and the conduct of parenting more generally. The main directions of the New Labour project for families are considered in the next section. Although the Labour Party failed to retain power in the General Election of 2010, these initiatives helped create the policy infrastructure and frame the cultural values that may now be continued or reshaped by the UK Coalition government.

The National Childcare Strategy

The main themes of the National Childcare Strategy (DfEE, 1998) included reference to transformations in paid employment, especially the labour market participation of women with children, and changing family patterns that meant many families could not rely on informal care alone but would need access to affordable formal childcare provision. Specific attention was focused on the position of lone parents tied in to the welfare-to-work agenda to encourage more lone mothers to return to work or education (Ridge and Millar, 2011). The strategy highlighted themes of quality, affordability and accessibility of childcare and included proposals to tackle gaps. There was to be increased investment to expand childcare places alongside the introduction of a new childcare tax credit to help with the matter of affordability. All of these proposals were to be taken forward at the local level through new Childcare Partnerships based on the Early Years Development Partnerships. It was claimed that the success of the National Childcare Strategy would be seen in relation to both better outcomes for children and the opportunity for 'more parents with the chance to take up work, education or training because they have access to diverse, good quality childcare' (DfEE, 1998: para. ES2).

The National Childcare Strategy could, therefore, be seen as a vehicle to advance wider employment and educational agendas in the context of welfare restructuring. As Gill Scott argues, this amounts to 'an intentional shift in the work, family, state triangle on the part of the state' (1998: 522). The intention to support families in combining work and childcare was also tied in to an agenda to ' "make work pay" ' (Lewis and Campbell, 2008: 528) and with a view to reducing welfare spending. The framing of childcare policy in relation to economic goals has profound implications in relation to its capacity to meet parental preferences and enhance family well-being; this claim will explored later in the chapter.

The Inter-Departmental Childcare Review, *Delivering for Children and Families* (Strategy Unit, 2002), identified further plans for the transformation of childcare policy. The twin themes of alleviating child poverty through promoting employment opportunity and improving outcomes for children through early years education and childcare remained the focus for discussion. It was noted that, despite progress, problems with the availability of childcare remained, especially in economically deprived areas. The review proposed further investment in childcare including the creation of new children's centres (Lewis et al., 2011) providing a range of services for children and families and the expansion of childcare in and around schools. In addition, a new inter-departmental unit was proposed that would draw together responsibility for childcare, early years education and Sure Start.

In *Choice for Parents, the Best Start for Children: A Ten Year Strategy for Childcare* (HM Treasury, 2004) the government set out how it would build on the achievements of the National Childcare Strategy and the Sure Start programme. As noted earlier, the National Childcare Strategy had identified that the development of childcare should be based on the principles of 'quality', 'affordability' and 'availability'. In the ten-year strategy a fourth principle of 'choice' was added so that 'parents are better supported in the choices they make about their work and family responsibilities' (2004: para. 1.10: 4). The capacity of policy to support parental choice was one of the themes for discussion in the interviews with mothers, fathers and policy officers. Their perspectives on how far policy has been able to deliver this commitment to supporting choice will be reported in Chapters 3, 4 and 5.

The Childcare Act 2006 progressed the ten-year strategy and introduced further regulation of the childcare and early years sectors. However, some sections applied only to England whereas others impacted on the responsibilities of local authorities in England and Wales. The Act placed a duty on both English and Welsh local authorities 'to secure sufficient childcare for working parents'.[1] In this way the framing of childcare as a service primarily for those seeking work, or engaged in education or training, to provide a route into work was embedded in the legislation. Childcare policy in Wales, however, has been developed in the context of devolution and changing governance arrangements through the National Assembly for Wales and the Welsh government and will be considered further in Chapter 2.

Research into the progress of the National Childcare Strategy (Daycare Trust/NCSR, 2007) revealed that, nearly a decade after the strategy's launch, significant weaknesses persisted in terms of quality, affordability and choice of childcare and its suitability for supporting maternal employment. The study raised questions regarding the capability of a childcare market based on demand-led provision to cater for the diverse needs of parents living in different neighbourhoods. Some of these issues will be explored in Chapter 4, where the three areas of the study are compared in relation to service provision and the capacity of local services to meet parental needs.

Supporting families?

The National Childcare Strategy was presented as one part of a package of government support for families (Rahilly and Johnston, 2002). In November 1998 the UK government published the Green Paper *Supporting Families* (Home Office, 1998) based on the deliberations of the Ministerial Group on the Family chaired by the Home Secretary. The Green Paper claimed that the government's intention was to introduce measures that would support families and thus strengthen family life. The 'family policy' outlined in the Green Paper focused on five areas linked with specific proposals that it claimed would help families: 'Better Services and Support for Parents', 'Better Financial Support for Families', 'Helping Families Balance Work and Home', 'Strengthening Marriage' and 'Better Support for Serious Family Problems' (Home Office, 1998).

The conflicts and ambiguities evident within this Green Paper support claims that the New Labour project was inherently contradictory (Lister, 2001; McRobbie, 2000). The devotion of an entire chapter to the matter of 'Strengthening Marriage' provides one example to support this claim of ambivalence. Martin Durham (2001) has argued that the ambiguities that were evident in this Green Paper reflect divisions within the government with regard to the principles that should underpin family policy. The Green Paper favoured traditional perspectives regarding family structure and roles, such as 'Strengthening Marriage', that seemed to be at odds with other progressive policies associated with the New Labour project.

The discourse surrounding family support was also often couched in terms that appeared to be critical or punitive towards parents who were perceived as failing to cope. Proposals that aimed to change parental *behaviour* through education and advice or through particular sanctions were evidently preferred to more fundamental structural changes to address problems parents may face (Rake, 2001). Support for parents was thus directed towards those perceived to be a risk to their children, meaning that specific target groups were identified; for example, teenage parents, who have persistently been portrayed as a social problem in need of intervention by government (Duncan, 2007). Moreover, although government discourse uses the convention of referring to particular categories of parent, in reality the main care-givers tend to be women, meaning that mothers are the focus of attention (Featherstone, 2006; Nixon, 2007). Simon Duncan observes that this conception of a 'parenting deficit' (2002: 306) takes place in a policy context 'of seeing paid work as a moral duty while demoting unpaid caring work' (2002: 306). Yet at the same time a shift towards the greater regulation of parenting practices (Edwards and Gillies, 2004) is tied in with a reassertion of the moral responsibilities of parents towards their children. This represents a tension in the framing of policy that reflects the claim that in a society such as the UK, where participation in paid work is seen as the 'key to citizenship' (Lister, 1997: 139), the contribution of those providing unpaid care is devalued (Kittay, 2001; McKie et al., 2001). Whilst legislation and social policy in the UK has started to support, indeed encourage or require, women's labour market participation, it has done less to support women's caring role or to challenge the gendered nature of caring (Lewis, 2007; McKie et al., 2001). The next section will question the degree to which gender equality, work–life balance and family-friendly policies have made progress with these issues.

Gender equality, work–life balance and family friendly policies

> Women increasingly want to work and have careers as well as being mothers. Many fathers want more involvement with their children's upbringing. (Home Office, 1998: 2)

> The Government welcomes women's greater involvement and equality in the workplace and wants to ensure that all those women who wish to can take up these opportunities. (DfEE, 1998: Para 1.6)

Supporting Families (Home Office, 1998) signalled the UK government's intention to help families balance their work and home responsibilities. In 2000 the government launched the work–life balance campaign to encourage employers to recognize the benefits of flexible working. Alongside this have been various developments with regard to parents' employment rights. According to Simon Duncan, New Labour policy discourse on 'the reconciliation of work and family life' (2002: 305) represents a broadening of understanding of gender equality policy focused previously on promoting equality of opportunity in paid employment. However, this is mainly as a consequence of European Union (EU) policy directives that posed a dilemma for New Labour because, 'while the British government may be ideologically more attracted to the liberal US model of "flexible" labour, it is bound by EU law to implement a more corporatist gender equality model' (Duncan, 2002: 305).

The attention to work–life balance matters and parental rights in the context of EU policy directives has led to some (limited) improvements in (some) parents' rights in relation to employment.[2] In December 2000 the Department of Trade and Industry (DTI) published the Green Paper *Work and Parents: Competitiveness and Choice* (DTI, 2000), which outlined proposals concerning provision to help parents balance work and home responsibilities. In March 2001, the UK government subsequently announced increases in Statutory Maternity Pay, an extension of the period for which maternity leave would be paid, new rights to paid paternity leave, paid adoption leave and an increase in the Sure Start Maternity Grant. Consultation on parental leave also took place during 2001, leading to changes in the regulations in January 2002. A Work and Parents Taskforce was set up in June 2001 and this focused on issues relating to flexible working. New employment rights were introduced from April 2003 for employees with young children to request flexible working. This was part of a wider package of measures relating to maternity and paternity rights and the introduction of the new child tax credits (HM Treasury and DTI, 2003). These changes have been widely criticized for not going far enough and for offering little more than minimal compliance with EU policy directives (Dean, 2002; Dean and Shah, 2002; Lister, 2002). Ruth Lister has argued that the Green Paper (DTI, 2000) was 'written with one eye on what business will accept, making clear, in particular, the Government's reluctance to introduce payment for parental leave' (Lister, 2002: 523). In this sense, the needs of business have retained priority over the needs of parents.

The debates about work–life balance have continued following the DTI consultation *Work and Families: Choice and Flexibility* (DTI, 2005) and proposals that were set out in the Ten Year Childcare Strategy (HM Treasury, 2004). The Work and Families Act 2006 extended the period for maternity pay and adoption pay, extended the right to request flexible working to carers of adults and improved rights to paternity leave. Although this represented some valuable improvements in rights to time away from paid work for care, it has been argued that these developments did more to facilitate women's opportunities for time away than to encourage a shift in the distribution of care between women and men:

> What is notable in terms of engendering policy is that leave policies were predominantly directed at women, rather than at men and women as a gender equality strategy intent on redistributing the burden of formal and informal work. (Annesley et al., 2010: 397)

UK childcare and family policy certainly reflects ambivalence over issues of gender. As Jane Lewis and Susanna Giullari have observed, where policy refers to gender equality it is 'often defined in a particular, partial and instrumental way' (2005: 78). Gender equality is largely defined in relation to paid work opportunities, thus evading its connection to the distribution of labour in the home and in relation to who conducts caring duties. Policy texts refer to the generic needs of parents and, therefore, employ a gender-neutral discourse (Lewis and Campbell, 2008) but this 'effectively disguises the continuing gender divisions of caring labour' (Rake, 2001: 223). This is a concern explored by Brid Featherstone (2006) in an analysis of the usage of the term 'parent' in New Labour policy texts including those relating to childcare. The usage is problematic in that the terminology only serves to obscure actual power differentials between mothers and fathers, reducing the capacity of policy to effect meaningful change.

Welfare reform, childhood poverty and social exclusion

The New Labour UK government sought to use policy to tackle the problem of childhood poverty (Piachaud and Sutherland, 2001). Policies relating to families, parental support and childcare were driven particularly by the concern of the UK government to pursue the welfare-to-work agenda (Rake, 2001). This agenda has been advanced through a wide variety of initiatives to tackle social exclusion and childhood poverty (Cabinet Office, Social Exclusion Unit, 2001; DSS, 1998; Labour Party, 1997). The government set out its intentions to change the emphasis of social security policy in a Green Paper, *A New Contract for Welfare,* in which it declared that it would 'rebuild the welfare state around work' (DSS, 1998: 23). The main emphasis of policy has been to encourage welfare benefits claimants to move into employment and this is based on the philosophy that this is the most effective way of tackling poverty and the problem of social exclusion. A variety of welfare-to-work programmes were implemented for eighteen- to twenty-four-year-olds, for the long-term unemployed and for lone parents and disabled people who are in receipt of welfare benefits. Measures to 'make work pay' (Gray, 2001) included the introduction of a national minimum wage, the working families tax credit and support for the costs of childcare through the childcare tax credit (Rahilly and Johnston, 2002). The assumptions underpinning welfare-to-work have attracted considerable criticism supported by a substantial body of research that reveals flaws in the argument. The claim that the approach will ensure children are lifted out of poverty, for example, has been challenged on the grounds that a large percentage of poor children live in families of which at least one adult is in paid employment (Parekh et al., 2010).

During the last period of Labour government, the Secretary of State for Work and Pensions asked for a review of welfare-to-work policies and this was carried out by David Freud, reporting in 2007 (Freud, 2007). In his critique of the Freud Report, Chris Grover (2007) considers the continued focus on moving lone mothers into paid employment. This not only devalues their caring labour but is likely to fail as a measure to lift them out of poverty because of persisting gender inequalities in labour markets and the forms of paid work likely to be available. Those who are heavily engaged in unpaid care may find it difficult to access suitable paid employment (Lloyd, 2006) that is compatible with their caring duties.

Sure Start

Alongside the targeting of parents on low incomes through welfare-to-work are those funding streams that target support towards specific geographic areas of poverty and deprivation, including provision of support for parenting and childcare. The Sure Start programme (Glass, 1999; Tunstill et al., 2005) is of particular significance here and the present research included two neighbourhoods where Sure Start projects were being offered to families. Introduced in 1999, following a review of early years provision, the programme's aim was to improve the life chances of children living in deprived communities (Gustafsson and Driver, 2005). It has been directed specifically towards children aged from birth to four years of age and their families. The programme seeks to provide better access to 'early education and play, family support and advice on nurturing, and health services specifically aimed at children' (Bagley et al., 2004: 598). Multi-agency collaboration is encouraged through Sure Start partnerships and an effort to secure local involvement in programme delivery (Gustafsson and Driver, 2005). The programme rests on the view that early intervention when children are young can help to break cycles of disadvantage (NESS Research Team, 2004). Following on from the Sure Start local programmes, Children's Centres began to be established in England from 2004 onwards with a view to offering integrated early childhood services (Lewis et al., 2011). Comparable area-based anti-poverty programmes have been introduced in Wales and will be considered in the next chapter.

Placing children at the heart of social policy

New Labour social policy has claimed to place children's needs and interests at the heart of its concerns; to make children one of 'the central subjects' (F. Williams, 2004a: 406). This trend towards paying children particular attention has been analysed as part of the emergence of a 'social investment state' (Dobrowolsky, 2002; see also Lister, 2003, 2006) whereby children are constructed as future 'citizen-workers' within liberal welfare states. Hence, the centre staging of children within social policy is not confined to the UK (Dobrowolsky and Jenson, 2004). Moreover, the claims to be child-centred are linked intimately with economic agendas:

> One of the dominant characteristics of the social investment state is the investment in the child as citizen-worker-of-the-future, achieved through anti-poverty and education measures in which a notion of partnership of the state with parents, business and the voluntary sector, is central. The overall aim is to maintain competitiveness in the global economy. (F. Williams, 2004a: 408)

A compelling claim is made by Ruth Lister that child-focused policies may serve to sideline gender issues in that 'children are de-coupled from their mothers so that it is no longer a case of "women and children first" but "children (not women) first"' (2006: 315). A similar process has been identified by Rianne Mahon (2007) in her analysis of the changing politics of childcare policy in Canada, revealing a shift from linking support to gender equality matters to a focus on addressing child poverty. The commitment to framing policy in relation to a programme for children can be seen to use children's needs as a potent frame or master narrative securing support from a wide range of stakeholders. In comparison, a master narrative pertaining to women's rights might be less likely to build consensus between competing interest groups.

Specific policy measures that focus on children and young people have been wide-ranging. Some relate to the UK as a whole, whereas others have followed different routes in England, Wales, Scotland and Northern Ireland. Policy measures relating to Wales are discussed in detail in Chapter 2. The Green Paper *Every Child Matters* (DfES, 2003) called 'for the biggest shake up of statutory children's services since the Seebohm Report of the 1960s' (F. Williams, 2004a: 406). This Green Paper included proposals that would ensure services would focus around the needs of children and young people and would be more effective in safeguarding their interests. *Every Child Matters: Change for Children* emerged as an ongoing programme of action designed to transform children's services and the Children Act 2004 provided the legal framework that underpins this programme. Whilst the *Every Child Matters* Green Paper contained proposals mainly for England, the Children Act 2004 had implications for both England and Wales.[3]

The Children Act 2004 introduced similar provisions for England and Wales although specific measures were detailed separately because of differences between children's services in each country. The overall goals of improving the well-being of children and young people, and securing partnership and integration in children's services, are common to both England and Wales. Legislation to create an office of children's commissioner for England was also contained within the Children Act 2004. However, Wales had already provided a lead in this regard by the appointment of the first of the UK's four children's commissioners in 2001. There are important differences in the role and remit of the Commissioners for Wales, Northern Ireland, Scotland and England (Rees and Chaney, 2011; J. Williams, 2005). Interest in securing the participation of children and young people in policy processes has also occurred at different levels of government across the UK (Tisdall and Davis, 2004).

Cutting across all these policy agendas is a set of assumptions that child poverty and social disadvantage can best be tackled through combining economic and educational goals. Opportunities for people to access paid work or training and for their children to benefit from early years services were fundamental to the Labour government's social inclusion and social justice agenda (Cabinet Office, Social Exclusion Unit, 2001; Levitas, 1998) and were thus linked into childcare policy and funding streams. At the same time the National Childcare Strategy embraced other priorities including those relating to work–life balance and the promotion of equality and gender mainstreaming.

Overall, New Labour did shift the policy landscape relating to childcare and parental support, linked in to wider agendas to address economic matters and child poverty. Prior to an assessment of the impact of this national policy arena, it is important to recognize that the terrain has changed again with the transfer of UK government in 2010. This discussion will, therefore, now move to a consideration of UK Coalition government policies and their implications for families in a climate of severe economic austerity.

THE COALITION, THE 'BIG SOCIETY' AND WELFARE REFORM

> The Big Society is our positive alternative to Labour's failed big government approach, and it runs consistently through our policy programme. Our plans to reform public services, mend our broken society, and rebuild trust in politics are all part of our Big Society agenda: these plans involve redistributing power from the state to society; from the centre to local communities, giving people the opportunity to take more control over their lives. (Conservative Party, 2010: 1)

In May 2010 the UK General Election failed to return a majority government. Subsequent talks between the Conservative Party and the Liberal Democrat Party resulted in the formation of a UK Coalition government and their leaders, David Cameron and Nick Clegg, became Prime Minister and Deputy Prime Minister respectively. The research presented in this book was completed prior to the change in UK government. The consequences and long-term future of this landmark shift in party political leadership and partnership remain uncertain. However, it is important to consider how this significant period of change in the political environment at UK level is likely to impact on policymaking in Wales and the possible consequences for mothers, fathers and children living in Wales as well as in other regions of the UK.

The discussion in Chapter 2 and interview material with policy officers in Wales will point to some differences between Labour values in Wales and agendas pursued by New Labour in Westminster. Nevertheless, the divergence between policies made by the Welsh Government and agendas pursued by the UK Coalition government is more pronounced in view of party political differences. There are deep ideological differences with implications for the future trajectory of legislation and policy and for the likelihood that different social policy agendas will be pursued in the devolved nations. In order to explore the degree of continuity or ideological fissure following the change of UK government, the concept of the 'big society', associated with David Cameron's leadership, warrants critical scrutiny.

The idea of the 'big society' was presented within the Conservative Party's 2010 election campaign as an overarching philosophy that could summarize the party's vision for change and with implications for the range of Conservative policies. The concept is essentially a political slogan that has since been pursued under the UK Coalition government and subject to increasing criticism, if not outright mockery, in the wake of the cuts agenda. In a response to the concept, the Young Foundation offers a summary of its problematic status:

> The Big Society is a loose and rather baggy concept. Its short-term purpose was to signal to the right that a Conservative government would be willing to shrink the state, and to the left that it would care about society. It's already proved somewhat baffling to the public and has been much criticised for vagueness, for intellectual vacuity and for being blind both to history, and to what civil society is already doing. (2010: 3)

The Office for Civil Society within the Cabinet Office is charged with translating this policy idea into practice. Ideologically, the concept is close to neo-liberal political, social and economic priorities relating to the creation of a small state, privatization and minimal welfare support. However, it is presented in terms of a declaration of commitment to community empowerment, reform of public services and the encouragement of localism, understood as a culture of responsibility led by neighbourhood groups, charities and social enterprises. As UK Coalition government policies take shape, however, the economic strategy including deep cuts to public funding is giving rise to considerable alarm and critique (Dolphin, 2010a). The evidence shows that the most vulnerable in society will be hurt the most; this has implications for families with children and for the progress of poverty, inclusion and equality agendas (Daycare Trust, 2010; Dolphin, 2010b; UK Women's Budget Group, 2010). The deficit is being used as a platform from which to seek justification for cuts, a slashing of welfare state protection for those who need support and the reduction of the public sector. There are implications for those who rely on the welfare state for their employment or for service provision. Under current UK government agendas it seems certain that social divisions and inequalities are about to become deeper and more entrenched.

The most far-reaching changes announced by the UK Coalition government concern the radical reform of the welfare system set out in the *21st Century Welfare* consultation (Secretary of State for Work and Pensions,

2010a) followed immediately by the launch of the White Paper on *Universal Credit* (Secretary of State for Work and Pensions, 2010b) and the *Welfare Reform Bill* (Secretary of State for Work and Pensions, 2011). These proposals sit alongside planned deep and immediate cuts to welfare expenditure that are claimed to be essential in order to cut the fiscal deficit. The intention to target welfare expenditure was announced by the Chancellor of the Exchequer in the Emergency Budget of June 2010 and in the Comprehensive Spending Review in October 2010. As the Welsh Government does not have powers in relation to the benefits and tax credits system, these changes will impact on Wales as elsewhere in the UK. Indeed, in response to the UK Coalition government's Comprehensive Spending Review and budgetary measures, the Welsh Government published a report on the likely impact on Wales (WAG, 2010a). The report claimed that, given it is anticipated that the benefits and tax measures will be regressive across the UK, this will also be the case in Wales but with deeper impact because of existing high levels of poverty, including child poverty, and reliance on welfare benefits. In addition, the cuts to government departments will mean cuts to public services, and the Welsh Government observed that this will affect the living standards of those on low incomes, who are most reliant on those services. However, where its powers permit, and as a consequence of the block grant, the Welsh Government has some opportunity to mitigate some of the impact within very narrow parameters. The Welsh Government has, for example, declared continued commitment to the economically disadvantaged in relation to policies such as free breakfast clubs, free prescriptions, education maintenance allowances for school and college students and support for students studying in higher education.

Prior to the change of UK government, concern had been expressed that the global economic crisis of 2008 and its consequences were a threat to the social policy agendas of concern in this book: childcare, anti-poverty, social justice and gender equality. In the field of childcare provision, for example, the Daycare Trust was briefing policy-makers on the potential impact of the recession on the childcare market. As Joe Caluori observed in a Daycare Trust briefing paper:

> The weakness of demand-led finance is already being exposed by the recession as job losses are quickly followed by the loss of tax credit based funding to parents struggling to pay fees. If there are questions over whether it is possible to deliver a universal childcare offer in a mixed market, then the credit crunch will provide some of the answers. (Caluori, 2009: 4)

One of the policy recommendations that flowed from this briefing was for parents on lower incomes to receive 100 per cent of their childcare costs through tax credits rather than 80 per cent. However, the reforms to the tax credit system pursued by the UK Coalition government have moved in an opposite direction so that from April 2011 working parents have been able to claim only 70 per cent of their childcare costs. This is a move that will most affect working parents on the lowest incomes. It is a development that appears to be in tension with UK Coalition government claims that new policies will further incentivize work over reliance on welfare state benefits.

In a talk to Compass and the Fawcett Society in May 2009, Ruth Lister explored the impact of the economic recession on women. Women in families with children would be particularly vulnerable in view of their role as 'poverty managers' (2009: 1). Lister called for welfare benefits to be offered at adequate levels and highlighted the importance of women having access to financial resources in their own right. This is significant in view of planned cuts to universal welfare benefits including child benefit, which is usually paid to the main carer, so that women in particular will be affected by this historic shift in policy. Not only have rates of child benefit been frozen for a three-year period from April 2011, but from January 2013 the UK Coalition government has proposed to restrict eligibility and reduce child benefit where there is one parent earning over £50,000 in the household. In addition the Welfare Reform Act has introduced a benefit cap on the amount any family may receive from the welfare system, which will be imposed regardless of the number of children in a household. The cap includes child benefit in the calculation and will mean families with several children, and those facing high housing costs, may not receive current levels of financial support. Concern continues to be expressed by children's charities and others campaigning against these proposals that this will impact on children living in poor families, leading to an increase in child poverty levels and to problems such as homelessness for families with children.

The impact of economic austerity on women is a theme explored by Katherine Rake (2009) in a Fawcett Society report where she offers three major factors that influence how women will be affected by recession. First, the rise in female employment over the last thirty years means that more women will be affected as employees than in previous economic downturns. Second, the increased labour market participation of women and the increase in lone mother households mean that more families rely on women's income for their economic well-being and survival. Third, continuing inequalities between women and men mean that the recession will have a gendered impact:

> A number of factors make women less likely to be able to withstand the impact of the recession – women are more likely to live in poverty, especially in old age, have fewer financial assets, more likely to manage a household budget and act as shock absorbers when this changes, are more likely to experience violence, and as mothers and carers will need to make a complex set of decisions about their family and work life influenced by – among other things – the cost of childcare, the tax and benefit system, etcetera. (Rake, 2009: 4)

These are issues that should be held in view as UK Coalition government welfare policies start to bite. It seems likely that a different interpretation of 'political motherhood' and the role of the welfare state in providing support for childcare will take shape in this climate and will reinforce and deepen existing social class and ethnic divisions amongst mothers. However, these concerns also reveal that New Labour policies had failed to offer robust protection to families with young children, to women and to those living in poverty, since they were the first to be affected when the banking crisis and the economic downturn impacted the most vulnerable. In the concluding section New Labour policies will be assessed in relation to this claim and with regard to the legacy that was left as a new UK government with different ideological priorities took office.

CONCLUSION: WHO BENEFITS FROM CHILDCARE POLICY?

An assessment of 'who is benefiting and who not from existing care policies' (F. Williams, 2001: 487) can be illuminated through use of the framing concept introduced earlier in the chapter. This section will raise some initial questions and identify some themes that can be explored further through the personal accounts of mothers and fathers and the responses of policy officers in Chapters 3–5.

Childcare and family policy draws together a variety of different agendas, meaning that it is possible to find a range of master narratives or frames (Ball and Charles, 2006) within the policy texts. This complexity is partly an outcome of historic factors relating to policies for young children. There have been three main areas of policy and provision for young children: nursery education, childcare for working parents and welfare care for children in need (Penn, 2000). Whilst all three areas were re-examined under New Labour policy reform, these services cater for different, yet overlapping, needs and are based on different practices, philosophies and modes of regulation. In addition, New Labour reforms of each area were led by different government departments, albeit with the intention of achieving integration of services for children (Penn, 2000).

There are at least *four* different agendas that may frame how childcare was viewed in New Labour policy texts, which are being extended or revised as UK Coalition government policies take shape. These master narratives can be described as economic, children's needs/rights, 'work–life balance'/ gender equality and supporting parents. These four master narratives or frames are outlined next.

The *economic* frame constructs childcare mainly as a service for parents in paid work and as a mechanism for stimulating economic growth and encouraging people into the labour market. The frame links with the 'welfare to work' agenda (Lewis, 2002), thus connecting it to concerns over poverty and social exclusion as well as efforts to reduce welfare spending. By framing the role of childcare in this way, the possibilities for offering *universal* childcare for all parents and children that want it is closed off. Simultaneously, the focus on paid work as the route to tackling poverty restricts choices for parents, especially those on low incomes, who would like to care for their children at home. Arguably, it is this frame that is paramount in policy texts and the other frames identified here all intersect with, and are subservient to, economic priorities. The neglect of the value of unpaid caring work in policy undermines claims made within the other frames. In addition the focus on *social inclusion/exclusion* rather than on inequality positions problems of poverty, wealth and economic disadvantage in specific ways. This is a point made by Ruth Lister, who advised us to be wary of the shift 'from equality to social inclusion' (1998: 215) in welfare policies within New Labour's emerging agenda when it first took office:

> while we have a government committed to promoting *social inclusion*, it appears to have abandoned the goal of promoting greater *equality*. The question has to be whether, in the context of entrenched structural inequalities, genuine social inclusion, including the eradication of poverty, is possible without greater equality. (1998: 224)

What was missing from the New Labour economic agenda was a commitment to tackling poverty through *redistribution* of wealth and material resources, a model suggested by Levitas (1998). This had profound implications for the way in which New Labour could then meet some of the claims made in the context of the other frames identified later in this section. Where redistribution did occur, this was confined to the use of benefit and tax credit policy as the key mechanism for change (Harker and Oppenheim, 2010) and it is significant that this area of policy came under immediate attack by the UK Coalition government. With the transfer of power to the UK Coalition government in May 2010, there has been little protection in place from the ideological onslaught on the welfare state and on society's most vulnerable citizens currently evolving at significant pace.

The *children's needs/rights* frame focuses on meeting the interests of children. As Helen Penn and Vicky Randall observe, 'the child and child poverty constitute a positive, acceptable symbol for the government's overall social policy, as well as a rallying point for different strands within the Left' (2005: 83). Whilst this discourse may include claims of concern for the wellbeing and rights of all children, it is often directed towards children deemed to be vulnerable or at risk because of family poverty or perceived failure in parenting. It may be linked to a commitment to early years education and encouraging healthy child development based on the belief that early intervention will help address a wide variety of social problems later. The principles underpinning Sure Start and other area-based anti-poverty and community regeneration programmes share this view (Glass, 1999). The belief that it is necessary for social policy to break the 'cycle of deprivation' through tackling childhood poverty drives these programmes (Deacon, 2003). However, it is pertinent to ask how an agenda that is so cautious about the redistribution of wealth, and places so much emphasis on paid work as the antidote to social problems, can claim a universal commitment to children. Nevertheless, its symbolic role has been important in harnessing support for some progressive initiatives and will remain important for those wishing to challenge the potentially harmful impact of UK Coalition government reforms on families with children. It is significant that the debate in the House of Lords during January 2012 concerning the proposed benefit cap to families in receipt of welfare support was couched in relation to the concerns of some peers over the likely harmful impact on children. Despite objections, the benefit cap was retained in the Welfare Reform Act 2012.

The *'work–life balance'/gender equality* frame (Duncan, 2002; Glover, 2002; Lewis and Campbell, 2007) expresses an interest in enabling both mothers and fathers to undertake paid work and participate in care and leisure activities. Where gender equality is referred to in policy texts, it is generally confined to issues of work–life balance and to promoting equality in paid work opportunities. There has been less focus on how gender equity may be progressed in the domestic realm. Nevertheless, the frame offers opportunities for securing some rights for mothers and fathers and will need to be asserted strongly in the current climate, in which the public sector jobs that have traditionally offered important rights in this regard are being cut.

The *supporting parents* frame focuses on the role of government in providing assistance to, and working in partnership with, parents. In common with the other frames, this may embrace diverse discourses and policy agendas (Rake, 2001) and address different 'recipients' of policy initiatives. It may address the need to encourage *parent participation* in policy delivery, such as in local Sure Start programmes (Gustafsson and Driver, 2005). Alternatively it may relate to the expansion of the *parenting education* 'industry' (Miller and Sambell, 2003), embracing a view that (certain) parents may benefit from professional expertise if they are to discharge their role effectively. The childcare policy agenda includes both concerns whilst also espousing *parental choice* with regard to work–life balance and decisions over the kind of (formal/informal) childcare to be utilized. Alongside claims to provide various sources of support for parents, there is a strong emphasis on parental responsibilities couched in a moralizing rhetoric (Rake, 2001). In addition, the impact of differing parenting initiatives will be mediated by existing structures of privilege and disadvantage so that some parents will be more strongly placed to take advantage of opportunities based on 'choice' while others will be vulnerable to intervention if perceived to be failing.

These four policy frames – economic, children's needs/rights, 'work–life balance'/gender equality and supporting parents – have each presented the function of childcare policy in specific ways. The weakness of the New Labour project lay in the positioning of policies concerning care, support and well-being in relation to an *economic* agenda that celebrates 'paid work as the key route to citizenship' (Rake, 2001: 209) and as part of the shift from passive to active welfare (Lewis and Giullari, 2005). The interview material will illustrate the failure of this model to capture the needs, circumstances and wishes of parents in their diversity. Nevertheless, those agendas have offered some opportunities and benefits for (some) parents that are now being eroded by the UK Coalition government.

This chapter has provided an introduction to New Labour's, and the emergent UK Coalition government's, social policy agenda with regard to childcare and families. In the justification of childcare as an issue for policy attention, claims have been made that policies will extend well-being for mothers, fathers and children in a variety of ways through (a) the provision of choice for parents; (b) the extension of support to parents; (c) the promotion of gender equality and work–life balance; (d) the expansion of services in the interests of all children. It would be difficult to disagree that these promises make policy appear to be attractive and with something of benefit to all. Yet if we look beneath the surface a more complex picture emerges.

The 'master frame' that dominated New Labour childcare policy constructed it as an *economic* issue and as part of the welfare-to-work agenda (Ball and Charles, 2006). This limited the possibilities for the realization of claims around the principles of choice, support, equality and children's interests. These principles act as symbols designed to achieve broad-based political support but they are overshadowed by the 'master frame' driven by economic and moral priorities. This has left the way open for the UK Coalition government's current welfare agenda based on a punitive approach to the needs of families in poor and modest circumstances and with deep cuts to the public sector that will further limit choice, support and equality.

The linking of childcare and parenting policy so closely to the welfare to work agenda has to be questioned if social policy is to act as a vehicle for parental choice and support, gender equality and children's well-being. Pressures towards work intensification and the intensification of expectations concerning the conduct of parenting may contribute towards increased stress and hardship for many mothers, fathers and children. Those least able to negotiate those stresses for themselves because of existing inequalities, lack of support and material hardship may be subject to intervention couched in a moralizing framework.

The purpose of this research was to explore how mothers and fathers in different socio-economic circumstances organize childcare on a daily basis in the context of this shifting policy landscape. In response to the question that was posed earlier regarding who benefits from policy and who loses out

(F. Williams, 2001), the chapter has indicated some possibilities. However, this is no substitute for exploring these questions directly with mothers and fathers. Following and extending Dorothy Smith's claims that research should begin from women's experiences in order to better understand how these are 'socially organized' (1997: 393), the empirical chapters will explore the question of benefit and loss and the principles of choice, support, equality and well-being in the context of interview material. The research will add to the growing body of empirical research into parents' perspectives on childcare (Duncan et al., 2003; McDowell et al., 2005; Rahilly and Johnston, 2002; Vincent and Ball, 2001; Vincent et al., 2008) through exploring these within the context of Wales.

The National Childcare Strategy (DfEE, 1998) was launched by the UK government prior to devolution and the creation of the National Assembly for Wales in 1999. The strategy was, nevertheless, intended for implementation only in England; policy relating to the development of childcare in Wales was, at this time, delegated to the Secretary of State for Wales (DfEE, 1998; Welsh Office, 1998). Similar arrangements for delegation with respect to childcare policy applied also to Scotland and Northern Ireland. Following devolution in Wales in 1999, the National Assembly for Wales took over responsibility from the Welsh Office for childcare policy. The Welsh Government has since been able to prepare a regional childcare agenda for Wales but within limits pertaining to the reserved powers of the UK government. The differences in policy priorities between the UK at national level and the devolved nations are becoming more pronounced with the election of the UK Coalition government with an agenda for reform that has proved highly contentious during the early years of office. The next chapter will explore what devolution means for the making of social policy in Wales within this changing political terrain.

2

Devolution, Gender and Childcare: A Distinctive Policy Agenda in Wales?

INTRODUCTION

Policy agendas in Wales following devolution and the creation of the National Assembly for Wales (NAfW) in 1999 are the focus in this chapter. Policy documents and interview material with regional and local policy officers are analysed in order to explore the making of childcare policy in Wales. The chapter pursues the question of how much scope there is for doing things differently in Wales with reference to the making of childcare policy and the Welsh Government's commitment to the key political values of equality, social justice and inclusion, and children's rights. Policy officers' perspectives on devolution, the role of the Welsh Government and opportunities for creating 'made in Wales' policies will be presented. Claims that Wales has been able to create a distinctive social policy agenda will be evaluated. In Chapter 5 policy officers' understanding of childcare policy and its connection with other Welsh Government policy agendas will be analysed and their views on issues of childcare policy delivery, achievements and challenges will be presented.

These perspectives help to point to some of the emphases in policy. In Chapters 3 and 4, through interview material with mothers and fathers, the book will proceed to illustrate how those emphases may not always connect with parental preferences, needs and circumstances with implications for family well-being and access to support.

POLICY INNOVATION IN POST-DEVOLUTION WALES: KEY POLITICAL VALUES

In Chapter 1 an overview of childcare, parenting and family policy was offered with reference to the national level in the UK. This picture is moderated once we move to policy agendas in Wales following devolution and the creation of the National Assembly for Wales in 1999.[1] This created a space for the making of childcare policy at a regional level and with regard to the needs and preferences of parents and children in Welsh communities. Policy development is also informed by overarching priorities referred to as 'themes' and 'strategies' by the Welsh Government. Policy is thus connected with the Welsh Government's social justice agenda and its commitment to mainstream equality of opportunity and gender equality across all policy developments (Chaney and Fevre, 2002; Day, 2006; NAfW, 2004; Winckler, 2009). Childcare policy has also been linked to the Welsh Government's agenda in extending the rights of children and young people (WAG, 2004a). In Chapter 1 it was argued that, although New Labour had connected childcare to gender equality/work–life balance, children's needs, supporting parents and social inclusion agendas, it was *economic* matters that were intended to drive policy. With the emergency budget and the spending review, fuelled by the austerity drive of the UK Coalition government, economic matters continue to direct social policy allied to a different ideological agenda. The scope for regional childcare policy divergence will be modified by national economic policy but the question remains how far there is political will and opportunity to pursue alternative policy routes within Wales. This chapter seeks to examine this question.

What then is the scope for 'doing things differently' in Wales (Drakeford, 2005) in relation to childcare and parenting support policies? How does policy divergence link to the political values of gender equality, social justice and children's rights? Comparative research in the field of childcare, parenting and gender regimes tends to compare the UK as a whole with other European welfare states (Himmelweit and Sigala, 2004; Leon, 2005; Mahon, 2002). Yet this may not be the appropriate unit for comparative analysis in the context of devolution. The Welsh Government has powers to develop and implement policy in a number of key areas including education and training, health, housing, social services and local government. The UK government has retained control over other areas such as employment, social security and financial and economic issues, and the Welsh Government has had neither primary legislative nor revenue-raising powers (Ball and Charles, 2006). However, as devolution has unfolded, the Welsh Government has gained new powers with regard to proposing and developing legislation which may be passed by the National Assembly for Wales. The Government of Wales Act 2006 established the formal separation of the legislature and the executive that commenced after the National Assembly election of May 2007. The Act also introduced a new category of legislation for Wales in Assembly Measures but the National Assembly for Wales had to seek legislative competence from the UK Parliament in order to pass those measures within the devolved areas or subjects. More recently, devolution has progressed further following the referendum in Wales in March 2011, in which the Welsh electorate delivered a majority in favour of the extension of the Welsh Government's law-making powers.

This means that the Welsh Government can develop and propose law on all issues within the twenty devolved areas and the National Assembly for Wales has the power to pass new laws in those areas without having to seek agreement from the UK Parliament.

Devolution is an interesting arena for social policy analysis given that 'the degree of devolution is greater in social policy areas than in matters of economic policy' (Mooney et al., 2006: 487). This remains the case despite the changes following the referendum because the Welsh Government still has no powers to make law in relation to taxation or welfare benefits. Childcare policy connects with a range of both devolved and reserved issues, so the Welsh Government is able to be innovative but within significant limits. The question remains how far the UK government's control of employment policy, taxation and benefits has encouraged the economic framing of childcare that has been identified at the national level to reign supreme also at the regional level in Wales.

Devolution and the creation of the National Assembly for Wales in 1999 brought into being a new stakeholder in politics and this is relevant to the book's concern with the relationship between the state, childcare and gender. Some gender theorists have seen the state as offering potential for political engagement despite claims that it acts in patriarchal and capitalist interests (Connell, 1990). A framework is required that does justice to this for, as Nickie Charles points out with regard to gender politics, 'feminist social movements engage with the state by confronting it *and* by working within it; it is experienced as both enabling and constraining, as oppressive and responsive to pressure for change' (2000: 28). In viewing the state as a site of struggle and as contradictory, there is scope for progressive movements to exploit loopholes and reshape policy. The delivery of welfare policies, including those concerning childcare, is one arena that may offer opportunities for political activity, providing potential for reshaping the 'gender regime' that comprises divisions of labour, sites of bureaucratic power and structures of emotional attachment (Connell, 1990). The structure and culture of gender relations within the Welsh Government as a regional state institution is potentially distinct from that of the UK national state although contained by it in many ways. The picture is further complicated in that responsibility for the delivery of childcare policy lies with local EYDCPs (Tanner et al., 2006), meaning there is scope for variation across local authority areas in Wales. Localized and culturally based conceptions of the relations between childcare and gender may prevail, with implications for policy.

This section explores childcare and parenting policy in Wales in relation to the commitment to gender equality, social justice and children's rights claimed by the Welsh Government. Through critical analysis of public policy texts, the chapter examines the connections between childcare and these wider themes and values. The concept of 'framing' that was introduced in Chapter 1 is used to guide policy analysis once more. What is significant is that devolution may have provided a space for alternative policy discourses to achieve hegemony in Wales. The chapter thus seeks to analyse the framing of policy in public texts in Wales and outline the delivery mechanisms and funding streams. This will provide the basis for a consideration of the degree to which devolution has enabled the makers of childcare policy to pursue an agenda that is distinctive and shaped towards the needs of mothers, fathers and children in Wales. The chapter will offer a framework against which it will be possible to assess the perspectives and experiences of mothers, fathers and policy officers in subsequent chapters.

This analysis is based on Welsh Government policy texts relating to three arenas that have been claimed as a priority. These arenas are significant in that they represent guiding principles or political values that are claimed to drive the policymaking process across the whole range of agendas for which the Welsh Government is responsible. The concept of 'inclusiveness' has been very significant in the way in which devolution has been understood in Wales as an opportunity for a new way of doing politics (Laffin and Thomas, 2000; McAllister, 2000) and in the Welsh Government's policy agenda (Chaney and Fevre, 2001). The three guiding principles selected for discussion in relation to childcare can all be linked to this attention to 'being inclusive'. These priorities are, first, those concerning gender equality; second, those relating to social justice and social inclusion issues; and, finally, those addressing children's rights. Each is discussed in turn.

Gender equality

According to Rees, the National Assembly for Wales was set up with 'a clear intention to avoid the Westminster style of government' (2002: 62), with implications for gender politics and issues of inclusive participation in governance (Chaney and Fevre, 2001). The progress of the Welsh Government in pursuing equality of opportunity and gender equality gives some grounds for optimism and lends support to the claim that 'devolution offers an unprecedented opportunity for the furthering of equality in Wales' (Charlotte Williams, 2001: 57). There is evidence of political values and initiatives that may reshape the political opportunity structure (Ball and Charles, 2006; Charles, 2004; NAfW, 2001a) and this can be seen in part as an outcome of feminist struggle.

When the National Assembly for Wales was established through the Government of Wales Act 1998 this legislation included a statutory duty that it should:

> make appropriate arrangements with a view to securing that its functions are exercised with due regard to the principle that there should be equality of opportunity for all people. (Government of Wales Act 1998: Section 120)

The inclusion of the equality clause was the result of successful lobbying by equality campaigners including those active in the women's movement (Chaney, 2004; Chaney and Fevre, 2002). This duty to promote equality is enshrined in the structure and operations of the Welsh Government. It means that all policies and practices have to be reviewed by the Welsh Government to ensure they fulfil the equality duty. As Chaney observes, the Duty 'is singular in its non-prescriptive phrasing and all-embracing scope and is an *imperative* that applies to *all* people and *all* functions of government' (2004: 66). The statutory duty should be considered in relation to further legislation at the UK level with implications for the pursuit of equality, including the Race Relations Amendment Act 2000, the Disability Discrimination Act 2005 and the Equality Act 2006.

Changes in the patterns of women's political representation in Wales in the context of devolution have also attracted some interest (Edwards and McAllister, 2002; Mackay, 2004). In 1999 the first elections to the National Assembly for Wales were held and a high proportion (40 per cent) of women representatives was returned. In 2003 this proportion increased to 50 per cent, which was hailed by the *Guardian* newspaper as a 'world record' for a legislative body (Watt, 2003). This reduced to 47 per cent in the election of 2007 (Rees and Chaney, 2011). Some of the women who were elected to the Assembly had previously been involved in equality issues (Rees, 2002; Charlotte Williams, 2001). Both the Labour Party and Plaid Cymru had adopted policies designed to improve the representation of women for the Assembly elections (Charles, 2010; Edwards and McAllister, 2002). This new gender balance in political representation, coupled with the Statutory Duty, raised expectations about the development of policies that would address women's issues. Further confirmation of the Welsh Government's commitment to the promotion of equal opportunities was the inclusion of this as a cross-cutting theme and value in its first strategic plan *www.betterwales.com* (NAfW, 2000a) (Chaney and Fevre, 2002).[2] The key principle driving developments is that of mainstreaming equality, including gender equality, in all policy developments (Edwards, 2004; NAfW, 2004; Rees, 2002).

The European Union and New Labour as well as the Welsh Government are all committed to mainstreaming equality (Beveridge et al., 2000; Duncan, 2002). The policy review report on 'Mainstreaming Equality' (NAfW, 2004) proposed the following definition of 'mainstreaming':

> 'Mainstreaming' equality is about the integration of respect for diversity and equality of opportunity principles, strategies and practices into the every day [sic] work of the Assembly and other public bodies. It means that equality issues should be included from the outset as an integral part of the policy-making and service delivery process and the achievement of equality should inform all aspects of the work of every individual within an organisation. The success of mainstreaming should be measured by evaluating whether inequalities have been reduced. (NAfW, 2004: 6, para. 2.3)

This definition of mainstreaming remains open to competing interpretations, particularly with regard to how a reduction in inequalities is to be measured. How, for example, would the Welsh Government measure a reduction of inequalities with regard to childcare and parenting policy? This question can be examined in relation to the distinction between role equity and role change issues (Gelb and Palley, 1982). Role equity issues can be accommodated within the discourse of liberalism and underpin policies directed towards equal rights and social justice such as campaigns for equal pay and equal access to existing opportunities. Role change issues, however, are more challenging as they involve a redistribution of resources and a fundamental review of existing gendered practices (Ball and Charles, 2006). Mainstreaming may be limited to the issues of equal pay and equal access associated with a role equity agenda. However, if gender mainstreaming addresses role change issues this would entail a challenge to the 'bread-winner/home-maker gender contract' (Rees, 1999: 179) and would seek to redistribute labour at home as well as in paid work.

Childcare and parenting policy offers an ideal arena in which to explore how gender mainstreaming operates within the Welsh Government in practice, especially with regard to the declared goal of achieving a reduction in inequalities. Devolution, the statutory equality duty and support for gender mainstreaming provide a specific context for the pursuit of childcare policy in Wales and there is the potential to raise some important questions about gender relations in caring for children. The emphasis on gender equality as a guiding political value may act as a 'policy window' (Marshall, 1999: 64) for activists wishing to ensure that gender claims are addressed in key areas.

Social justice issues

The Welsh Government established the promotion of social justice and social inclusion as a key priority during its first term of office. Following devolution, in the first strategic plan *www.betterwales.com* (NAfW, 2000a) the guiding principles of 'A Made in Wales Agenda' were proposed. One of the three major themes identified was 'Tackling Social Disadvantage', involving 'the development of an inclusive society where everyone has the chance to fulfil their potential' (NAfW, 2000a: 7). In the *Plan for Wales 2001*, 'Social Inclusion' is identified as one of the guiding principles (NAfW, 2001a: 3). This focus takes place in a context in which poverty levels in Wales exceed those in the UK overall (Bransbury, 2004) and the problem of low pay for those in work has been a long-standing concern (Brooksbank, 2001). The focus on social justice and on tackling high levels of poverty continued as a priority following the Assembly elections of May 2007 that led to a coalition between the Labour Party and Plaid Cymru. The *One Wales* (WAG, 2007) joint party agreement referred to equality within the context of establishing a fair and just society. However, there was a notable absence of focused attention in this document on the matter of gender equality.

Tackling social disadvantage has been addressed in partnership with local government and funded through the Communities First initiative, which targets the most deprived areas of Wales for community regeneration programmes in which a variety of agencies work with local communities to tackle local problems. In addition to this targeting of specific geographical communities, all local authorities are charged with a duty under the Local Government Act 2000 to develop a 'community strategy' for their area in collaboration with local communities and organizations in the public, private and voluntary sectors. Among other things, these are expected to consider the issues of poverty and social disadvantage (NAfW, 2001a).

The discourse of social inclusion examined in Chapter 1 appears to be as prominent in Wales as it has been in England, which suggests that New Labour had achieved hegemony in the political language and 'master narratives' adopted to drive welfare reform. There has certainly been considerable passion in the way the Welsh Government has progressed the commitment to 'inclusiveness' (Chaney and Fevre, 2001). In Chapter 1 the early concern that the New Labour focus on social exclusion could sideline issues of equality and redistribution (Lister, 1998) was highlighted. The Welsh Government has declared itself to be committed to *both* tackling social exclusion *and* pursuing equality. In this sense there is the possibility that social inclusion/exclusion has been understood in different ways in Wales from England. There may be greater support in Wales for a redistributive egalitarian understanding of social inclusion (Levitas, 1998) and this represents a difference in the framing of social justice issues that could provide opportunities for anti-poverty social movement organizations seeking to influence policy. However, in the absence of Welsh Government control of employment, taxation and welfare benefits policy, this could remain largely a difference of style and vision rather than practice. With the formation of the UK Coalition government and the extension of the Welsh Government's law-making powers there could be greater social policy divergence between the national and regional levels of governance in the future. In view of high levels of material disadvantage in Wales and the priorities of the Welsh Government to tackle poverty, a policy theme to be considered further in this chapter, the scope for conflict between these layers of governance could be considerable.

As Paul Chaney and Ralph Fevre observe, 'if "inclusiveness" is to be anything more than an effective word for conjuring up the *Zeitgeist* of devolution in Wales post-1995, further conceptual clarity is needed' (2001: 43). With this in mind the interviews with policy officers at regional level explored understandings of inclusion and it was suggested that there was a difference of emphasis in Wales, confirming claims that different political values have been a priority for Labour in post-devolution Wales (Sullivan, 2004).

The Welsh Government's anti-poverty and social inclusion work has particularly focused on child poverty (Bransbury, 2004; Winckler, 2009) and can be allied to New Labour's commitment to end child poverty. The *Report of the Child Poverty Task Group* went out for consultation in June 2004 (CPTG, 2004) and the Welsh Government subsequently launched a Child Poverty Strategy for Wales, *A Fair Future for Our Children* (WAG, 2005a). The Task Group had identified improved childcare provision as a route to tackling child poverty and subsequently made recommendations in relation to the need for flexible employment policies, for the provision of accessible and affordable childcare and quality childcare provision for disabled children. The Child Poverty Strategy for Wales referred to early years services, Sure Start, and Childcare and Family Support as arenas that would form part of the framework to tackle poverty and promote the well-being of children.

One study relating to children in Wales (Crowley and Winckler, 2008) estimated that 13 per cent of all children in Wales live in severe poverty. The report identified the provision of routes into employment as one strand of a policy response to tackle child poverty. This was linked strongly to recognition of the parenting role and the importance of improving childcare provision with regard to affordability, accessibility and flexibility. The authors also point to the need to maximize income for families, including through improvements to the delivery and take-up of welfare benefits and tax credits. However, this report was confined to exploring the potential of policy measures open to the Welsh Government, meaning that proposals to increase the national minimum wage and the levels of benefits and tax credits were acknowledged as an area of potential relevance outside the study's brief.

Although the Crowley and Winckler report accepts that routes into sustainable paid employment can be a major way of reducing child poverty, it is also acknowledged that this must be done in ways that are compatible with parenting: 'it would be a major policy failure if measures to tackle child poverty by encouraging more parents into work resulted in poorer parental support for those children' (Crowley and Winckler, 2008: 31). The report provides useful insights into the childcare problems faced by parents when moving into work which corresponds with some of the issues reported by parents in this research that will be presented in Chapter 4.

Commitment to reducing child poverty in Wales has been reaffirmed by the Welsh Government in the *Child Poverty Strategy for Wales* (WAG, 2011a). The Strategy is linked to the *Children and Families (Wales) Measure 2010* (WAG, 2010b), which placed a duty on the Welsh Government to publish a Child Poverty Strategy for Wales. The measure also introduced a requirement for each local authority and public body in Wales to develop a strategy to address child poverty. The updated Strategy continues to focus on tackling child poverty through providing pathways for parents into employment. In recognition that low-paid employment may not resolve the problem of family poverty, there is also a commitment to skills investment to help families on a low income progress into well-paid employment. This commitment is set out at the same time as there is recognition that the impact of the recent economic recession and current fiscal cutbacks may operate in an opposite direction. The Strategy revisits the need for more accessible and affordable childcare to enable more parents to enter the labour market. The Strategy recommits to the same key goals and mechanisms as before whilst acknowledging that the economic and political climate will pose a challenge. This regrettably makes for unconvincing reading in that there is a clear tension between commitment, strategy and the current direction of wider economic and political change.

Children's welfare and children's rights

New Labour claimed to place children's needs and interests at the heart of its policy agenda. This child-centred approach has been, and continues to be, highly visible in Wales. At times the Welsh Government has claimed the focus on children and young people as one of the ways in which Wales is following a distinctive route. The making of childcare policy in Wales can be understood in relation to this celebration of children's rights.

Wales was unique in the UK in that it was the first country to appoint an independent Children's Commissioner, the late Mr Peter Clarke, who took up office in March 2001. This is an approach supported by the United Nations Committee on the Rights of the Child in promoting the implementation of the United Nations Convention on the Rights of the Child (UNCRC) (J. Williams, 2005). At the time that the Welsh Government made a commitment to appointing the Children's Commissioner, the UK government was unwilling to go down this route (Bransbury, 2004). According to Lynda Bransbury, the Welsh Government's decision 'was therefore an immediate demonstration of the possibilities created by devolution. It was also tangible evidence of a rights-based approach and the promise of new and more collaborative governance in Wales' (2004: 178). It is significant that the first Act of Parliament specific to a devolved Wales was the *Children's Commissioner for Wales Act 2001*, which extended the powers of the Children's Commissioner for Wales (Catriona Williams, 2003). According to the first Children's Commissioner for Wales, this Act represented 'a small piece of legislative history' in that this was 'the first time that a public official has been charged with certain particular responsibilities under the United Nations Convention on the Rights of the Child' (Clarke, 2002: 288). Although there are now Children's Commissioners for Wales, Northern Ireland, Scotland and England, their role and powers are defined in different ways. Wales also remains exceptional in that the Children's Commissioner 'has the most extensive powers to provide advice and assistance and to deal with complaints and investigations in individual cases' (J. Williams, 2005: 41).

The Children's Commissioner is independent and has powers to review the policies and activities of the Welsh Government itself. The establishment of the Office of the Children's Commissioner was a firm example of the commitment of the Welsh Government to affirming the welfare and rights of children and young people in ways that may be distinctive for Wales. This was also seen as an indication of the commitment to a style of governance that is open, inclusive and accessible (Catriona Williams, 2003).

In placing children and young people at the heart of its policy agendas the Welsh Government also adopted its Core Aims for Children and Young People (WAG, 2004a). These are informed by the principles of the United Nations Convention on the Rights of the Child and the core aims are intended to underpin all services for children and young people. Policy in Wales has evolved within this framework of concern for meeting children and young people's needs *and* rights and ensuring policies are integrated. The Welsh Government's Core Aims for Children and Young People are to ensure children and young people:

1 have a flying start in life and the best possible basis for their future growth and development
2 have access to a comprehensive range of education, training and learning opportunities, including acquisition of essential personal and social skills
3 enjoy the best possible physical and mental, social and emotional health, including freedom from abuse, victimisation and exploitation
4 have access to play, leisure, sporting and cultural activities
5 are listened to, treated with respect, and are able to have their race and cultural identity recognised
6 have a safe home and a community that supports physical and emotional wellbeing
7 are not disadvantaged by child poverty

(WAG, 2004a: 1)

The emergence of policies for children and young people in Wales following devolution had implications for service delivery locally; they set the foundations for the arrangements at the local authority area level of governance today. The publication of *Extending Entitlement: Supporting Young People in Wales* (NAfW, 2000b) and *Children and Young People: A Framework for Partnership* (NAfW, 2000c) started a process directed towards improving services for children and young people and ensuring their participation in developments (NAfW, 2001b).

In July 2002 the Welsh Government issued a guidance set entitled *Improving Services for Children and Young People: A Framework for Partnership* (WAG, 2002b) containing proposals designed to integrate policies and services for children and young people and to secure their involvement in service delivery at the local level. The priority was 'to make the planning and delivery of services for children and young people by local agencies more coherent and cross cutting' (WAG, 2002c: 1, para. 1.1). The guidance proposed the establishment of local *Children and Young People's Partnerships* (CYPP) charged with the task of developing a strategic framework for all services for children and young people aged from birth to twenty-five years. The framework would take the form of a five-year strategy for children and young people that would also link to the local authority's *Community Strategy*. It also proposed that there should be two sub-groups. One sub-group would be a *Children's Partnership* for children aged from birth to ten years with a role to improve services in the context of guidance issued in *Early Entitlement: Supporting Children and Families in Wales* (WAG, 2002d). The Children's Partnership was to produce a Children's Plan for the local authority area. The other sub-group would be a *Young People's Partnership*, which would have a comparable role for the eleven to twenty-five years age group in the context of the *Extending Entitlement* (WAG, 2002e) guidance. This Partnership would be expected to develop a Young People's Strategy for the area.

The Welsh Government also introduced a new funding stream called *Cymorth*, the Children and Youth Support Fund (WAG, 2002f), beginning in 2003. This was a replacement for five funding streams that had previously been separate (Sure Start, Children and Youth Partnership Fund, National Childcare Strategy, Youth Access Initiative, Play Grant) and responsibility for administering the fund was placed with the local CYP Partnerships. The key aim of Cymorth was 'to make targeted services more effective in breaking the cycle of deprivation that affects children and young people's life chances' (WAG, 2004b: 6). Significantly, in the context of this research, family and parenting support was identified within the areas of priority for Cymorth funding.

Whilst it will be clear that the Welsh Government was providing a strong lead in matters relating to the well-being of children and young people in Wales, there were also developments at UK level that were presented in Chapter 1, including *Every Child Matters: Change for Children* (DfES, 2003), which became an ongoing programme of action designed to transform children's services, and the Children Act 2004 provided the legal framework that underpins this programme.

The *Every Child Matters* Green Paper contained proposals mainly for England, whilst the *Children Act 2004* had implications for both England and Wales.[3] The Act introduced similar provisions for England and Wales with specific measures to reflect differences between children's services in each country. The goals of improving the well-being of children and young people, and securing partnership and integration in children's services, are common to legislation and policies in England and Wales. Part Three of the *Children Act 2004* is specific to Wales:

- *Section 25* of the Act introduced a duty for each children's services authority (the local authority) in Wales to make arrangements to ensure cooperation between the authority, relevant partners and other relevant bodies to improve the well-being of children in the area.
- *Section 26* of the Act gave the Welsh Government the power to require local authorities to develop a plan for services to children and young people.
- *Section 27* of the Act concerns the requirement that local authorities each appoint a lead director for children and young people's services and designate an elected member as the lead member for those services.
- *Section 28* of the Act concerns arrangements to safeguard and promote the welfare of children and applies to key organizations that have contact with children and young people.[4]

The Act has thus enabled the Welsh Government to build on the original framework arrangements by putting them on a statutory footing. Each Children's Services Authority is required under the Act to 'have regard to the importance of parents and other persons caring for children in improving the well-being of children' [Children Act 2004: Section 25 (3)]. Parents are taken into account in the planning process but only in relation to the needs of the child. The focus is on the child or young person first rather than the family as a whole. This may not always be helpful in relation to addressing the needs of any adults with caring responsibilities for the child; this consideration will be explored later with reference to the research material. Nevertheless, there is recent indication that the Welsh Government has recognized the value of designing services that address the needs of the whole family alongside meeting the needs of the child or young person. The new *Child Poverty Strategy for Wales* (WAG, 2011a) and the *Children and Families (Wales) Measure 2010* (WAG, 2010b) that preceded it both use a discourse that celebrates the need for 'integrated services' for families based on the offer of 'holistic support'. The main centre of attention for this 'whole family' approach appears to be those families most affected by poverty or where there are safeguarding concerns for the child:

> There is emerging consensus, and evidence from Flying Start, that the best way of supporting families, particularly those families in poverty, is through an integrated, whole-family approach. (WAG, 2011a: 25)

Initiatives that have flowed from this shift of focus from the child to the whole family include the *Integrated Family Support Services* (IFSS) policy for vulnerable families and *Families First* for families living in poverty.

Three areas of Welsh Government policy have been reviewed: gender equality, social justice and children's welfare/rights. These were also areas addressed in New Labour social policy at UK government level and discussed in Chapter 1. However, these values may be understood in different ways in Wales and this is a matter for further consideration with regard to the research material to be presented as the book unfolds.

THE SHAPING OF CHILDCARE POLICY IN WALES, 1999–2012

To what extent are the policy processes around childcare and parenting driven by the Welsh Government's principles of gender equality, children's rights and social justice? In order to explore this question, this section begins with a historical reconstruction of the evolution of childcare policy in Wales during the period from 1999 to 2012. The major policy texts and initiatives are summarized in Table 2.1.

Following devolution, policy-makers in Wales have been free to develop their own agenda for childcare but within limits. Certain limits are a result of the reserve powers of the UK government in areas such as taxation, welfare benefits and maternity rights. Other limits come from the power of dominant discourses to shape what can be imagined. Childcare policy in Wales has primarily been shaped by New Labour's agenda for childcare set out in the National Childcare Strategy (DfEE, 1998) but with some evidence of divergence in relation to the Welsh Government's key values.

Table 2.1: Childcare policy in Wales, 1999–2012

Date	Policy document
1998	*The National Childcare Strategy in Wales*, Welsh Office
1999	*Childcare in Wales*, Welsh Affairs Select Committee
2001	*National Childcare Strategy Task Force Report*, NCTSF
2002	*Childcare Action Plan*, WAG
2003	Childcare Working Group established by Welsh Government chaired by Deputy Minister for Economic Development and Transport
2004	*Childcare Working Group Interim Report*, WAG CWG
2005	*The Childcare Strategy for Wales: Childcare is for Children*, WAG
2006	*Childcare and Early Years Provision in Wales: A Study of Parents' Use, Views and Experiences*, Bryson et al., research commissioned by DfES and WAG
2010	*Childcare and Early Years Survey Wales 2009*, Smith et al., report by NCSR for WAG
2010	*Children and Families (Wales) Measure*, WAG
2011	*Nurturing Children, Supporting Families: Our Policy Priorities for Childcare*, WAG

By tracing the process of policy change in this area, it is possible to identify which social movement organizations sought to influence policy and how the political and discursive opportunity structures influenced their framing of claims in relation to childcare and associated agendas. The analysis of childcare policy in Wales is based on Welsh Government policy documents and debates pertaining to gender equality, social justice and childcare. The Welsh Affairs Select Committee report on *Childcare in Wales* (1999) also provided a starting point in illuminating potential themes and tensions in the policy processes surrounding this issue. In June 1998 *The National Childcare Strategy in Wales* (Welsh Office, 1998) was published. This consultation document attracted considerable criticism from interested parties and, according to the Welsh Affairs Select Committee, 'was a disappointment to many' (1999: Introduction, para. 1). Critics claimed that it remained too close to the English strategy in the proposals, did not reflect Welsh differences and did not incorporate views put forward during consultation in Wales and by the Childcare Strategy Task Group that had been set up by the Welsh Office. As a consequence, the Select Committee on Welsh Affairs undertook an inquiry into childcare in Wales. Its report was published in May 1999. The select committee provided an opening in the political opportunity structure at a crucial point in the history of Wales, shortly before the transfer of power to the National Assembly for Wales. Social movement organizations with an interest in childcare had an unprecedented opportunity to express their views at a time of considerable optimism about the future of Welsh politics. This chapter will consider those organizations which gave evidence, how their arguments were framed and their subsequent involvement in the policymaking process. A wide variety of organizations took the opportunity to submit evidence, including organizations from the voluntary sector, industry and employment, early years education and childcare. There were three submissions from bodies with an obvious concern with gender equality issues: the Equal Opportunities Commission (EOC) in Wales, Chwarae Teg (Fair Play) and the Minority Ethnic Women's Network (MEWN). The Equal Opportunities Commission was set up by the sex discrimination legislation in the 1970s and was a quasi-governmental organization that was replaced by the Equality and Human Rights Commission in October 2007. Chwarae Teg was established in 1992 with the aim of improving the economic circumstances of women in Wales. It has sought to expand childcare provision and has been involved as a manager of various childcare projects. MEWN was established in 1991 on the initiative of the then director of EOC Wales and the Welsh Women's European Network in order to redress the low representation of minority ethnic women in the voluntary sector. The other organization that was very influential in the development of childcare policy was the Welsh Local Government Association (WLGA). Feminist activists were key to these organizations, either because they had been involved in setting them up (as with Chwarae Teg) or because they occupied key positions within them. With the exception of WLGA, there is a sense in which they emerged from social movement organizations or were established as a result of social movement activity; thus, although they play key political roles, they are positioned within the political opportunity structure as both insiders and outsiders.

The EOC's submission framed childcare within equal opportunities discourse and related it to economic needs; its main focus was on the achievement of gender equality through participation in the labour market. This can be seen as an example of strategic framing, with arguments being articulated in a way that will resonate with dominant cultural frames and, consequently, have a chance of influencing policy development. Chwarae Teg's submission concentrated on making an economic case for childcare and its interest in gender equality was expressed in terms of removing barriers to women's entering paid work. In both these submissions childcare was framed within a role equity discourse in relation to paid work and the needs of the economy. MEWN was the only organization that framed childcare in relation to the specific and different needs of women. Whilst the organization would not describe itself as feminist, it does support and provide women-only training as part of a positive action strategy. In its submission it outlined its interest in the provision of women-only training in childcare to meet the cultural and religious preferences of some Muslim women. Its arguments were, therefore, articulated in a way that did not resonate with the dominant discourse of gender equity and mainstreaming. The framing of childcare needs in terms of gender difference and separatism poses a challenge to dominant discourses of equality, and MEWN encountered some resistance from members of the select committee. In this instance, only through reference to cultural and religious differences was MEWN able to sustain an argument that women may have needs that are different from men's.

The WLGA argued for a child-focused policy that located childcare within a wider package of initiatives for children. The discourse it mobilized was one of children's rights. In most of the other submissions childcare was not linked to questions of gender equality and/or the needs of women, and those organizations that did state this as a priority were more likely to be taken seriously when the link between childcare and gender equality was located in a role equity and economic efficiency discourse. It is significant that feminists who had been active in the women's movement of the 1970s were amongst those framing the arguments for childcare both in terms of equal opportunities and economic efficiency and in terms of children's rights. Arguments constructed in terms of difference, such as those advanced by MEWN, were subsequently marginalized.

Following devolution, the National Assembly for Wales had to take the National Childcare Strategy forward and in February 2001 the Minister for Health and Social Services established a National Childcare Strategy

Task Force (NCSTF) with a brief to develop a new childcare action plan. A significant number of those organizations that had submitted evidence to the select committee were represented as members of the task force. Hence there was a sense of continuity in the kinds of organizations that have been able to influence policy development; those that framed childcare in ways that resonated with a role equity discourse were rewarded with further incorporation into policymaking arenas.

The National Childcare Strategy Task Force presented its report in November 2001 and this laid the foundation for subsequent childcare policy in Wales (WAG, 2002g, 2005b). The report placed emphasis on putting the needs of children first as part of an extensive programme of measures for children. This indicates that the political and discursive opportunity structure has been open to organizations that articulated their arguments in terms of children's rights and/or in terms of economic efficiency. This resonated with the discourse of equality institutionalized within the Welsh Government. Thus the minister for health and social services, in her fore-word to the report, wrote:

> we continue to recognise that an effective strategy for childcare can improve the opportunities of many people to access employment and training. *Women in particular – although not exclusively – are likely to benefit in this respect. An adequate supply of good quality childcare therefore helps to meet the Assembly's economic aspirations and promotes equality of opportunity.* (NCSTF, 2001: 2, my emphasis)

Here childcare is seen as enabling women to participate in the workforce. The link between expanded childcare and opportunities for women is taken to be so self-evident that the difficulties and challenges involved are glossed over. Childcare is seen as a means of enabling mothers to combine caring for children with paid employment and as a means of social inclusion. It is framed as an economic issue and as part of the welfare-to-work agenda of New Labour. The discourses that have resonance within the new political and discursive opportunity structure in Wales, therefore, are those of children's rights, equal opportunities and social inclusion through economic opportunity. The alternative discourse of women's rights and gender difference has been abandoned. Thus demands for childcare are now framed in terms of children's rights, equal opportunities and the economic benefits of childcare both by feminist campaigners within the Welsh Government and by organizations external to it. The voices of those, such as MEWN, who mobilize a discourse of difference are marginalized and a more radical framing of childcare that challenges domestic divisions of labour and the gendering of care work has been replaced by one that resonates with liberal notions of equality and equal rights. Thus there is little sense that either devolution or the statutory duty has encouraged childcare policy in Wales to be thought about in ways that are distinct from the New Labour vision.

With regard to connections between childcare, social class and material disadvantage, the Welsh Government has made a commitment to providing increased funding for childcare through European structural funds, through Cymorth and through a programme called *Flying Start* (WAG, 2005c). The aim of the programme is comparable to Sure Start and has targeted funding towards children aged from birth to three years in areas of disadvantage. The funding delivers part-time childcare for children in designated areas in order to improve child development outcomes, enable parents to access work or training and 'deliver respite for parents not in work who are having difficulty in coping with parenting' (WAG, 2005c: 2, para. 11). This, therefore, remains an initiative for children living in areas of high poverty and for parents who disclose difficulties in coping. It therefore fits with the New Labour discourses and policies that stigmatize certain (poor, working-class, lone) parents. It fails to recognize that *all* parents are likely to go through periods when they do not cope very well and that this cuts across social class, geographic location and other aspects of family diversity. Clearly there is a challenge in targeting limited resources towards those in greatest need in ways that do not stereotype or stigmatize.

In connection with the focus on *parenting support* and the interest of New Labour to address the needs, rights and responsibilities of parents, as discussed in Chapter 1, the Welsh Government also turned its attention to this policy arena and, following consultation, published its *Parenting Action Plan* (WAG, 2005d). This proposed support for parents across a range of areas including information and advice, promoting positive parenting, encouraging parental participation in service planning and ensuring that services such as education work in partnership with parents. Some areas of support are of relevance to all parents, for example local Children's Information Services (CIS), whilst others are targeted towards specific groups of parents, for example parents with disabled children. The action plan 'recognises that the needs of mothers and fathers, of male and female carers, are not always the same' (WAG, 2005d: 8, para. 1.12) and refers to the Fatherhood Development Project run by Children in Wales and Fathers Direct. This has the potential to offer a 'policy window' (Marshall, 1999: 64) for raising questions about the distribution of unpaid care and the matter of gender equity as well as some of the issues facing fathers that will be identified in the book's conclusion.

The impact of the Welsh Government's childcare and early years policies was explored in studies conducted by researchers at the National Centre for Social Research commissioned by the Department for Education and Skills (DfES) and WAG to survey parents' use of provision (Bryson et al., 2006; Smith et al., 2010). The reliance of many parents on informal childcare was raised in the studies, revealing this was for reasons of affordability and flexibility but also because parents preferred a home environment with trusted family or friends for their child. There is a need for government initiatives on childcare and early years provision to address the role that informal care can play. This is a matter that also featured strongly in this research and will be illustrated in later chapters with reference to the mothers' accounts of the contribution informal care could make to their capacity to manage.

The *Children and Families (Wales) Measure* (WAG, 2010b) gives local authorities powers to offer parental support services, to be offered free of charge, narrowly defined as services that offer training in parenting skills or other provision to facilitate effective parenting. The measure also includes a duty for local authorities to make available free childcare provision for pre-school children from a prescribed age up to entry to compulsory education. Both of these elements are presented within the part of the measure focused on the eradication of child poverty, suggesting a link between parent support services, the provision of formal childcare at an early age and tackling poverty.

The Welsh Government policy statement on childcare, *Nurturing Children, Supporting Families: Our Policy Priorities for Childcare* (WAG, 2011b) reaffirmed earlier commitments to affordable, accessible, high-quality provision. Childcare continues to be linked to a wide range of agendas including rights for children and young people, family and parenting support, work–life balance, increased employment and tackling poverty. The document links childcare to other current strategies such as the new *Child Poverty Strategy for Wales* (WAG, 2011a) and specific initiatives such as *Families First*. In addition, the current situation with regard to fiscal tightening and the UK Coalition government plans for major welfare reform are acknowledged as factors to be addressed: 'Our vision is for families to have access to the childcare they need at a price they can afford, but we recognise that there are significant challenges ahead' (WAG, 2011b: 15). Disappointingly, the new policy statement does not work through the links between childcare and gender equality other than with regard to increasing female labour market participation, presented as a positive choice for both mother and child. This failure to integrate childcare policy and gender in creative and thoughtful ways will be revealed later in other contexts.

POLICY OFFICERS' PERSPECTIVES: DOING THINGS DIFFERENTLY?

So far, this chapter has connected childcare policy in Wales since devolution with certain key political values that have been celebrated by the Welsh Government as potent interpretive symbols. These have been presented as markers of distinctiveness in the pursuit of a social policy agenda for Wales. The reading of policy texts provides a foundation from which to explore policy officers' perspectives on the prospects for a 'made in Wales' policy agenda and for progress towards the key values of gender equality, social justice and children's rights. The views of policy-makers and professionals involved closely in the development and delivery of childcare policy and services are examined.

The Welsh Government's commitment to a different style of politics based on inclusivity, accessibility and openness (Laffin and Thomas, 2000; Catriona Williams, 2003) has been welcomed and, according to Catriona Williams, the 'working methods of the Welsh Assembly Government have been extremely conducive to the involvement of outside bodies in the development of policies' (2003: 250). It was, therefore, important for this research to include regional policy officers inside and outside the Welsh Government who would be in a position to reflect on partnership working. Six regional policy officers were selected for interview. The sample included two officers (a senior advisor and a cabinet member) located within the Welsh Government, three officers from regional public bodies that had been active in the childcare policy-making process and one officer from a public body representing children. This is obviously a small sample and cannot represent the full range of political and policy interests in this regard. However, all six regional officers were well placed as 'key informants' to provide some important insights into regional level policy agendas and all occupied senior and influential positions.

Childcare policy, made at the national and regional levels, is delivered locally (Penn and Randall, 2005; Randall, 2004), resulting in 'extraordinary diversity in existing patterns of provision' (Randall, 2004: 4). In order to capture this point, this research included attention to the local authority level and how city partnerships were seeking to address childcare issues in the context of national and regional priorities. Eight local policy officers drawn from the city's children and young people's services and partnerships were interviewed. This included members of the Early Years Development and Childcare Partnership, which had representation from the statutory, voluntary and private sectors. Further insights were gained through meetings with local practitioners working either across the city or in one or more of the three areas selected for the neighbourhood case studies.

The interviews with policy officers covered a variety of issues including those relating to how childcare policy is thought about and talked about, and those relating to the delivery of policy and some of the challenges of making policy work in practice. The focus was thus on finding out how different policy officers understood childcare and related policy arenas, in the context of devolution, in relation to the Welsh Government's key values and policy delivery. The material in this section will reveal that many policy officers were sensitive to the need to redistribute economic resources towards families in poverty, focusing on achieving this through paid work opportunities. However, they had not fully worked through how redistribution might link with gender and with the need for the cultural recognition of the value of care work. This is a matter to which the book will return in Chapter 5 following the presentation of mothers' and fathers' perspectives on care.

The analysis in this section is organized around three key themes. First, the policy officers' perspectives on devolution and the scope for policy divergence in Wales are presented. Second, the policy officers' interpretations of childcare policy are related to the key values expressed in New Labour and Welsh Government texts. Third, their perspectives on the challenges involved in policy delivery are offered.

Devolution and 'doing policy differently' in Wales

Regional policy officers were all supportive of devolution, a finding perhaps to be expected given their proximity to the Welsh Government as key insiders or as partners. All identified areas of significant achievement in the Welsh Government's agenda. According to Mike Davies (Welsh Government advisor), devolution had meant that policy-makers could tailor programmes and services to local needs:

> I think that devolution does mean that you are more able to be in tune with some of the things that mean the difference to people in the way that services are provided.

He also referred to the possibility of having ' "made in Wales" solutions for problems that exist, or are more important than they would be elsewhere'. This was a view that was shared by Alison Connor (officer, regional equality body 1):

> There is an awareness of the need to be Welsh in policy thinking so they [the Welsh Government] are quite good on researching what the differences are, why it is different in Wales and why UK policy may not fit the needs of people in Wales.

Policy officers also referred to the Welsh Government's association with a different *style* of governance as one of the markers of being distinctive. They identified partnership and cooperation between the different public, voluntary and private bodies involved in specific policy agendas as a significant achievement:

> I think the Welsh Assembly Government are a very, very listening Government . . . it is a huge willingness to make change . . . And there is this willingness to consider children's rights. And, of course, being Wales, it is much easier to get unity in this way . . . And things that come in, you can put

the issue straight to the people who are making the resolutions. (Paul Waters, officer, children's organization)

Concerning childcare policy, for example, Mike Davies claimed that this improved communication meant that there would be considerable interaction between civil servants and ministers within the Welsh Government and the people working in the local Early Years Development and Childcare Partnerships.

Regional policy officers were also generally positive about the achievements of the Welsh Government in relation to the policy agendas and political values concerning equality and social inclusion. The achievements of the Welsh Government with regard to children's rights and gender equality were praised. Speaking about gender equality, Liz Spencer (officer, regional equality body 2) was very enthusiastic about the lead provided by the Welsh Government:

> Absolutely fantastic! In terms of elected members, in terms of Cabinet. In terms of flagging up gender inequality . . . in other organizations in Wales, then, of course, the [Welsh Government] is the shining exemplar and working hard to mainstream equality in everything that it does.

Similarly, praise was raised with regard to the Welsh Government's stance on children's rights. Paul Waters (officer, children's organization) observed that the establishment of the Office of the Commissioner for Children 'was a very, very brave move for the Welsh Assembly Government'. He continued 'because they established an Office and have given Peter [Clarke] power to criticize the Government and he is completely independent in doing that'.

In summary, regional policy officers supported devolution, felt that there had been a transition towards a more open and listening form of government and agreed that some significant developments had been made in relation to specific policy arenas and key values. Nevertheless, some also offered reflections on the limitations to devolution. These related to a shared perception that the Welsh Government's agenda was too ambitious to be practical and this could create problems for partners responsible for the delivery of policy. As Alison Connor (officer, regional equality body 1) put it, 'they are trying to juggle [policies], five hundred things they are trying to deliver'. Concerns were also shared about the constraints facing the Welsh Government in what could be achieved in a policy arena such as childcare because of the reserved powers of the UK government in relation to taxation and the benefits system. These matters will be discussed further in Chapter 5.

Many *local* policy officers were in agreement with opinions expressed at regional level concerning the willingness of the Welsh Government to consult, to engage in partnership with other agencies and to listen to different viewpoints:

> I think the [Welsh Government] has created a shift of more about a culture of discussing with people what the policies should be before they are implemented. (Sarah Wilson, officer, voluntary sector/EYDCP)

However, local policy officers expressed the view that the Welsh Government's energetic style of operation was difficult to handle at the local level, where commitments had to be delivered:

> I think they have done some things too fast for a quick fix . . . and I think it is trying to mean everything to everybody. (Rita Daniels, senior officer/local authority/EYDCP)

Some policy officers felt that the Welsh Government issued conflicting guidance in areas such as childcare that cut across the responsibilities of different departments. It was further suggested that there was a failure to 'join up' policy and that guidance would not fit together for those attempting to interpret it at the local level. As Nicholas Peters (senior officer, local authority) explained:

> what the [Welsh Government] is trying to do is right . . . it isn't joined up enough. So we have to try to join it up here which is very difficult so we just end up sending plans to the [Welsh Government] all the time.

Other concerns related to the perception that the Welsh Government did not always provide resources to match its ambitious agenda and that at the local level people were already overstretched:

> The other thing about the [Welsh Government] is how much we get resources to do these things because unless we get more resources, people are pretty committed, often overcommitted and as well as deciding to fund a new service you have to spend time working out what that might be. (Chris Coleman, senior officer/local authority)

In addition, some officers reported that staff within the Welsh Government did not always have a firm understanding of some of the strategies and principles that were being encouraged. Chris Coleman felt that the principle of planning services for children and young people through partnerships was an example of this:

> The other bit of the muddle is that they are mixing up the planning that you do when you have clear targets and resources and the planning that you have to do when you don't have resources and you are coordinating agencies which do and have their own lines of accountability.

All the local policy officers were generally supportive of devolution and were convinced of the commitment of the Welsh Government to the policy arenas addressed in this research. However, as the partners responsible for the delivery of the Welsh Government's agendas at the local level, they held reservations about how these could be realized in practice.

Childcare policy frames and inclusive values

Earlier in the book it has been argued that there are certain dominant frames used to 'package' childcare policy and these celebrate particular political values. In Wales, these political values are connected to the Welsh Government's commitment to 'inclusion' (Chaney and Fevre, 2001) and the interviews with policy officers provided an opportunity to delve into this further. Different ways of framing childcare policy indicate distinct understandings of the purpose of childcare, whom it is for and how it should be provided. The interviews explored how officers understood childcare with reference to those agendas highlighted in the earlier analysis of policy texts. How did policy officers make sense of the connections between childcare and economic matters, social justice and inclusion, children's well-being, gender equality and parental support?

In the interviews with regional policy officers it was childcare for the economy and childcare for children's well-being that were emphasized. What was especially significant was that these two frames were generally viewed as *compatible* and *mutually supportive*. They were often linked together in terms of the social justice and inclusion agenda through a concern for tackling child poverty. The goals of childcare for gender equality and for parental support/parental choice were subsumed within these other frames and this meant that recognition of their relevance was muted.

Childcare was linked by regional policy officers to the economic frame, presenting childcare mainly as a service for parents in paid work and as a mechanism for stimulating economic growth and encouraging people into the labour market. The frame thus linked in with dominant discourses around 'welfare to work' (Lewis, 2002) and achieving 'work–life balance' (Duncan, 2002; Glover, 2002) articulated by the UK government. The Assembly Working Group on Childcare had been chaired by the Deputy Minister for Economic Development and this had signalled clearly that this was the key driver behind childcare reform at the regional level. According to key policy officers within the Welsh Government it was intended that the lead should come from an economic perspective:

> The Childcare Working Group that we have within the [Welsh Government] is actually chaired by Brian Gibbons who is the Deputy Minister for Economic Development. It is not an accident from the [Welsh Government's] point of

view that the Chair of all that isn't from the Education Minister or the Health Minister or whatever but it is the Economic Development side of things that is taking the lead in doing that. (Mike Davies, Welsh Government advisor)

[Chair of the Working Group] is an Economic Minister, so to a certain extent there is a message in that, that this is being led by an Economic Minister rather than an Education Minister or a Social Care Minister. So the economic issue is an important issue. (Keith Hall, Assembly Member)

Childcare was also linked with economic priorities through the 'welfare to work' agenda and this seemed to be a particular concern for those officers located within the Welsh Government. Policy officers linked to the Welsh Government stressed particularly high levels of economic inactivity in Wales. Mike Davies and Keith Hall both argued that Wales faced a more significant problem of economic inactivity than other parts of the UK and explained that improved childcare provision had been identified as one way of tackling this. Economic inactivity was thus distinguished from unemployment to signal that the problem is seen in terms of the ability and willingness of those not currently working to take the paid jobs that are available. There was a need to:

Bring more people back into thinking that work is something that would be good for them and they would want to do and so on. Often these are people who are out of the workplace for health related reasons but as well there are people who are not looking for work because they have family obligations including childcare. (Mike Davies)

This shift of attention from *unemployment* to *economic inactivity* (used to describe a situation in which it is felt more people who are currently not undertaking paid work must be persuaded to do so) reveals a discursive sleight of hand. The construction of 'family obligations' as a barrier to paid work rather than an area of valued activity in its own right echoes directly the narrow framing of childcare in New Labour and Welsh Government policy texts. Furthermore, Mike Davies believed there was the potential for those who were economically inactive as a consequence of unpaid caring duties to be persuaded to convert their skills into something of value in the labour market:

One of the things that I think that we have to do is to persuade people in that position is that actually the things that they have been doing when they have not been formally working give them skills and experiences and are very directly relevant to what the marketplace needs. Most often they seem to me to be in the caring type areas.

He continued:

> So, from an economic development perspective, the interest in childcare is both because we need it in order to persuade people who are economically inactive to become active, but also because I think those people represent an untapped pool of talent that means some of those people will be able to become the providers of childcare.

This is far removed from the vision of an 'ethics of care' (F. Williams, 2001) in which care within the domestic realm is valued in its own right, thus meeting claims for cultural recognition. Those who provide the bulk of unpaid care, namely women, are merely to be encouraged into a social care sector characterized by low pay, insecurity and unsatisfactory working conditions (Osgood, 2005). Moreover, women already make up the majority of paid care workers in this employment sector (Scott et al., 2002). The proposal to 'tap into' this pool of talent is hardly a strategy to promote gender equality. There is little evidence that childcare policy has been examined through the lens of gender mainstreaming geared towards a reduction in social inequalities. This seems disappointing in view of the involvement of officers from gender equality organizations in the regional policy process and partner networks.

Beyond the Welsh Government, the other regional policy officers also stressed childcare in relation to an economic frame. Liz Spencer (regional equality body 2) linked childcare to both an economic frame and a gender equality frame, taking the view that these were intrinsically linked. Her organization had been closely involved in the making of childcare policy at various stages and she commented 'we were pleased to see a section of that first Childcare Strategy document that dealt with childcare and the economy or childcare and employment'. Similarly, Alison Connor, working for a different regional equality body, explained 'we have been working with [Welsh Government ministers] Jane Hutt and Jane Davidson to engage childcare as an economic productivity issue as much as an equality and fairness issue'. Lesley Thomas (officer, regional public body) also approached childcare from an economic frame by seeing it as a personnel and trade union matter of potential benefit to public service employees, as she said: 'It is just part of the Human Resources agenda really. Around recruitment and retention, flexible working, improvement to services, all those kinds of issues. And equalities as well'. These interviews thus confirm that regional policy officers from gender equality bodies working in partnership with the Welsh Government were mainly utilizing role equity discourses in their contributions to policy development. Yet this did not fully engage with the issue of the lack of cultural recognition for unpaid care or the need for a redistribution of resources to support those who perform childcare duties. Nor does the role equity discourse embrace an agenda for changes to the division of labour at home so that men also play an active and equal caring role in a society that values care responsibilities as a basis for citizenship (Lister, 1997, 2006).

The role equity discourse may be in tension with the existence of 'gendered moral rationalities' (Duncan and Edwards, 1999) that do value care but on terms that may reinforce traditional gender differences in who provides this care. This moral economy of childcare shapes the decisions that mothers (and fathers) make about the organization of paid work and care. Local case studies can form a valuable resource in exploring the decisions that mothers make about work and childcare and how these are shaped by social context. As Duncan and Edwards (1999) demonstrate, local social and cultural expectations may be as important as the character of the local labour market in the decisions that mothers make. These are claims that can be explored further in this research.

As Fiona Beveridge and her colleagues have argued, many gender equality initiatives are lacking in that 'they identify the problem of women's inequality as a labour market problem and measure progress in terms of such factors as women's labour force participation' (2000: 385). The restricted understanding of gender mainstreaming at the regional level in Wales that was revealed in the interviews with policy officers demonstrates their claim forcefully.

Regional policy officers also emphasized childcare for children's well-being and for the promotion of social justice and inclusion:

> Interesting that the response from most childcare organizations and, indeed, all the other partner agencies, is please, please, please, on this agenda make sure that what we are talking about first and foremost is children's and families' rights but especially children's rights and the rights of young people under the UN Convention. (Liz Spencer, regional equality body 2)

Regional policy officers focused on the perceived role of childcare in tackling poverty both now and for future generations. Childcare and early years education were viewed as a form of early intervention that would help address a wide variety of social problems later. In this sense the celebration of children is effectively harnessed to the economic agenda. The symbolic placing of the child at the centre of policy is utilized to draw support for measures that have other objectives. Mike Davies, for example, was candid in explaining that at times presenting a policy as a 'children's needs' issue in terms of education or child poverty could make it more attractive to partners. He provided an example in relation to the Welsh Government's commitment to provide breakfast clubs in schools (WAG, 2004a), an initiative also introduced elsewhere in the UK (Shemilt et al., 2003):

> Free breakfasts in primary schools is essentially an anti-poverty and

educational policy. I think there is a bit of fear here that if we talk up the childcare side of it too much then it could cause difficulties with the teacher unions and other people that we are having to persuade to come along and help us with this policy. (Mike Davies, Welsh Government advisor)

Some views chimed with the notion of investing in children for the future (Lister, 2003) and tackling a variety of social problems believed to be associated with exclusion:

If you have got a situation in which the parents are working, children are having quality childcare that they are benefiting from, then their academic achievement will improve, their role as young citizens will improve, hopefully antisocial behaviour will decline so there should be a community benefit as well. The line we are using is childcare for children, parents and communities. So we want to make sure children, parents and communities all benefit from it. (Keith Hall, Assembly Member)

And childcare is an important part of what many Communities First partnerships have concentrated on. They do it for a lot of these reasons . . . because it helps people become economically active, because in a Sure Start sense it provides a set of socializing experiences. (Mike Davies, Welsh Government advisor)

The discursive frames propounded by the former New Labour government that simultaneously claim childcare as a benefit for all whilst targeting those labelled as social problems were thus echoed by insiders within the Welsh Government. The notion of childcare as a *universal right* for all children is thus sidelined despite the children's rights agenda claimed as a marker of distinctiveness in Wales. In addition, the well-known limitations of area-based anti-poverty/social inclusion programmes need to be signalled more clearly, for, as Gordon Jack observes:

appropriately designed community programmes should be able to achieve some improvements in children's lives but, on their own, they are unlikely to be able to combat the stronger influences of structural inequalities and individual characteristics. Furthermore, it is important to realize that most disadvantaged *individuals* do not actually live in disadvantaged *areas*. (2005: 295)

Alison Connor (regional equality body 1) proposed an alternative understanding of the connections between childcare, the economy and an anti-poverty agenda. She recognized that tackling childhood poverty raised issues of *gender* too. In her view, the economic case for childcare was linked to both gender equality and antipoverty issues and she argued:

childcare provision is absolutely the critical key to moving children and

> women out of poverty . . . children enter poverty because of their mothers,
> there is definitely a gendered link to child poverty and if we want to tackle
> that you need to tackle the values . . . economic activity is the best route out of
> poverty to independence for women.

Some regional policy officers, as this extract illustrates, were seeking to ensure gender issues were not sidelined. However, this is a view that may fit uneasily with those 'gendered moral codes' that place mothers at home with their children, an issue that we saw Sheila was facing and which is to be explored in greater depth through the mothers' narratives in Chapter 3. Here, this policy officer appears to be taking for granted that the welfare state is moving towards a dual adult earner model and that this is to be encouraged in the interests of women and gender equality. Yet comparative work on welfare states and gender can offer alternatives which equality bodies could consider, such as payments for carers. Cultural recognition for the massive economic and social contribution made by those who care for children could lead to a fairer distribution of economic resources so that this contribution is rewarded. In addition, the assertion that economic activity may provide the means of moving women out of poverty must be tempered with the recognition that the female labour market can be characterized by low pay and insecure work (Grant, 2009).

The regional policy officers did not all share an understanding of the centrality of gender in discussing childcare. Concerns with gender equality appeared subservient to the economic frame, meaning that full attention to the interaction between gender, care and work was lacking. Regional policy officers were asked to comment on how childcare could connect with the Welsh Government's gender mainstreaming agenda. Alison Connor (regional equality body 1) argued that gender mainstreaming had not happened in the childcare policy arena. When asked if the gender equality agenda was integrated with childcare policy, she replied:

> No, I don't think they are, I don't think they are and I think there is a general
> lack of awareness of the issues between the two and there is a general lack
> of understanding of child poverty and the gendered nature of child poverty
> . . . I think the lack of understanding of how those things interconnect has
> seriously damaged policy.

Whilst those with gender expertise raised some concerns, it was evident that some of the insiders to the Welsh Government were not confident in discussing the issue of gender equality. Keith Hall, for example, claimed that the issue was dealt with by the fact that the membership of the Childcare Working Group (CWG) was predominantly made up of women, some of whom had a 'track record' in this area:

So the equal opps [sic] people, the fact that they are not, you know, to a certain extent, *I think we just take it as read*, it is not an issue of contention, really. And I'd say, it does not guarantee anything but two-thirds of the group are women, if not more, so I mean, many have a long track record on equal opps [sic] activity. So people who are involved on the Committee have probably spent their political life dealing with gender issues and equal opportunities issues. [my emphasis]

Nevertheless, Chwarae Teg was the only organization represented on the Childcare Working Group that has a specific brief to address gender equality and its focus is on economic development. It has been taken for granted that women will benefit from an expanded childcare market in terms of removing barriers to paid work for all:

We will take the view that certainly everybody who wants to be able to partake in the labour market should have all the obstacles that can affect that removed from them. So, I think we are coming at it from that way. I mean obviously the [Welsh Government] is completely signed up for the equal opportunities agenda. (Keith Hall)

This is a restricted view of the connections between childcare and gender equality and ties in with the emphases of New Labour and Welsh Government policy texts. In this sense it is possible to identify how dominant textual discourses regulate and set limits to social action and tie social action in different localities to the economic apparatus (Smith, 1990a). Those partners that achieve access to regional policymaking are those that support favoured discourses and are able to use them effectively to further their particular interests (Ball and Charles, 2006). Kim Hoque and Mike Noon have considered claims that equal opportunities policies can sometimes be merely 'empty shells' and 'exercises in image management' (2004: 482). Put another way, Simon Duncan has argued that gender mainstreaming can be rhetorical and can result in gender policies that are ' "broad and shallow" rather than "narrow and deep" ' (2002: 312). These reservations are supported in this analysis of the making of childcare policy in Wales and its connections to gender.

The delivery of policy at regional level, achievements and challenges

The economic frame and the child-centred frame can be said to be brought together through the Welsh Government's child poverty strategy. This will mean that the needs and rights of many children living outside areas of deprivation or living in households that do not meet the thresholds for welfare benefits or tax credit support may fail to get attention. Indeed, the

Cymorth fund for supporting children and young people has reflected this tension between declaring universal rights for children whilst targeting limited funding only to certain geographical areas or communities of need.

At the same time, the use of a child poverty/disadvantage frame offers the benefit that all officers claim to agree with it and believe that childcare has a crucial role to play in the interests of children. It therefore seems to have significant symbolic power in drawing together officers in different locations in the spheres of politics, gender equality, children's rights and public services. Whether they frame the goal of improved childcare provision in terms of the economy, justice/inclusion or children's rights, the claim that childcare policy can help to tackle child poverty has something to offer them.

Local policy officers, in contrast to those at regional level, tended not to interpret childcare mainly as an economic issue, although some were supportive of the welfare-to-work agenda. The *children's needs* frame combined with the *anti-poverty frame* became the master narratives now. Overwhelmingly, childcare was referred to in the context of helping to support parents and children, especially those living in difficult social conditions:

> We know how hard it is to identify someone to offer childcare. So we tend to say, well we will sort that out, bring them with you. And, obviously, as well, whether it is [local Family Centre] or our own crèche there is a lot of stimulation that goes on in that childcare, which their child might miss out on if they are with other people. (Erica Bell, Sure Start officer)

> I think there should be creative opportunities for parents. In the fully Integrated Centre we can access, you can have the course for you, maybe something to prepare you, or maybe offer you the opportunity to do Playwork, to get accreditation . . . You have got one child in nursery, you have got the other child in childcare or crèche, while you can access that. And it is about self-esteem for parents. (Rita Daniels, senior officer/local authority/EYDCP)

Local policy officers seemed more likely to identify potential tensions in policy agendas than those at regional level, illustrating the gap between those who 'make policy' and those who have to 'make policy work'. The emphasis on meeting the needs of families, especially those living in poverty, also led to a different understanding of the links between childcare and gender issues. We have seen that the regional policy officers mainly connected gender and childcare in terms of providing equal opportunities to access paid work. The local policy officers understood childcare policy as providing support for (vulnerable) mothers and their children. This also incorporated recognition that women in minority ethnic communities might have particular needs for support resulting from inequitable access to services. This echoed some of the concerns presented by MEWN to the select committee:

> The first report we did was research into why [minority ethnic] women weren't accessing the key sections of social services, health. That was very eye-opening evidence. (Debra Mason, officer/local authority/EYCDP)

Narinder Begum (Sure Start officer) also raised the issue of the isolation of the minority ethnic women with whom she was working in the local community: 'With the women because they are at home with the children, they don't have the external environment for them to learn English or how to pay bills or fill in forms'.

Many of the local policy officers involved with the EYDCP and Sure Start Partnerships talked about the relationship between parenting and childcare in terms of some of the difficulties facing mothers and fathers. The traditional division of labour between mothers and fathers was generally taken for granted but some recognized the stresses that mothers confined to the home or seeking to balance too many responsibilities could face. There was an appreciation that childcare did not provide an automatic route to equality for women and that, where women do work, this can be a double burden and a source of guilt:

> I think it is one in five children is raised without a dad and here the woman has to be in a high enough job to be able to access childcare. But more and more women are, I suppose, career-minded and I think they are caught in the middle, really. They would like to stay at home to care for their children but equally they have got all the other areas. (Debra Mason, local authority/ EYDCP)

> [W]omen still predominantly take over responsibility for childcare, whether they are doing it themselves or organizing it and also a lot of domestic . . . sometimes organizing the childcare as well as going out to work as well as doing all the domestic, sometimes it is just one more burden. (Sarah Wilson, voluntary sector/EYDCP)

This understanding of how women, especially those with access only to low-paid employment, may experience the pressures involved in combining work with childcare seemed to be missing at regional level, which ties in with the strategic and operational split in policymaking. It also relates to professional and social class differences between women. Regional policy officers, although claiming to act on behalf of all women, seemed to be articulating a role equity discourse that may speak more to the interests of middle-class, professional women. In contrast, local policy officers, focusing their work on women and children living in poverty and low-income households, recognized that this discourse may not seem to be relevant to their circumstances. There was also some recognition that there was a need to consider the role of men, including those fathers caring alone or living apart from their children. The Sure Start Partnership had appointed a 'dads' worker and Sure Start officers stressed there was a need to expand this work due to huge demand from fathers. Some of the fathers who were in touch with Sure Start projects were interviewed during this research and their perspectives are presented in later chapters.

Whilst some local policy officers did refer to the gendered nature of childcare in their responses, there was no evidence that this was in the context of a strong gender equality policy or commitment to further the Welsh Government's mainstreaming agenda at the local level through the partnership arrangements. As one member of the EYDCP observed, attention to gender equality 'hasn't been a role that it [EYDCP] has taken on and I'm not sure I could see it doing so in the near future' (Sarah Wilson). This finding is echoed in Vicky Randall's research in six English local authorities, leading her to conclude that 'Where gender politics is concerned, even in the politics and discourse of the most generous daycare providers, avowedly feminist concerns and formulations have been muted in their expression' (2004: 17). Although the Welsh Government has placed gender equality as a key political value on the map in Wales, it cannot be assumed that this has encouraged a shift at the local level of governance, where social justice interests focus on issues of social class and deprivation.

Some of the differences between regional and local policy officers in the framing of childcare have been highlighted. This is really a difference of emphasis and alternative selections from the various frames that are available rather than evidence of conflicting priorities. These differences seem to be a result of where officers are placed in the system of governance and policymaking with a broad distinction between childcare for economic development and regeneration (regional level) and childcare for children and family needs (local level) as the master narratives. Childcare policy tries to reconcile competing interests in a single package in which economic priorities dominate. The limited extent to which this can address the day-to-day childcare needs of mothers and fathers will become evident in Chapters 3 and 4, where the personal accounts of parents are presented. The book will then return to the interviews with policy officers in Chapter 5 in order to explore their understanding of the gaps between policy and what ordinary families would value.

CONCLUSION: DISCONNECTIONS IN POLICY?

The Welsh Government is distinctive in its allegiance to particular political values and styles of policymaking (Chaney and Fevre, 2001; Chaney et al.,

2000). There is a commitment to developing 'citizen-centred services' and ensuring democratic accountability so that the Welsh Government in partnership with local government takes the lead. Devolution has also led to the creation of new structures to support partnership, which Paul Chaney has described as significant as they 'provide a further key mechanism whereby equalities policies at the Assembly level can be transferred to other areas of economic and political life' (Chaney, 2010: 46). The interviews with regional and local policy officers suggest that there is an understanding and appreciation within the policymaking community of these values and style of approach. However, it remains to be seen whether the parents in this study feel that this has made a difference in their daily lives and whether they feel that childcare offers them 'citizen-centred services'. The next chapter begins to explore their perspectives.

The Welsh Government makes policy with its hands tied in relation to powers reserved by the UK government such as taxation, welfare benefits and employment legislation. In this sense childcare policy in Wales can be distinctive only in limited ways. The power of dominant policy discourses to set limits to what can be imagined may also shape how policy officers approach the issue of childcare. Despite the adoption of the statutory equality duty and support for gender mainstreaming by the Welsh Government, this does not appear to be the driving force behind childcare policy. Rather childcare policy is presented as an 'investment' in children's future, as part of a package to secure children's rights and as a means to promote inclusion and social justice through ensuring both mothers and fathers are available for paid work. The claim that women, in particular, are likely to benefit from childcare policy remains untested and diversity amongst women is not addressed. If the Welsh Government is to take its statutory duty for equality seriously, it must consider the accounts of ordinary mothers and fathers about how paid work, unpaid care and their attention to children's needs interact in their lives. This claim will be illustrated in Chapters 3 and 4.

There is evidence that, as Welsh childcare policy has evolved, children's rights, social justice and gender equality have been a priority but they have been framed and connected with each other in relation primarily to *economic* goals. In this sense the overall *substance* of policy in Wales does not appear to be distinctive even if the *style* of making policy appears to be inclusive. Nevertheless, the existence of both the Office of the Commissioner for Children in Wales and the statutory duty continue to offer 'policy windows' (Marshall, 1999: 64) for activists seeking an alternative vision. This research tells a story that is still evolving as devolution is understood 'as a fluid and dynamic process' (McAllister, 2000: 592) rather than a one-off event. The 2011 referendum in Wales delivered a clear majority in favour of increased law-making powers for the Welsh Government and vividly underlines this potential for further change.

3

Mothers' Perspectives on Childcare, Gender and Social Support

INTRODUCTION

The narratives of the mothers presented in this chapter expand the theme of the interaction between personal decisions, cultural expectations and public policy illustrated by the case study of one mother, Sheila, in the Introduction to the book. These interviews illuminated the mothers' daily childcaring practices, the social relations of care and their shaping through material and emotional concerns. The methodology for linking the mothers' narratives to a wider theoretical analysis and to an assessment of policy is informed by the ideas of Dorothy Smith (1988, 1990a, 1990b, 1997). Smith developed the method of 'institutional ethnography' to explore the everyday worlds of women and the method is ideally placed to illuminate personal accounts of mothers and their relationship to the moral economy of care. It is well known that this moral economy of care is gendered and the notions of 'sensitive mothering' and 'intensive mothering' have been used to describe the performance of childcare by women. This study, therefore, follows Smith (1988) in beginning with mothers' accounts of their daily lives in relation to care of children, including their reflections on the role of fathers and wider networks of support.

Mothers from diverse backgrounds and occupying contrasting material circumstances were interviewed and this diversity is reflected in the cases selected for discussion.[1] Yet this study seeks to go beyond documenting multiple standpoints on mothering. The intention in drawing on the accounts of the mothers as they see their social world is to understand how social structures and social relations extend their grip. Smith's methodology is powerful in linking personal experience with its *social* character. Her view is that the researcher can start from women's everyday experiences with attention to the private realm of home, family and domestic life. The aim is to explore how mundane activities that are taken for granted are shaped by wider social processes and how those activities simultaneously support what Smith calls 'the relations of ruling'. The state is a key player within the 'relations of ruling' and occupies a central place in the 'construction of the world as texts' (Smith, 1988: 3) that mediate dominant discourses and create ways of thinking about gender that are thus naturalized.

The claim that ways of thinking about the maternal role are naturalized was supported during the research process. It was often difficult in the interviews to encourage mothers to reflect on activities perceived to be mundane and indisputable. Yet as the research progressed it also became increasingly clear that childcare practices represent a highly sensitive topic (Renzetti and Lee, 1993) for many mothers. Questions around mothering, care and domestic labour pose challenges for those conducting interviews because of their association with the 'natural' abilities of women and because, as Jane Ribbens observes, mothering occupies an 'intensely moral space' (1998: 32). Indeed, the practices of mothers can be so 'taken for granted' that often the mothers in this research appeared taken aback by some of the questions. They had never been asked before *why* they decided to organize childcare and domestic arrangements in a particular way, nor did they perceive caring for children as 'work'. Many of the mothers would not discuss their decisions about the balance between paid work and care or the distribution of domestic labour through the language of 'choice' or 'constraint', as they often perceived their situation as one that had evolved naturally. This simultaneously presented a difficulty in encouraging the mothers to reflect on their circumstances whilst also confirming the themes emerging in literature about the conditions of motherhood and the status of care (Glenn et al., 1994; Hays, 1996).

The first section begins with the mothers' accounts as they reflected on the social relations of childcare, their daily caring practices and the material and emotional concerns that shape these practices. Material is presented on the transition to motherhood, mothers' narratives on their care routines and the impact of gendered moral codes (Duncan and Edwards, 1999) that emphasize the importance of 'being there' for their children. The accounts of the mothers concerning how they 'do childcare' will be revealed as 'socially organized practices' (Smith, 1997: 393) that are gendered and justified with reference to moral codes. This chapter thus seeks to document personal choices and investigate how these are related to family circumstances as a basis for assessment of public policies on childcare.

As revealed by Sheila's narrative in the Introduction to the book, mothers place considerable emphasis on their *educational* role in their children's lives and this shapes how they place themselves in relation to other roles, such as in paid work. In the second section, the interview data will thus illustrate how mothers interpret their role as an educational one and why this may conform to certain contemporary policy agendas whilst being in tension with other agendas. The narratives will also reflect claims that the narrow framing of gender equality, in terms of advancement in paid employment, has meant that there has been less progress towards gender equity in the performance of care within the home.

Although there was considerable common ground between mothers from different family and economic circumstances in their narratives about care, those material differences did matter in relation to issues of family well-being and their access to support. This is the focus in the third section, where the mothers' accounts of crises, loneliness and isolation will be examined. The important role of informal care as a form of social and emotional capital that can mitigate these sources of stress will also be indicated.

In the conclusion to the chapter the case study messages are addressed through a theoretical lens concerning motherhood as an institution, social practice and source of identity. A variety of themes are presented, which are explored in relation to understandings of the gendered moral economy of care (Duncan and Edwards, 1999; McDowell et al., 2005), the regulation and self-surveillance of mothering (Hays, 1996; Walkerdine and Lucey, 1989) and the importance of access to social and emotional capital (Edwards and Gillies, 2005; Reay, 2005).

MOTHERS' REFLECTIONS ON CARE: FROM SENSITIVE TO INTENSIVE MOTHERING?

Three noteworthy themes emerged from the mothers' accounts of care. First, the transition to motherhood had changed their lives and shaped their well-being and opportunities in momentous ways. Second, the daily routines involved in childcare were usually talked about by the mothers as though they were inevitable and taken for granted, although there were differences between mothers in whether their arrangements were more or less traditional or egalitarian. Third, the mothers' accounts reflected strong moral codes relating to their caring role and these cut across differences based on material circumstances, social class and ethnicity.

Transitions to motherhood: benefit and loss

The mothers reflected on how the transition to motherhood had impacted on them. In the majority of cases the mother had been in paid work prior to the birth of her eldest child and most of them had made changes in their paid work as a consequence of motherhood. Sally, for example, was a young lone parent living in Tinbury with an eighteen-month-old son. She was no longer in paid work because of health problems. Her health had created difficulties in maintaining paid work during her pregnancy and she now was involved in voluntary work:

> before I became pregnant with [son], for a few months I went back to work in a nursing home. And I was enjoying that but when I fell pregnant with [son]

> I kept vomiting every day for the whole nine months! I was ill all the time . . .
> And since I have had him I haven't gone back to work except at [centre where
> she is a volunteer]. (Sally, single parent, one child)

Natalie was a middle-aged mother with a seven-year-old son. She had
divorced and her son had occasional contact with his father. She had
moved to Tinbury when she was rehoused and was now working as a part-
time teacher:

> I was clerk in a school so I was working full-time and after I had [son], I
> mean, you know it was cheaper to stay at home for the small salary that I had
> at the time than to pay a crèche. It wasn't worth it with everything, paying
> transport, crèche. And in a way I enjoyed it more as well! (Natalie, single
> parent, one child)

The transition to motherhood was analysed in terms of perceptions of
benefit and loss. Generally the mothers' ambitions for a career or financial
independence took a secondary role in their assessment of what was 'best'
for their children, an issue reported by F. Williams (2004b) and discussed
later in the chapter. However, the women differed in terms of how much
power they had to decide how they organized their paid work and childcare.
This was shaped by their conditions of employment, by their material circumstances, by whether it was perceived to be practical to combine work
and care, by (where appropriate) their husband or partner's paid work and
by whether they felt that they could cope with both working and caring.

Many of the mothers changed their work arrangements over time as they
tried to find a balance between work and care that suited their needs. Lowri
was a middle-aged mother living in Shaw with two sons aged seven and
six years. She was in full-time professional employment now her children
were of school age. She had separated from her husband, who had regular
contact with the children:

> I have always worked full-time. I used to work in [city] for the same company
> that I work for now . . . I was acting manager. I went on maternity leave with
> my eldest child for four months, and I returned using a nursery in [city] for
> three days a week. My husband at the time then, he worked shifts, so he had
> the children the other two days a week. I did that for four months and it got a
> bit much. Then I reduced my hours to working three days a week.
> (Lowri, single parent, two children)

Lowri became pregnant with her second child at a point when she was being
encouraged to apply for promotion within her company for a full-time job
that would involve relocation. She took this option and returned to full-
time work following the birth, whilst her children were cared for by their
father on his days at home and otherwise attended a private day nursery

on a part-time basis. Lowri was unusual in relation to the other mothers interviewed in that her then husband shared responsibility for care during these early years and her pregnancy did not prevent her company from offering her opportunities for promotion. However, despite the opportunity to share care and take a promotion, Lowri had found the pressure during the children's early years to be too much. She took the option to reduce her working hours in order to cope. This case illuminates a gap in policies designed to facilitate women's continuation in paid work through the expansion of childcare: they fail to acknowledge a basic problem, that the demands involved may be too much to manage at particular points in time.

The transitions experienced by Gail and Becky further illustrate the compromises that may follow maternity. The two mothers provide an interesting contrast although they were similar in that they were white, middle-class women married to men in full-time employment and living in Shaw in comfortable material circumstances. Both had held full-time professional posts prior to motherhood. Yet the following extracts reveal that, whereas Gail felt that she had lost status and an interesting job following maternity, Becky relished the freedom of being at home and did not wish to return to work.

Gail had continued in full-time paid work as a team manager for a large company following the birth of her eldest child. She had planned to continue on a full-time basis following the birth of her second child but:

> They made it so awkward when I went back, I was going back all along, I was going back full-time all along. Then I went for a meeting before starting back, about four weeks before I was due to start back and they had disbanded my team, so I didn't have a team to manage and they wanted to absorb me into someone else's team.
>
> They wanted me to retrain . . . and I was quite annoyed at the fact that when it suited them they wanted me to do it, when I had asked eight years beforehand *when I didn't have any children and I could really commit myself to it,* that's what I wanted to do. *And I thought it is not the right time for me to do it with two young children and the travelling.* [my emphasis]

It is the *combination* of unfavourable circumstances at work and the responsibility for young children that led to Gail's decision to accept a redundancy package following the birth of her second child. A more vigorous equality policy could have protected her status while on maternity leave so that she did not relinquish her management role. Yet this might not have been enough to encourage Gail to stay in work, as her reflections suggest the stresses of travel and meeting the needs of two young children influenced the decision. She had been experiencing poor health on account of the travel and the stress. This case reveals the multiplicity of factors that may impact on a mother's decisions on how best to organize paid work and the care of children. Like Lowri, Gail found that her health was being compromised by the stresses of combining a demanding professional role with the early years of caring for children.

Becky, although sharing certain characteristics and circumstances as Gail, provides a point of contrast in her perception of the transition to motherhood. She had been a civil servant before the birth of her eldest child and returned to her post on a part-time basis when he was two years old. When pregnant with her second child she took the option to take a career break and she had since given birth to a third child. She had been on the career break for four years when interviewed. She could take a maximum of six years, by which time all of her children would be in school. In reflecting on her future plans she explained:

> When I do go back to work there is a good chance that I could plan to go back part-time, term-time. And be with the children school holidays. Thirteen weeks! Plus I get a condition so I could arrange my working day only part-time within school hours so I wouldn't have to employ a childminder myself.

Becky further explained that she would also be able to return to the same job at the same grade. She was currently working part-time as an unregistered childminder. She talked about how much she enjoyed being in this position and being able to spend time with the children:

> I enjoy most of it! It is very demanding, very, very demanding. I think I am much busier than actually going out to work for an employer . . . Out of the two I prefer to be with the children. And I always had the intention that when the children did come along, that if we could afford it, that I would like to be with them. And I don't think there is anything wrong with that.

As a consequence of her enjoyment at being home with her children, Becky said she was unlikely to return to her previous post irrespective of the offer of family-friendly conditions. In this case, Becky perceived the position of her husband, who was in full-time well-paid work, as something that was to her advantage, as she commented: 'I think I am very fortunate actually. I don't know any of my friends who are in that position. I think, from a financial point of view I am lucky as well'.

Becky was able to exercise a choice to stay home while her children were young because her employer offered appropriate parental leave and her material circumstances were secured. She was willing to forgo the status and independence afforded by her paid employment in order to do something that she found more fulfilling. Her perception that she was fortunate was accurate, if compared with Gail, in that she retained a choice to return to her paid work in the future should she wish to do so. In contrast, Gail felt a sense of loss, feeling she had been forced out of a job that she enjoyed through a combination of work-related, health-related and practical factors. Both women were now dependent on male breadwinners as a consequence of changed circumstances following motherhood and neither expressed unease in this regard. Both talked about the joys of spending time with young children. Nevertheless, for Gail, the circumstances of motherhood had involved certain costs and a sense of loss. Despite her strong commitment to using her professional skills in paid work and her willingness to use formal childcare, she found herself conducting low paid, part-time unskilled work as an evening supermarket cashier in order to fit in with the children's needs and her husband's full-time job. The stresses of travel, demotion in her professional work and childcare were too much to negotiate.

The themes of benefit and loss and maternal well-being or stress emerged from the mothers' accounts of the transition to motherhood. These themes continued to be significant as the mothers reflected on how they managed childcare on a daily basis.

Daily routines: managing care, domestic work and paid employment

It was not unusual for the mothers to represent domestic labour and care as not counting as 'work'. This theme supports Smith's claims that 'institutional ideologies' are influential as mothers account for their experiences of care. As Smith argues, women's relationship to the ruling apparatus is expressed in their 'work', which 'has been both necessary to and unrecognized by it' (1988: 153). Women generally do not see the value in their caring work at a *societal* level as the discourses of family life and motherhood articulate that value only in *individualistic* ways. This means mothers place value on 'being around' for their children and 'keeping on top' of domestic tasks as their contribution to their family. Gendered moral codes (Duncan and Edwards, 1999; Duncan et al., 2004) operate as mothers simultaneously express pride in and enjoyment of their role as 'mother' and 'homemaker' and frustration, guilt and stress when they find it hard to cope.

This ambivalence was expressed both by mothers participating in largely traditional domestic arrangements and by those who felt that they shared duties with their husband or partner. The perception of whether care and domestic tasks were shared fairly or equally also varied, meaning that some mothers reporting what appeared to be a traditional division of labour perceived that their arrangements were egalitarian. Mothers rarely expressed the view that husbands and partners could make a greater contribution to care and domestic work. Although this could be down to a reluctance to divulge those feelings publicly, it seems more likely that the 'taken for granted' nature of care and gendered moral codes explain this lack of concern for achieving a redistribution of caring labour. In order to illuminate the variety of perspectives expressed by the mothers, some contrasting cases will be presented. Some of the mothers' accounts described a fairly traditional division of care and domestic tasks whereas other mothers' arrangements came closer to a shared model of care.

The traditional 'breadwinner–homemaker gender contract' (Rees, 1999: 179) retained partial hold for some mothers, including women who were also engaged in paid work. It was common for the mothers to claim that their husband or partner worked harder than they did. Stella was married and living in Tinbury. She was a part-time nurse, working night shifts, and her husband worked full-time during the day as a manual worker. They had a four-year-old daughter. Stella reflected on her reasons for taking responsibility for all the childcare and household duties:

> Well, because he [husband] is working full-time, I just feel he is more tired than me. Even though I'm working two nights and I don't sleep before or after, other than those two hours. I just feel he works harder than what I do.

Even though Stella worked long hours on night shift twice a week and would then have sole responsibility for caring for her child during the day, her perception was that it was fair that she undertook all the domestic duties.

Gail, who was introduced earlier, had sole responsibility for her two children during the day and worked as a cashier in the evening once her husband arrived home from work as a manual worker. There was a sense of rush and urgency in the way she described her daily routine and this seemed to be partly because she felt she had to have dinner ready before she left for her evening job:

> It is quite difficult then if anything upsets the routine and everything goes to pot then. It is quite stressful thinking, I have got to have everything ready for five o'clock and he comes through the door starving and I have got to have a meal before I go to work as well and make sure the girls are all right as well.

While she acknowledged the pressure of this situation, this had not apparently led to any negotiation with her husband around who should cook the tea. When invited to reflect on these arrangements she remarked:

> Basically it was the deal when I gave up work! [laughing] He'll say, 'oh, you're at home all day, you can do the cooking, the cleaning and the ironing and everything'. *And, I think it is fair enough.* If he's at work all day, he can't come home and cook his own tea. So, it's just the way I see things . . . As he's been working so many hours I just keep the house going.

Gail continued:

> He'll get the hoover out if he can. But the last couple of months because he

has been working so many hours, he's got to have a rest somewhere as well. *I don't class mine as a working day as strenuous as his* but it is in other ways, not physical but on the go. [my emphasis]

Gail thus accounted for a traditional division of labour on the grounds that her husband's paid work was perceived to be harder and more physically demanding than her work in the home. These extracts support claims that the mother *does not count* her role in care and domestic labour as work of equal importance to the paid work undertaken by her husband or partner. These are cultural practices in which the value of unpaid care is not fully recognized.

Throughout the interviews there were difficulties in encouraging many of the mothers to reflect on their arrangements because of the 'taken for granted' nature of their role in the home. In many cases they seemed to want to present an image of 'being on top' of their role and not making a fuss about it. Stella's response was typical of many of the mothers:

> I just take it for granted . . . all in my stride, as I said, and just get on with it. I have always had to get on with it so I mean I just do it.

Joy was not in paid work at the time of the interview. She was a young, married mother living in Tinbury and her husband was a self-employed manual worker. They had one son aged nineteen months. Joy had been on a government training scheme shortly before her pregnancy and had given this up after getting married because she was no longer eligible for remission of the course fees as she was now assessed according to joint income with her husband. This offered a poignant example of ways in which marriage can limit independence and opportunities for women. Joy and her husband shared fairly traditional views about the role of mothers:

> I would want to go back to work eventually. At the moment we are lucky I don't have to, there's no need for me to work because [husband] is one of these people who prefers me to be at home with [son] while we can manage it rather than me go out to work as well and [son] not see either of us.

In describing the daily routines, Joy said she took main responsibility for care of their child during the week when her husband was at work but there was a sharing of domestic duties:

> We tend to share quite a bit of the cooking but if it is teatime meals I normally cook them, but on the weekend we tend to share. Ironing, neither of us like to do it, so if it needs doing, it gets done when it needs it. Cleaning, we tend to share between us if there is stuff I haven't been able to do during the week.

Joy described a very busy routine of entertaining her son during the week and described how this took priority over the performance of domestic tasks. Hence, her routines were a mix of both traditional (full-time mother for child) and more egalitarian/liberal (shared domestic labour but no fixed routine).

Despite there being some aspects of Joy's daily routines that she perceived to be egalitarian and fair, some more traditional views influenced her perception of her arrangements in that she expressed gratitude towards her husband for being willing to help:

> I think to a certain extent [husband] does more than most people I know whose partners do. Because [husband] will come in from work and play with [son] and help me get [son] ready for bed and bath him. [Husband] does an awful lot for the amount of time he works as well. Like I suffered from depression for a long time and I get very tired in the afternoon and so he will come in from work and have [son] for the hour or so for me to go and have a sleep. He has just done a full day's work himself, so I think he is very good.

The contribution of her husband to childcare and domestic labour was not taken for granted but was seen as exceptional. This expression of gratitude when a husband or partner contributed to domestic tasks also emerged in other interviews. Other mothers referred to a husband or partner as being 'very good' when they contributed to domestic tasks, suggesting this should be seen as unusual and praiseworthy rather than to be expected.

Turning next to some instances in which mothers seemed to be moving away from more traditional ways of organizing care, Hameeda provides one example. She was a married Bangladeshi woman living in Crossland with her husband and their son, who was aged fifteen months. She provided an example of care practices believed to be egalitarian and shared with the father. She worked full-time during the day as a community worker in the voluntary sector, whereas her husband worked evenings as a chef. They shared childcare without any use of formal provision or the regular involvement of wider family. As her husband began work after four o'clock, her employers had agreed that the child could play in her place of work after being dropped off until Hameeda finished work. Hameeda expressed concern that Bangladeshi girls, including those within her own extended family, were not treated equally with the boys and were relied on by family to help with care of younger siblings. She was determined that she was going to conduct her own care arrangements in what she perceived to be a more egalitarian manner:

> I am working and my husband is working and I have only got a nuclear family . . . I get away with it as my in-laws aren't here. As a Muslim, it would

be the duty of the housewife to look after the elders. My husband does have quite a large family and I went back to Bangladesh and visited them. They had never seen me before.

Hameeda stressed that their division of labour was equal and that her husband was better at some aspects of care and domestic work than she was:

I have problems because I am a bit messy! Like with the nappies, my husband is better at doing it than I am. All our daily routines have been divided up between us. When my husband is doing one thing, I am doing another.

Hameeda's narrative suggested that she had a strong commitment to paid work and did not wish to be confined by traditional views of the mothering role. Her narrative also revealed that she interpreted this in relation to a questioning of cultural expectations of mothers within the local Bangladeshi community. She perceived her situation to be distinct from that of other mothers within the community.

Christine also described childcare based on non-traditional arrangements. She was a white, working-class mother with three children aged seven, five and three years. She was married, living in Tinbury with her husband, and was the only mother in the sample who described her husband as a 'housedad'. Both Christine and her husband had a history of doing low-paid, unskilled work since having their children. They had each moved in and out of insecure low-paid employment, trying to fit around each other so that one of them was available to care for the children:

We had our child. Then I got a job in a call centre and then I moved to another job in another call centre. Then I had the baby, stopped work as my husband got a job then. So I was at home then with the three of them. We both got a job then in the new [supermarket] and both of us were working so it was like six trips back and forth and it was too much. So my husband stopped, so it was just me going out and then I got a job in [shop] in [area of city] and then I moved to [nursing home].

Christine had decided to apply for a college course in nursing studies combined with experience in a nursing home to move away from this pattern of unpredictable employment. However, she was unable to drive and lived in an area where public transport was reported to be poor. She therefore relied on her husband to do the school and nursery run and to take her to college and her place of employment. This routine was making it impractical for him to seek work:

The way we are at the moment is because I want to go to college. So with the baby down at nursery, my husband can't get a job because he is trying to fit it round the hours. So he is at home and I am working. When I finish college the baby will be at nursery and he will go and get a job then as he won't have to worry about me having to get to college.

In justifying why her husband was currently not in paid work, Christine appeared to be suggesting the role of 'house husband' was not perceived as natural and was not expected to continue. It is also possible that this effort to justify the arrangement was influenced by political and policy discourses concerning welfare entitlement whereby the idea of the 'hardworking family' is celebrated. It is argued that this idea has a moral component:

> the discourse invokes an idea that families *should* be 'hardworking'; families *should* contribute to the economy; they *should* pay their own way (i.e. they *should not* live on state benefits); and so on. (Ribbens McCarthy et al., 2012: 122)

Christine described a routine in which tasks such as cleaning, washing laundry and tidying up were shared, cooking would be her responsibility unless she was working and looking after the needs of the baby fell to her. Her narrative illustrates the potential for traditional and egalitarian roles to be combined and to shift over time in relation to the demands of paid work or study.

Being there and liking it: moral codes and childcare

> [T]he predominant image of the mother in white Western society is of the ever-bountiful, ever-giving, self-sacrificing mother . . . a mother who lovingly anticipates and meets the child's every need. She is substantial and plentiful; she is not destroyed or overwhelmed by the demands of her child. Instead she finds fulfilment and satisfaction in caring for her offspring. (Bassin et al., 1994: 3, cited in Turney, 2000: 47)

There is pressure on mothers to view the care of children as natural and enjoyable and this sets the scene for some of the reflections presented in this section. All the mothers appeared to be influenced by moral discourses around motherhood and expectations that they should demonstrate their competence in this role. Some mothers would distinguish between domestic tasks that they shared with partners and the personal and emotional care of their children, for which they tended to retain responsibility. One example of this was provided by Sheila, whose personal account was discussed in the Introduction to the book. This commitment to playing an educational, creative and involved role was common in all the mothers' accounts regardless of how they combined paid work and care and irrespective of class or ethnic background. This material provides firm evidence that the mothers were influenced by the messages underlying the models of 'sensitive' and 'intensive' mothering that were introduced earlier.

Mothers generally presented the time spent with their children as an enjoyable experience and were often reluctant to discuss what they did not enjoy. Mothers also made comments about the need to 'be there' for their children and to make time for them. When mothers were asked what they most enjoyed doing with their children they generally responded with passion. Gillian was a married mother living in Tinbury with her husband and four-year-old daughter. She was working part-time in the civil service and her husband was a full-time civil servant. She described how she had become a first-time mother in her early forties and perceived that this impacted on her wish to make the most of a joyful and unexpected experience:

> The sheer enthusiasm and eagerness for life and we see things that she sees for the first time. When she is in awe of things, I think that is magic. She will talk to you and she will ask you questions. But everything is exciting to her. I am seeing things through her eyes. And I like the close contact. (Gillian)

However, when asked directly if there were any aspects of childcare that the mothers did not enjoy, many of the mothers appeared reluctant to comment. Gail, for example, stated 'Well, if you don't like anything what can you do about it anyway?' while Stella said 'No, I just take it all in my stride! I'm quite happy with everything'. These comments revealed once again the taken-for-granted assumption that childcare is something that is natural and that mothers should demonstrate that they are on top of it. There is a taboo regarding complaining about it. Although some of the mothers did mention specific things that were difficult – for example, establishing eating routines and coping with tantrums – these are referred to as insignificant problems within the context of a generally fulfilling experience. These examples of difficult aspects of childcare are those which are recognized in childcare manuals, women's magazines and parenting websites and are age-related. Hence, mothers may feel they can speak about these issues so long as they do this in a matter-of-fact way in which they portray this as something to be expected and that they can handle. The resonance of the mothers' responses with wider policy and parent education discourses supports Smith's claims that social practices may be shaped by textual discourse (Smith, 1990a).

It was more unusual for a mother to express feelings about the whole routine being difficult as in the next extract:

> Just the mundane, the mundane things. It's doing the wash on the weekends and doing the ironing and cooking and still having to do the reading when all they want to do is go and play really. (Lowri)

It had been expected that expressions of frustration and being worn down would have been more widespread. Where mothers did express feelings of stress, this usually emerged at other points in the interview rather than in response to a direct question about what they did not enjoy about childcare. In particular, questions about use of services and perceived gaps in provision could sometimes prove more effective in elucidating accounts of the stressful nature of childcare. That material will be presented in Chapter 4.

Some mothers found that motherhood had changed their attitudes towards paid work. It was not unusual for them to say they enjoyed being home with their children more than being in paid work, even when they had previously valued a career. Kelly, for example, was a white, middle-class mother living in Shaw with her husband and two children aged seven and four years. Her husband held a senior position in the local hospital. She also worked in a highly qualified role in the health service and was now working for three days per week:

> To be honest, I think my life is a lot more enjoyable, splitting it between the children and work. I did drop a grade, which I might not have needed to do. But, you know, I think I have got the best of both worlds. I am not sure I want to get up to that level again. There is a lot of stress involved.

This view points to an issue that those focusing on ensuring women have equal access to paid work do not recognize. Some of the mothers expressed a view that paid work was not necessarily enjoyable or fulfilling, but on the contrary that it was stressful and demanding. This could be true of mothers who had been in professional occupations as well as those in lower-paid or more routine work. In this context some expressed a preference for being home with their children over success in paid work.

Gillian, introduced earlier in the chapter, provided a further example of this changed perspective on paid work. She was married with one child. She had worked for the civil service for many years and had continued in her job on a part-time basis after the birth. However, she had recently given up this job for a new part-time post closer to home and with hours that would fit in better with childcare. She explained how her priorities had shifted:

> I could easily give up work now whereas before I went to work and it was my social life, to see all my friends. Since I had my [daughter], my whole thing about work has changed. I go to work, do my stuff and then come home and put my family first. I waited so long for [daughter] that I don't want anything to take the time that I spend with [daughter].

These examples suggest that, if childcare policy is to meet parental preferences and mothers' perceptions of what is in their children's best interests, more will need to be done to support those who wish to spend time at home with their children for a period, with the opportunity to return to paid work later and with conditions that recognize their experience and qualifications gained prior to maternity. Becky, whose opportunity to take an extended career break was discussed earlier in the chapter, was unusual in the sample of mothers in her employment rights in this regard.

There were other mothers who stressed that they liked being able to work, who strongly supported the 'work ethic' and who were in favour of efforts by the government to encourage mothers to engage in paid work. This revealed a wide diversity of preferences amongst mothers regarding the balance they wanted between care and paid work. This is an issue that is discussed further in the next chapter in relation to the use of formal childcare.

Alongside the presentation of childcare as being enjoyable and fulfilling, the notion of 'being there' emerged repeatedly during the interviews and in a variety of contexts. This is a strong theme in other research into motherhood: 'mothers and children in a range of Western societies may define a key aspect of caring for children in terms of "being there"' (Ribbens McCarthy and Edwards, 2002: 210). Continuing this theme, Deborah Lupton and Virginia Schmed found in their study of Australian mothers that the concept of 'being there' could be used to explore their accounts:

> The women . . . were not simply speaking of a number of domestic and childcare chores that needed to be done, when they spoke of their desire to 'be there' for their children. They were describing emotional shift work, which, in their view, would need to be done by them, regardless of whether they worked or not. (2002: 467)

This was also true of the mothers interviewed during this research. Those mothers who had changed their conditions of paid employment following childbirth would often justify this in terms of wishing to give time to their children. Gail, who was introduced earlier in the chapter, spoke of this in terms of being able to manage her childcare arrangements without having to rely on others:

> I've been there for them! You know, see them off in the morning, pick them up at night and nobody else is doing that. It has been quite lucky that since [youngest child] has gone to school I haven't had to rely on anyone else to pick her up or drop her off.

Danielle had separated from her husband and was living in Tinbury with her seven-year-old daughter. She was in part-time work with two jobs as a teacher and skilled craft worker. She described her work as interesting and fulfilling but was clear that she wished to work part-time in order to have sufficient time to be with her daughter:

I just try to fit it in. I didn't want to spend too much time too far away from [daughter]. To work ten hours per day and then I didn't see [daughter]. That is something that I didn't want to do because they give you so much.

Two of the mothers, Becky (Shaw) and Margaret (Tinbury) were working as childminders and both pointed out that this was a source of income that enabled them to 'be there' for their own children. As Margaret points out:

I wouldn't like to go back to work. If I had to go to a job I wouldn't, I would rather stay home. At the moment I have got the best of both worlds. I am home with my children and getting paid. But I don't think I would like to go and work in a shop and leave my children.

Similarly, there were some mothers who were concerned that their paid work was impacting in a negative way on their ability to be there for their child and fulfil the mothering role in the way that they wished. Sheila was a mother who provided the strongest case for this, as discussed in the Introduction to the book. Her narrative revealed that *emotions* about childcare and work can be more influential here than *practical* considerations; this has implications for policy that seeks to offer genuine choices for parents. In this case, the option to take a long career break and then return to her job would have helped to resolve Sheila's dilemma. This case revealed some of the tensions that may exist between feelings about being there for their children in order to secure emotional and educational benefits on their behalf, and asserting the rights of women to achieve financial independence, have a fulfilling career and show commitment to their paid work. The impact of discourses of 'sensitive mothering' and 'intensive mothering' is firmly illustrated in these accounts. The strong commitment of the mothers to supporting the education of their children is also reflected these discourses and will be explored in the next section.

THE EDUCATIONAL ROLE OF MOTHERS: THE PRESSURE TO BE 'CONSTANTLY CREATIVE'

Mothers emphasized their educational role, expressed in terms of both the general socialization of their children and supporting the work of their child's nursery or school. The active role that mothers play in relation to their children's education (Smith, 1988) is well established, and adopting a pedagogical role at home is a central element within the ideal of the 'sensitive mother'. In recent years there has also been an intensification of the parenting role with regard to children's education, meaning that there are increased expectations with regard to what parents, usually mothers, are expected to do to support their child's schooling. This intensification is evident in policy texts produced by the state and in the expansion of parenting advice in childcare manuals, television programmes and other media. This provides a firm example of Smith's (1990a) claim that textual discourses may be especially important in guiding the social practices of mothers. Yet some textual discourses resonate more easily with mothers' gendered moral codes than others. Those that urge mothers to be involved educators fit more closely with the ideologies of 'sensitive' and 'intensive' mothering than those that now encourage them to be paid workers, putting their career aspirations first and competing equally with men. In the Introduction to this book, Sheila's account revealed the anxiety that the need to coordinate these competing expectations could create.

As Curt Dudley-Marling argues: 'The co-ordination and supervision of children's educational activities often demands a significant portion of mothers' waking hours' (2001: 184–5). Yet why do mothers appear to readily embrace this role in addition to, or even in preference to, other responsibilities? The method of 'institutional ethnography' can help us make sense of the relationship between mothers and the domain of education, in which mothers appear to be compliant. Smith (1988) calls for a broad understanding of 'work' that goes beyond what is generally understood by that term, so that, for example, caring practices are recognized as *work* and these caring practices are tied into wider institutional processes such as those pertaining to paid work and education. Mothers, for example, interpret their role through particular institutional ideologies and associated discourses, meaning the work of mothering is *socially organized*, yet this is obscured, being presented as 'natural'. The contribution of mothers in supporting the work process of schooling is one example of this claim. Schools are reliant on, and take for granted, many of the tasks that mothers perform on a daily basis. This will include tasks as varied as ensuring children arrive at school on time, supporting homework, making costumes for the school play and baking cakes for the school fete. However, 'the interpretive practices rendering mothering accountable in this context do not identify it as work' (Smith, 1988: 168). Wider institutional policies and discourses thus impact on the work of mothering and strive to regulate what mothers do in caring for their children. At the same time the work that mothers put in to supporting the school makes it possible for the education system to function efficiently but is not acknowledged as labour.

The extent to which mothers had accepted the expectation that they should continually find opportunities to prepare their children for school or support the work of their child's nursery or school directly was particularly striking in the interviews. Other sites of government, including the health service and social services, also regulate the performance of mothering. In the Sure Start areas covered in the research (Tinbury and Crossland) a variety of parenting programmes were targeted mainly towards those who were perceived to be failing to parent adequately. The professional and textual regulation of the performance of parenting (Hays, 1996; James, 2005) had clearly impacted strongly on the mothers, who often seemed to be reflecting on their role in ways that mirrored wider discourses. As Smith asserts, 'Textual realities are the ground of our contemporary consciousness of the world beyond the immediately known' (1990b: 83). This is not to claim that these texts necessarily carry a coherent message or that parents necessarily absorb advice contained within the texts uncritically. However, it is clear that the idea that mothering is something that comes naturally does not mean that its conduct is left to chance. On the contrary, it is a role that is encouraged to conform to certain ways of doing and being.

The following accounts illustrate how mothers from a broad range of backgrounds and living in a wide variety of circumstances nevertheless seemed to be speaking a common language with regard to their perceived educational role. When the mothers were asked about what they most enjoyed doing with their children, nearly all of them provided examples that suggested they were seeking to educate their children and do creative things with them.

One of the mothers, Joy, had been referred by her health visitor to a local community centre in Tinbury that offered classes for parents. She spoke of her enjoyment of the pedagogical aspect of her role and how this had been encouraged in the parenting classes she had attended:

> I love doing craft things with him, like a couple of weeks ago we made, you know, the shakers you can make and he loves doing things like that and I've started making a scrapbook for him with different things like photos and different receipts from outings.

The mothers represented this role as educator as an enjoyable aspect of their relationship with their children. Even when mothers had extremely busy routines or were facing significant stress in their life, they would go to some length to ensure that they were able to make time for the this educational role. The following examples provided by Diane and Tracey illustrate this claim.

Diane was living in Crossland with one daughter aged three years. She had recently separated from her daughter's father but shared care with him. She had a degree and had tried to build a career as a freelance artist alongside low-paid work. Since the birth she had not done as much freelance work but had found a job as manager of a small business. She was able to work part-time hours, making use of a private day nursery and relying on her former partner to share childcare duties. Nevertheless, her daily routines appeared to be very busy as she had to travel some distance to the nursery and her place of work on public transport. She described a routine in which she made a continual effort to turn mundane tasks into a creative experience for her child. This resonated with the image of the 'sensitive mother' very clearly and reveals how the construct remains relevant to a new generation of mothers despite diversity in their parenting and partnering arrangements. The task of getting to the bus station early in the morning was described by Diane as an opportunity for play:

> So we walk over and we normally end up playing on the way over and play games, chasing, singing, shouting in the tunnel. Get a bus to crèche and I normally get my lift to work then.

Diane explained that on those days when she had been in work all day she liked to make sure that there was some space to be creative with her daughter before bedtime:

> We do painting on a Monday night unless I am very, very tired. She comes and I have it all ready for her and she comes in, has her food normally. Then we do painting. Then we clear up. Bath, bed normally and a story in bed every night.

Diane said she thoroughly enjoyed taking on this constantly creative role in relation to her daughter and this is conveyed further in the following extract:

> I love doing the art stuff with her. We do it a lot, we love painting. I picked up pebbles from the beach . . . the other day and we painted those. So we do do a lot of art work. I love jigsaws as much as she does so we do jigsaws. I love taking her to the park, anything. I love being out and about weather permitting, obviously. I just love it all.

Even while this routine is one that Diane conducted with enthusiasm, it was also one that conformed to the messages conveyed in various parenting texts such as childcare manuals and supported by the advice of health visitors and teachers. Diane's daily routines seem to resonate with textual and professional discourses and are thus linked to the 'relations of ruling'. Like Sheila's, her interpretation of her role was shaped by the construct of the 'sensitive mother'.

In the next example, Tracey illustrates a case in which the professional expectations of maternal performance are reversed. Tracey was disabled and was also experiencing problems with her health. She was married and living in Crossland with two children aged five and three years. Her husband was in full-time work and her mother, who lived nearby, was regularly involved in providing support. Tracey also needed assistance from her local social services department in relation to the care of her children. In this case Tracey felt that she had faced a battle in being allowed to be a fully involved mother. Before her eldest child started at the local school nursery, Tracey had asked her social worker if she could have some help in getting him to school and collecting him later. Her social worker had told her that someone would come and do this for her:

> I didn't like that. I wanted to be involved. I basically turned round and said to her I wanted to be involved and I wasn't going to have children for someone else to be involved. I wanted to be involved as I could be in my children's lives. And I didn't see that it was fair that because I had a disability that I should miss out on any of my children's lives. Like their first day at school.

Tracey recounted how the social worker continued to argue with her by saying that she was also a mother and had to miss out on taking her own children to school herself as she was working:

> I turned round to her and said that the difference between you and me is that you choose to miss out because you are working. I don't choose to work and so, therefore, I don't choose to miss out on my children's lives!

Tracey pressed for a referral to a different social worker willing to support her wishes by providing assistance so that Tracey could walk her child to school. Nevertheless, Tracey stated she had had to be very assertive to achieve her wishes and to be an 'involved mother' on her own terms. She went on to talk about how she was particularly worried that she would not be able to support the children in their reading and writing in later years because of her disability, once again demonstrating the significance of the educational role of mothers. Tracey also believed that her children missed out as other mothers at the school arranged to meet up and get their children together out of school but excluded her:

> I think I rely on people to be friendly. When the mums are meeting up with other mums *(WB: Do the mums at the school do that?)* Well, they do with each other but they don't with me. I hear them at school and they join up at clubs. There are quite a few day groups and things in this area but I can't go to them.

Tracey expresses regret that she cannot perform the role of mother in the way that she would like and she fears that her children may suffer as a result. Her isolation is a reminder that, where support networks for mothers exist, there is scope for exclusion, and mothering can be a very competitive activity. The concepts of 'social capital' and 'cultural capital' are helpful for illuminating the wider context to Tracey's situation and expression of distress. The notion of social capital is utilized by Duncan and Edwards (1999) to explore the social networks of the lone mothers in their study. In this context, social capital is defined as 'those features of social organisation, such as norms, values, expectations and networks of social support, which facilitate co-operation and trust between people for their mutual benefit' (Duncan and Edwards, 1999: 65). With regard to the role played by mothers in social capital building on behalf of their children (Reay, 2005; Vincent and Ball, 2007), the ideas and social practices of 'sensitive' or 'intensive' mothering may privilege and celebrate particular ways of being a mother, which in turn will have currency in wider social networks. Participation in local social networks may thus help to either mitigate or reinforce structures of privilege or disadvantage.

The image of Tracey standing alone at the school gate, feeling excluded on account of her disability, provides a poignant example of how structures of inequality can develop around a seemingly mundane activity such as the school pick-up. So, to be clear, with regard to social capital, the informal gendered networks of support and friendship that mothers may inhabit (Bell and Ribbens, 1994; Ribbens, 1994) may also place some at an advantage whilst excluding others. They should not be interpreted simply as a benign complement to childcare.

Mothers may also be seen as taking a particular role in developing 'cultural capital' (Reay, 2005), understood as knowledge, values and ways of thinking associated with those forms of culture that are most valued by society. This claim is supported by research into parental involvement with the education system, in which mothers play a central role (David, 1993; David et al., 1993; Reay, 2005). However, the abilities and resources of mothers from white upper- and middle-class backgrounds to engage more easily with the education system and with the logic of 'sensitive' or 'intensive' mothering may confer advantages for their children. Tracey's personal account illustrates this point and reveals that she was profoundly aware of her exclusion, her limited capacity to involve herself with her children's schooling and its potential impact on her children.

Those forms of social and cultural capital relevant to the care of children are gendered and are managed especially by mothers (Edwards and Gillies, 2005) and can also be based on social class (Vincent et al., 2008). The socially negotiated 'gendered moral codes' that mothering networks may help to construct are thus embedded within deeper systems of social control, power and inequality. The social isolation that Tracey felt was considerable and expressed forcefully. The matter of social isolation as a potential feature of parenting will be considered further in the next section.

WELL-BEING, SUPPORT AND STRESS

When the focus of analysis shifts to the well-being of the mothers, differences of material circumstances, social class and ethnicity matter considerably, despite the mothers holding shared interpretations of the moral basis to childcare. Whilst childcare policy may be presented in a form that implies a desire to support parents and meet the best interests of children, it is also driven by the interests of the economy, as argued in Chapters 1 and 2. As an alternative, the research sought to explore what mothers had to say and to evaluate policy in relation to an 'ethics of care' (F. Williams, 2001) in which the well-being of all family members was central. Could the research illuminate what helped mothers to cope, and, conversely, where stress could occur? In this section some of the dominant sources of stress in the mothers' lives are explored. This theme is considered further in the following chapter in relation to matters concerning the organization of formal or paid-for childcare.

One 'low-level' source of frustration for many mothers was not having sufficient time to manage everything properly, to enjoy family life or to do their paid work to the standard that they would like. However, in addition to this general feeling of being constantly under pressure, some mothers identified deeper problems in coping with crises and facing social isolation and loneliness. Let us look in more detail at what mothers had to say about the relationship between childcare and triggers for stress.

Coping with crises

Mothers pointed out that their routines were so tight that it was difficult to cope if anything upset the balance. The illness of either children or themselves was a particular difficulty. Lowri, for example, was a single parent who worked full-time in a senior professional role. Although she shared care with the children's father, the school would always ring her if either child were taken ill, demonstrating the hold of gendered assumptions on the part of the education system. Although Lowri was in a senior position and her line manager would understand if she had to leave work to collect a sick child, some of her colleagues were resentful: 'Everybody just sees it as an excuse to go early and stuff. You get stressed about going as well as what you are doing'.

Because Lowri did not have any extended family available to care for her children, she had no choice but to take time off work despite feeling enormous guilt over this. This is a problem that has been given insufficient attention in policy debates. In contrast to Lowri, other mothers had access to informal support for situations of illness. Diane pointed out that illness of her child could be a problem but that she was able to rely on her mother for support in emergencies:

> I think I find looking after [daughter] really difficult if I am not well or if
> I am very tired. Obviously I have got less patience then. I was very ill last

weekend and I phoned my mum. And I said, oh, mum, please and she said bring [daughter] round and I will have [daughter] tomorrow as well.

The issue of dealing with sickness was discussed in all the interviews with mothers. Many working mothers relied on the support of family members when children fell sick. The connection between access to informal social support and the ability to manage childcare and paid work was striking. Others, such as Gail, whose narrative has been presented, had changed their paid work patterns so that there would always be someone available at home should illness occur. Where both parents worked similar hours or where mothers had sole responsibility for their children and there was no informal care available, they were reliant on having an understanding employer. In the majority of cases the mother said that it would be she rather than the father who would take time off work for emergencies. Hence some mothers expressed gratitude if they had an understanding employer rather than seeing time off to care as something they should be entitled to as an employment right:

> because of [husband's] job. He is the . . . manager. He is not in a position, really, not to go in to work. He has not got the flexibility that I have got. I can ring in and say that I have got a problem with childcare and they are quite accommodating. (Gillian)

> I have never felt bad, if the children, when [child] was ill, they didn't make me feel bad at all about having to have time off. Because I felt bad, but I also felt bad for [child] but they didn't put any pressure on me at all. (Kelly)

Where mothers perceived that their employer would not show understanding about illness, this was a source of anxiety. Natalie, who was divorced and now working part-time as a teacher, illustrates this claim:

> I do not feel confident to say that I am off for my [son]. I say it is me who is not well, I lie, because I feel if I say that I am off for my [son], then, I do not know how understanding they are. (Natalie)

Natalie had been on a teacher education course and had been advised by her tutor when her child was sick to inform her placement school that it was she who was unwell rather than explain that her child was ill. Greta, who was a nursing student with three children, felt that tutors were completely unsympathetic to those students with childcare responsibilities and would not take this into consideration in relation to illness or in arranging placements. Family-friendly employment policies and rights for parental leave can help mitigate these strains but these were not the norm for most mothers. Even where these employment rights are offered, it cannot be assumed that they are implemented vigorously and fairly in practice. This would suggest that it will be important for both the UK and Welsh governments to secure implementation of current policy in this regard and extend work–life balance policies for both mothers and fathers. Coping with any change to busy routines can create stress and where informal support is available this makes a considerable difference in the management of childcare. Conversely, those lacking informal support can be particularly vulnerable when crises and disruptions to routine occur.

Social isolation and loneliness

Some mothers were facing significant hardship, expressed feelings of finding it hard to cope or were depressed. Joy, for example, mentioned that she had suffered from depression following the birth of her son. Her health visitor had identified this:

> [Son] had his hearing test when he was about seven or eight months and the health visitor could see that I was getting a bit down. I was just stuck in all day with [son] and she said 'why don't you try the community centre and see what is on over there?' So I phoned them that day just after she had gone and it just happened to be the Tuesday when drop-in centre was there, and it was pouring with rain, but I put [son] in the buggy and I went straight over and that was over a year ago now.

Joy said that she benefited considerably from the availability of a local centre for parents that offered different activities every day and a crèche for parents attending classes. The availability of a facility that could provide respite, parenting advice and somewhere to meet other parents was influential in helping Joy overcome her depression. It seems important to recognize this positive aspect of parent support at a time when Sure Start family centres face the risk of closure in the current fiscal climate. It is being widely reported that UK Coalition government public spending cuts are impacting on services for families with children, including the closure of valued Sure Start Children's Centres in England (Daycare Trust and 4Children, 2011). Joy also appreciated the assistance that she received from her family, including her mother, who was present during the interview. As she was unable to drive, and she found taking a child on public transport very difficult, she was reliant on her husband and other family members to take her out.

Another mother whose narrative illuminated issues of isolation and lack of informal support was Sally. She was a young single parent with one child. She explained that she had experienced health problems since she was sixteen years old, involving a period in hospital. She was supported by a community nurse and attended a day centre for people with health problems. She was currently undertaking some work experience at the day centre:

> They give people a chance who go there as clients to work in the office if they think they can cope with it. Because it gives us something to do rather than staying in the house all the time or just doing things in the day centre.

During this work experience Sally was able to use a local crèche that was paid for by the day centre. In addition, she was paying for her child to attend on one other day from her own finances. She was very frank about the difficulties of being with a child all day:

> Sometimes I don't like it when I am on my own all day and all night with [son]. It is just me and [son] and I hate that when I don't see anybody. I take him out for a walk but sometimes there are not many places that he wants to go with me. And I find it hard when [son] is ill . . . and I am here on my own. I find that hard.

Sally commented on feeling constantly tired and that she was too tired to have a social life of her own. She also felt that she would find it hard to manage working more than one day per week because of all the demands of childcare:

> I couldn't work full-time. I would be much too tired and I don't think I could cope. And I do find it hard even working one day a week. You know, taking [son] to the crèche and stuff. It is a long time to be left really because somebody else picks [son] up for me . . . and then I don't get to see [son] until about half five, so it is like a long day for him. *I don't think anyone else can give the care for [son] that I do* . . . I find it hard like going to work. [my emphasis]

The feelings expressed by Sally revealed the considerable strains involved in combining childcare and paid work without access to regular informal support from family or friends.

Whilst access to informal help from family can assist mothers and help avoid isolation, in some cases a mother may find that the informal care that is offered creates its own pressures. Rashida, a Bangladeshi mother living in Crossland, was married with a three-year-old daughter and described herself as a full-time housewife. She lived with her husband, who was a full-time waiter working nights. She was pregnant with her second child at the time of interview. Rashida seemed to be very depressed and frustrated with her current situation. Although her husband had family living locally, she felt isolated because her own family lived in another city. She had worked for a national company in her home city and had been able to transfer to their local store when she moved. She had given up work with her first pregnancy and expressed some frustration over this:

> But the thing is that I have always been independent and now I think that I have lost my freedom completely. It took me a while, actually, to come round that. You know I have no freedom in a sense like something to do with my [daughter]. I mean I don't mind the love, obviously you adore your children. You put them first. And now I am expecting again and that doesn't make it any easier. Obviously now again I will have to wait another year or so. I daren't even think of going back to work.

Rashida held strong views about not using formal or paid-for childcare and stressed that she had no trusted family who could provide any support, commenting 'I can't see myself leaving my child with a stranger. If it was family, I can, but I couldn't do it'. Nevertheless, Rashida was sure that she would return to part-time, paid work once her children were in school. She seemed to see having children as a duty to be endured, saying 'I want to get them over and done so that I can get my life back'.

Throughout the interview Rashida would move from stressing how much she loved her daughter, whom she described as 'really good' and 'a quiet child', to expressing her loneliness and isolation:

> [Daughter] used to cry a little bit and I used to be really upset. But it is not to do with [daughter], I just get emotional for some reason. And then I think 'why am I crying?' but there is no answer. It is probably because things get on top of me and maybe I am homesick. Sitting by myself, day in and day out, seven days a week, just me and my [daughter] when my husband goes to work.

When Rashida was asked if she had any support from family locally to help relieve the situation that she was describing, she replied:

> Yes. And then we are surrounded by his family, not mine, they are not my friends. So it is not really . . . You know there is stuff I do with [daughter] but then again there is not much to do here. I can't drive and that is the disadvantage. If I could drive, I could go to the swimming pool, do more stuff with [daughter] and so my day would have gone and my evenings wouldn't seem long as they do now.

Rashida's isolation seemed to be shaped by a variety of factors. Her husband worked night shift and she had no paid work and no trusted family or friends living locally. She felt strongly that her husband's family was seeking to control her in relation to the maternal role rather than sustain her. She was angry that they had asked her to give up driving lessons during her first pregnancy in case it harmed the baby and now she was left unable to drive in a city that lacked the transport links she was used to in her home city. Her dissatisfaction was palpable:

> As I said, I will eventually get a job. I always had that in my mind. Maybe that is why I am more determined once I have had kids to go out. Some people are happy, don't get me wrong, once they have kids and they're a housewife, they don't mind it, but it is just not me.

Whilst, for some of the mothers, access to help from local family and community networks was a source of strength, for Rashida this was not the case. She talked about feeling under scrutiny with people 'poking their nose' into her business and said, 'As I said I am from [home city] and people have no time and don't care who is doing what . . . Here you just feel people have no lives'.

The mothers expressed hardship in relation to loneliness and isolation rather than in terms of material deprivation. Nevertheless, it was notable that the mothers who talked about feeling isolated and depressed were living in areas of socio-economic disadvantage and with high levels of child poverty. A significant factor in these examples was that none of the mothers were able to drive, exacerbating their reliance on a public transport system they perceived to be inadequate and expensive, or they needed the contribution of their extended family to get around with young children. Both Sally and Joy have revealed in their narratives how they valued local services for parents and children, and this theme will be considered further in Chapter 4, where the book turns to the parents' views on service provision in the city.

Mothering and informal care: social and emotional support

The availability of informal care provided by wider family or by friends and neighbours can be significant in helping mothers cope with pressures. Conversely, mothers such as Rashida who lack access to *trusted* informal support may feel especially vulnerable. This informal domain can be understood as providing access to social and emotional capital which can mitigate the impact of the demands of childcare for mothers. When mothers were asked whether they felt they managed childcare differently from other mothers, those who did not benefit from any informal care referred to it as a factor:

> I guess it is unique in that I am single and I am a foreigner . . . Because she goes to school in [area of city], people are very close to their relatives and often they have got a sister or mum living around. I don't have that. I miss that really. (Danielle)

I guess it is surprising just how many people can rely on family completely, you know, there seems to be an awful lot of people who do have their children taken to and from school every day! . . . . I have got a couple of girls at work after having babies and their mothers, you know, have got their babies permanently. (Lowri)

The significance of access to informal care for mothers is demonstrated in the following narratives of two of the Bangladeshi mothers, Zeena and Farah. Both mothers were engaged in paid work and neither was able to rely on income from the father of her children. Zeena, for example, lived with her extended family including her parents and siblings. She had one son aged six years. She worked part-time for the health service. Zeena's narrative revealed that she was very satisfied with her current situation. She emphasized the strong cooperation that she received from her family in relation to the care of her son and acknowledged that this enabled her to do a job that she really enjoyed. When asked how the birth had impacted on her life, she responded:

Well, it hasn't really affected my life because I have got my family to help me. Because my mum and my sisters have always helped me to look after [son] so I haven't actually stopped working. I used to work in my dad's [business] before that. So it is just helping each other.

Zeena argued that without family help she would adapt her working hours rather than make use of formal childcare:

That is the good thing about having family to help, you see. You don't worry, you know they will take care of your children properly, you know. Whereas if it was somebody else then you would really have to know the person well before you could trust them to look after your child properly. I think so anyway and I have never left [son] with any strangers and I don't think I could either. If it came to the fact that I had to leave [son] with strangers I think I would give up work.

Zeena also thought this was a particular issue within the Bangladeshi community in that 'It is not expected for a mother to leave her children to go to work and leave the children with strangers. It is not done'. This distrust of formal childcare was fairly common in the interviews and was expressed by some mothers from different social class and ethnic backgrounds. Whilst a number of workers within the Bangladeshi community, and Bangladeshi mothers such as Zeena, stressed family-based childcare as a *community* preference, the research indicated that this view is more widely held and is linked with the wider gendered moral codes that cut across class and ethnicity. In other words, the gendered moral codes expressed by some Bangladeshi mothers were very similar to those expressed by many of the white mothers from both working-class and middle-class homes in the area of Wales that provided the location for this research. The distrust of formal childcare is an issue that is known to policy-makers (WAG, CWG, 2005) and has been revealed in other studies of parental views on childcare (Ben-Galim, 2011b; Bevan Foundation, 2005). The role of informal care was discussed in the interviews with policy officers and is explored further in Chapters 4 and 5.

Zeena articulated a very strong commitment to paid work, commenting that she had worked in her father's business until the day before the birth of her son. She was also very enthusiastic about government 'welfare-to-work' schemes:

> I think it is good, it is really good because rather than being stuck at home feeling sorry for yourself. Going out to work, getting a chance. Because some people never got a chance because some people get married early or some people get pregnant or something like that and they don't get an opportunity to do what they wanted to do. So getting another chance, I think is really good. It is like me as well. I didn't get a chance to take my education further and now I am getting the chance so I am really grateful for that.

This narrative reveals an interesting position in relation to discursive frames relating to childcare. It has been argued that the economic framing of childcare policy so that the focus is on encouraging mothers to return to paid work may be in tension with gendered moral codes that place mothers at home. Zeena supported the trend for mothers to return to paid work and had accepted the way this was framed in welfare-to-work initiatives as relating to 'getting a chance', as being about individual mobility rather than an effort to reduce welfare spending. However, she held strong feelings that she would never use formal childcare under any circumstances. She would put her child's needs before her devotion to her work if her family could not help her. Zeena was able to reconcile the potential disjuncture between these competing frames because of her access to informal social support.

Zeena was aware that she was able to avoid the strains faced by many working mothers in that her mother carried out most of the domestic labour while she was at work and all the family helped each other in the evenings. Zeena said she was happy with her circumstances 'because going to work gives me a bit of free time. Like it is my time. It just gives me a bit of freedom rather than staying at home and doing the housework'. Zeena's well-being was enhanced by the degree to which she could rely on her family to provide support. The achievement of independence, personal well-being and role equity for some mothers is secured on the basis of gendered social networks of support in which an older generation of women continue to do the unpaid care. Zeena was in a very different position from working mothers who have housework to conduct once their paid work is finished, as illustrated in the next account.

Farah was married and living in Crossland with her husband and two children aged three and two years. She worked part-time in the education service and the family was entirely dependent on her income. Farah had wider family living close by in the area but took main responsibility for caring for her children and for domestic labour. She had one child in half-day school nursery and another who was cared for at home by his father until Farah returned from work. She had previously made use of formal childcare through a private day nursery but found that it was too expensive to sustain. Farah had been working full-time but had been able to cut down to part-time working once she received some advice about the working tax credit. She stressed that this had been 'a life-saver' for her as she had been so worn out attempting to undertake full-time work with two small children. This account is instructive in the context of the changes to eligibility for working tax credit that were introduced in April 2012. The working hour threshold was increased from sixteen to twenty-four hours for couples with children. This will mean that someone in a situation like Farah's will no longer be able to reduce their working hours without a significant financial loss.

Although Farah felt that the transition to part-time work had been positive, she still made frequent references to the constant worry of managing work and childcare:

> I would love someone, if someone could take [daughter] to school so that, the morning, I am driving like a maniac to get to my work and the traffic is terrible then. So that is the only reason why I get out at quarter past eight and park my car in such a way that I can just leave [daughter], drop [daughter] off and then just rush back and still I am late.

Although the school ran a breakfast club, Farah felt strongly that her four-year-old daughter was too young to be left there. This was a familiar value position amongst the mothers: that they would not make use of formal facilities that could relieve their stress if this was believed not to be in the best interests of the child. The pressures of this responsibility was mentioned throughout the interview, although Farah said she loved her job and wanted to work. Recent research conducted by Dalia Ben-Galim (2011b) revealed similar attitudes whereby parents expressed a preference for home-based family care for younger children and judged formal childcare quality in relation to whether their child was happy.

If Farah's position is considered in relation to the themes of childcare policy, it is clear that she is a mother who wished to undertake paid work and had also gained from the opportunity to work shorter hours as a result of the tax credit system. Contrary to popular, but potentially misinformed, views about the attitudes and circumstances of mothers in the local Bangladeshi community, she was willing to use formal childcare, did not feel that she could make too many demands on her wider family for assistance and was the sole breadwinner. The local childcare market was failing her in many ways. In addition to the high costs of private childcare, Farah also commented on the lack of flexibility:

> All these formal childcare venues, I find them very formal. You either put your child in for a time or not. Part-time has to be two or three days, they won't do less than that. Otherwise you are taking up space for another child. Or they won't do one or two hours a day, anything like that.

This account provides one example of a wider matter; for those mothers without cooperation from family, and who needed to use formal childcare provision, current services did not meet all their needs or protect them from the stresses of combining paid work and care. It is these gaps in the formal childcare system that tend to be plugged where possible by wider family, especially grandmothers. The book will return to the theme of the contribution of informal care in the next chapter.

CONCLUSION: PERSONAL ACCOUNTS AND PUBLIC POLICY

In this final section of the chapter, some of the themes that have emerged in the mothers' accounts will be revisited in relation to the literature on motherhood as a social institution. It has been argued that understandings of motherhood are socially constructed through a moral economy of care (McDowell et al., 2005). Childcare comprises three forms of work: practical care, educational development and emotional support (Reay, 2005). With regard to all three forms of work, it is well documented that this labour is gendered and that mothers are most intensely involved in performing it (Lawler, 2000). The concepts of 'sensitive mothering' (Walkerdine and Lucey, 1989) and 'intensive mothering' (Hays, 1996) were offered in the Introduction to the book as a means for exploring how motherhood is shaped in particular ways whilst being packaged as the 'natural' way of raising children.

Despite differences amongst the mothers in their domestic and childcare arrangements, there is firm evidence that their values and practices are indeed shaped by the ideologies of 'sensitive mothering' and 'intensive mothering'. Yet, like the mothers in Hays's research, they may seek to meet the cultural expectations of mothers embraced by the ideology in ways that fit their material circumstances. In doing so, they negotiate the contradictory expectations of the relations of ruling that now place women as paid workers, as creative educators and as nurturing mothers.

This process of negotiation in caring practices is located within wider networks of family and community support. The findings presented in this chapter support claims that gendered local networks may provide access to social and emotional capital (Edwards and Gillies, 2005) including informal care provision. These networks may be crucial for helping mothers negotiate the expectations that face them. The sensitive/intensive mother faces many pressures in reconciling the demands of employment and family policy and ensuring her children do well in an increasingly competitive and consumerist society. The *availability of informal care* and *social networks of support* are particularly important and, yet again, reinforce gender divisions and the unpaid contribution of women to the economy and education systems (Smith, 1988). The accounts revealed the contribution made by grandmothers and by other female relatives and friends (Gray, 2005; Wheelock and Jones, 2002), indicating the significance of gendered social and emotional capital (Edwards and Gillies, 2005; Reay, 2000, 2005) for childcare arrangements. In order for many mothers to be able to work and be willing to work, the informal care sector is essential. It is through utilizing informal care that many mothers negotiate the tensions between different ideologies in terms of the paid work ethic, the intensification of parental responsibilities and yet remaining true to the core principles of 'sensitive mothering'.

Many parents have to rely on informal childcare from relatives and friends either entirely or to plug gaps and may have a strong preference for informal care (Daycare Trust/NCSR, 2007; Rahilly and Johnston, 2002; Wheelock and Jones, 2002). The research by Wheelock and Jones (2002) showed that many prefer the use of informal care because it is perceived as the best quality, the best for their children and with people who are trusted. They conclude: 'A clear understanding of why working parents use complementary childcare is essential for any childcare policy that hopes to be attuned to what families actually want' (2002: 459).

Another study found a strong preference for, and reliance on, informal care among a sample of lone parents. They justified this on grounds of trust, commitment, shared understanding and the child's happiness (Skinner and Finch, 2006). The role of informal care deserves to be taken seriously in public policy but support for childcare costs under the tax credit system will meet the costs of only approved childcare. The UK government has determined that informal childcare provided by relatives, neighbours and friends will not attract state subsidy (Skinner and Finch, 2006). This provides further illustration that unpaid caring labour does not attract the public recognition that it deserves. The contribution made by those in these informal gendered networks of care is not fully recognized in government policy. In their research into family and kin relations in Swansea, Nickie Charles and Charlotte Davies found that 'at both the formal and informal levels of community the work women do is crucially important to whether or not communities exist' (2005: 688). Evidence of the value women may place on informal social networks is also provided by Jane Parry (2005) in her study of a south Wales coalmining community. Nevertheless, these gendered social networks 'also imposed restrictions upon their [working class women's] behaviour and limited social movement' (2005: 155). The care of children is an important service provided by women in these social networks. Yet both the reliance on informal care and the expectations placed on some women to conduct it may also be seen as potentially restrictive in relation to gender equity. This has led some commentators who have recognized the contribution of informal childcare, and who might otherwise support the idea of state subsidies to pay for it, to warn of potential pitfalls (Skinner and Finch, 2006; F. Williams, 2004b). The role of informal care is an issue that has been debated by those involved in the making of childcare policy in Wales and the book will return to this matter in conversation with policy officers in Chapter 5.

In linking mothers' accounts to childcare policies that celebrate the principles of equality, justice, the best interests of children and parental choice (HM Treasury, 2004; WAG, 2005b), some disconnections between policy and preferences emerge. The mothers' accounts reveal both diversity and inequalities in caring practices and some common concerns that reveal deep gaps in current childcare policy. Mothers expressed a variety of standpoints on how they wished to manage care and how far they felt they were exercising a choice in this matter. Perceptions of what represents an egalitarian or fair model of care and domestic labour are highly subjective and variable. The intention was to explore what worked to the apparent satisfaction of the mothers rather than to impose specific values.

The narratives support other research on the existence of a gendered moral economy of care (Duncan and Edwards, 1999; McDowell et al., 2005; Williams, 2004b) and this raises issues for feminists wishing to see a redistribution of domestic and emotional labour. Gendered moral codes may celebrate the role of mothers in providing care and yet also take this for granted. This means there is an incomplete cultural *recognition* of the social and economic contribution of domestic labour and the inequalities that result from this. In turn, gendered moral rationalities mean that the value of redistributing care between women and men will not be recognized and policies that seek to achieve this could be resisted. Many women cherish being with their children, feel they have a *moral* duty to be there for them and do everything they can to make paid work fit around this. The mothers' reflections resonated with the models of the 'sensitive' or 'intensive' mother (Hays, 1996; Walkerdine and Lucey, 1989), putting her child first and giving priority to the child's emotional needs and educational development. This cut across differences of geographical location, family circumstances, social class and ethnicity. Although mothers' material circumstances and childcare arrangements varied, these arrangements were justified with reference to these moral codes. Consequently gender divisions persist and often become more entrenched as a result of the transition to motherhood. In this sense, motherhood is tied up with deep-seated cultural and economic injustices.

The capability of mothers to manage the intensification of their role and to meet norms that celebrate white, middle-class values depends on social location. Indeed, this intensification is likely to be more easily managed by those families that still conform to the male breadwinner family model. In these circumstances mothers still retain time to mediate with the agencies that dispense advice, make themselves available to listen to and play with their children and support their child's education. The conduct of mothering thus takes place on an uneven playing field but this is not fully recognized; this leads to policy gaps that may reinforce existing inequalities between families.

The gendered nature of emotional attachments can help us understand the persisting role of women as primary carers and the ideologies that support this. The accounts discussed here show this theme of gendered emotions forcefully and correspond with other research studies (Duncan and Edwards, 1999). Unfortunately, family and childcare policy has not engaged with this issue (Barlow et al., 2002). Claims presented by those working within the UK and the Welsh levels of governance that childcare policy is designed to advance gender equality seem cynical and rhetorical in the absence of any deep engagement with these matters. There is a sufficient research and information base available for policy to embrace a more sophisticated understanding of the connections between childcare, paid work and gender. Liberal feminist efforts to provide women with access to paid work seem likely to benefit middle-class women in professional occupations especially. Yet we have long been aware of the limits to this agenda, which does little to challenge the gender- and class-biased nature of liberal welfare regimes.

Following the discussion of the ideologies of 'sensitive mothering' (Walkerdine and Lucey, 1989) and 'intensive mothering' (Hays, 1996) it will be evident that the regulation of child-rearing according to white, middle-class cultural norms pre-dates New Labour and extends beyond the formal boundaries of the state. Historically, modes of regulation have focused on mothers and rely on the capacity of mothers to engage in 'self-surveillance'. It can be argued that New Labour began shaping a discourse of 'intensive parenting' on the basis of international trends towards the intensification of work, education and family life. These trends are set to continue under the UK Coalition government within an adverse economic climate that will pose further challenges for ordinary mothers, fathers and children.

4

Different Neighbourhoods, Unequal Support? Local Childcare Services and Networks of Informal Care

INTRODUCTION

This chapter explores the mothers' use of local childcare and early years services. The small sample of fathers involved in the regular care of their child also provides a source of material in relation to the chapter's concerns. The relationship between targeted services and the case for universal childcare (Land, 2002a) has been a matter for policy debate and the chapter material provides opportunity to explore parental needs in this regard. The question of service targeting for children and their families is a matter for continued debate in the context of current deep cutbacks in public funding and UK coalition government priorities. The UK Coalition government has affirmed commitment to early years provision as a measure to tackle child poverty but in the context of more focused targeting:

> We will take Sure Start back to its original purpose of early intervention, increase its focus on the neediest families, and better involve organisations with a track record of supporting families. (HM Government, 2010: 19)

Responding to this announcement, the Daycare Trust has reaffirmed the importance of offering Sure Start as a universal service (Daycare Trust, 2010). Whilst the mechanism to achieve targeting on the 'neediest families' is not clear, it is apparent that arguments in favour of universality may not be heard at the national level of governance in the current context. Reduced public spending and reform to tax credit and welfare benefit systems are expected to create further pressures for parents seeking early years education and childcare (Ben-Galim, 2011b) and will impact on the childcare market. The degree to which the Welsh Government will use its powers to pursue an alternative regional agenda will be crucial for the well-being of Welsh families. This chapter sheds light on the issues involved as seen by mothers and fathers who use these services.

The three neighbourhoods in this city are described next with regard to service provision. The research material will illustrate how patterns of parental use of formal childcare and early years services can be understood in relation to mothers' and fathers' access to local networks of social support and informal care. This continues the theme developed in Chapter 3 with regard to the relationship between families and forms of social capital. Further insight can be gained through mapping the full range of services used and needed by families with young children. The socio-spatial inequalities of provision that have resulted from the creation of a childcare market are illustrated forcefully (Vincent and Ball, 2006).

Childcare policy has encouraged the development of childcare services to enable parents to access paid work and, in socially deprived areas, to provide socializing experiences for pre-school children (Glass, 1999; Millar, 2003). The scope and limits to childcare policy framed in these terms have been debated in Chapters 1 and 2. The parents' experience of the formal childcare and early years system is explored in relation to the issues of *support, choice* and *need* rather than solely with regard to labour market position. Services to support parents can be *universally* beneficial rather than serving only as a gateway to paid employment or a form of crisis management for families at risk.

Economically poor mothers are especially vulnerable to arguments that pathologize their caring practices (Krane and Davies, 2000; Scourfield, 2001) and some area-based anti-poverty programmes stigmatize those who are perceived to be unable to cope (Gillies, 2005; Kidger, 2004). Social work practitioners may engage in 'mother-blaming' (Turney, 2000) and the concept of 'neglect' is socially constructed and framed in relation to the gendered nature of care so that the focus is on mothers (Daniel and Taylor, 2006). Hence, mothers may be reluctant to articulate their caring practices in relation to feelings of stress or acknowledgement of economic pressures that undermine family well-being. This may help to explain why it was sometimes difficult to encourage mothers to talk openly about the day-to-day pressures of caring for children, an issue explored in Chapter 3. Nevertheless, when the focus was taken away from their caring practices to their perceptions of gaps in service provision, a different picture started to emerge, which the present chapter will seek to present.

The three neighbourhoods will first be introduced with regard to the chief kinds of formal childcare and early years services that are available for parents and children. This will provide an opportunity to indicate the socio-spatial inequalities in service availability resulting from the childcare market. Next, the parents' childcare arrangements are considered in relation to their values, perspectives on formal childcare facilities and access to informal care. This is followed by an examination of the other services that parents may utilize alongside childcare and early years education, and parental perspectives on gaps in service provision are explored. In conclusion, the benefits and drawbacks of current patterns of childcare provision are identified in relation to the criteria of *support, choice* and *need*. The conclusion also links the messages emerging from the research to current academic and policy debates on the relationship between families, locality, and social and cultural capital.

CHILDCARE AND NEIGHBOURHOOD INEQUALITIES

The research was conducted in three areas of a city in Wales with contrasting socio-economic and ethnic profiles, Crossland, Tinbury and Shaw.[1] The areas varied in the types of childcare and early years services available. The overview of service provision is organized with regard to what can be identified as three broad purposes for childcare: childcare for working parents, childcare to support child development and childcare to provide respite for parents (Brunel University, 2000). Childcare for the first category, by definition, relates to only those families where parents are in paid employment. However, it could be argued that there is a case for the delivery of free universal provision in order to meet the second and third categories of need (Daycare Trust, 2003). Current childcare policy in the UK, described in Chapters 1 and 2, directs resources primarily towards working parents, leading to inequalities for families with young children. Childcare policy to support paid work is based on the assumption that the market will respond to local demand whereas childcare policy to support child development and early years education is targeted mainly towards designated socially deprived areas through short-term funding. This means different kinds of childcare provision are available in different localities rather than a universal service capable of meeting diverse needs (Daycare Trust, 2003). Where an individual lives makes a profound difference in terms of access to support, inevitably leaving significant gaps for many parents and children. This undermines policy claims that 'childcare is for children' (WAG, 2005b). The needs of children are met within a volatile and divisive market in childcare leading to stark differences between areas in the availability of childcare for paid work, child development or parental respite.

In practice, childcare and early years education services also overlap (Penn, 2000; Rahilly and Johnston, 2002) and parents may use services outside the area in which they live for a variety of reasons. This was revealed in this research, which uncovered a wide variety of patterns of service use which reflected diversity in the childcare needs of parents and some distinctive value positions on why these services should be used or avoided. These factors interacted with the differences between the three neighbourhoods with regard to the availability of services and socio-economic indicators. What then were the defining characteristics of the three neighbourhoods in this study?

Shaw is an area with a mainly white, middle-class population with a high proportion of people in professional occupations. There are many private day nurseries including those based at the hospital and university that are located within the area. This is also an area that is well served by registered childminders. With regard to out-of-school care, the two largest primary schools in the area run after-school clubs with waiting lists due to high demand. There is also a state nursery school on the Tinbury/Shaw border that offers free, half-day provision for children aged three years and over.[2] There is a pre-school playgroup for children aged three years and above that charged fees and there is a fee-paying Welsh-medium playgroup.

In Shaw, six out of the eight parents in the sample had used formal childcare for the purpose of cover for paid work, and five of them (Janet, Gail, Lowri, Kenneth and Malcolm) had used childcare on a full-time basis. It was only in Shaw that the sample included parents working full-time. None of the parents in the Shaw sample articulated any unease over the use of formal childcare although some did express an intention to limit it. Some parents using formal childcare for paid work also believed that it was good for their child's development, valuing this as an added bonus. Many of the parents in this sample had the financial resources to pay for childcare for their own leisure and respite. Kelly, for example, a married mother with two children, had changed her pattern of part-time work and use of childcare to allow one day at home without her children to free up time for herself and to complete domestic tasks:

> I was working four days, by the time I finished work I was just picking up children and spending time doing things in the house . . . There was no time for me to myself . . . so eventually we changed it. The girls started school and I changed to three full days.

The Shaw sample included mainly parents in professional occupations with the economic means to buy childcare for work, child development and leisure purposes. However, for those parents living in Shaw and lacking these resources, there are no subsidized childcare services designed to provide respite free or at a low cost. Similarly, parents living in this area need to be in a position to pay for early years education until their child becomes eligible for part-time nursery education.

Crossland is a mainly working-class area with an ethnically diverse population. There is limited provision in the immediate locality for parents who need childcare in order to work. There are some private day nurseries bordering the locality, although they tended to be used by parents commuting to work from outside the immediate area. There is a college nursery in a neighbouring area that is accessible to people living in Crossland and had been used by some of the parents who were interviewed. There were no registered childminders offering a service in this area. Primary schools in the area offer half-day nursery provision. One school was operating an after-school club that was closed down during the fieldwork because the numbers using the facility were so low. In addition, Sure Start projects were operating in the area through the Minority Ethnic Women's Network, and these projects offered childcare provision for women attending education and training classes.

Three out of the nine parents in the Crossland sample (Emma, Diane and Farah) had used childcare while they worked on a part-time basis. None of the sample drawn from this area did so on a full-time basis. The three working parents who needed to use formal childcare each reported challenges in terms of accessibility and affordability of the childcare that had been used. The remaining seven parents living in Crossland (Hameeda, Sadiah, Tracey, Rashida, Zeena, Sunita and Aalam) had never used formal childcare to cover for paid work or to provide respite. This group included Tracey, who was unable to work and whose situation was influenced by her disability and health problems. The others were all parents from the Bangladeshi community and some expressed views that they would not be willing to make use of formal provision.[3] Both Rashida and Zeena expressed strong views against the use of formal childcare, describing this as leaving a child 'with strangers'. This position can be contrasted with the use of early years services for *educational* reasons, as all of the parents in this sample were eager for their children to benefit from the half-day nursery provision in the year before they reached school age. In contrast to the Shaw sample, none of these parents reported buying childcare services for the purposes of respite and recreation but some did have considerable support from wider family. Others, such as Farah and Rashida, who were not currently using formal childcare and felt they lacked family support, did report the strains and feelings of isolation that they faced. Their accounts were presented in Chapter 3. Although Farah had used formal childcare in order to work she had found it to be too expensive and inflexible to meet her needs. Rashida held strong views against using any kind of formal childcare facility.

Tinbury's population is mainly white and working-class and the area has significantly high unemployment levels and people living in local authority housing. Many lone parents and young families are housed by the local authority. There are no private day nurseries that provide care for a full working day. There is a crèche at the community resource centre that provides sessional care up to six hours per day. Hence, working parents can use the facility but it cannot cater completely for the needs of those working full-time. Many of the parents who use the crèche are students on college courses taking place in the community resource centre. There were no registered childminders listed in this area. Those parents living in Tinbury who require childcare in order to work full-time would need to look outside the area for registered childcare. In terms of out-of-school care, one school had looked into the possibility of providing an after-school club but had found there was little demand for it.

The area also had a school playgroup, offered in collaboration with the local family centre, for children aged two years and over, and full wrap-around care for children aged three years and over who attend the school nursery. The state nursery school referred to in relation to Shaw also serves the Tinbury area. Another school that serves the area had also developed a crèche for children aged two years and above with subsidized fees. However, the fees were reported to be still out of the reach of many local parents and the leaders were struggling to attract enough children to make the facility viable in the long term. Childcare provision is also offered at the local family centre through a playgroup and crèche while parents attend classes. Social workers and health visitors refer some families to the centre for parenting support and respite. There is further support available through several Sure Start projects and there is a health visitor for Sure Start based at the community resource centre.

In Tinbury, five out of the ten mothers interviewed individually (Natalie, Danielle, Gillian, Sally and Bronwen) used formal childcare while they worked on a part-time basis. They reported complex arrangements to cover for their time at work because of the need to access provision outside the locality or to use a combination of facilities so that their children could benefit from the free half-day nursery provision available in the area in addition to paid-for childcare elsewhere. The Tinbury parents that did not use formal childcare in order to work did use a local pre-school playgroup and nursery facilities.

If the three areas are compared in relation to the three key purposes of childcare, for paid work, child development and parental respite, the differences between the areas are profound. In terms of *childcare to support working parents*, those living in Shaw have access to appropriate provision in the private sector through a choice of day nurseries, out-of-school care and registered childminders. A buoyant private market in childcare has developed as a result of demand from parents in professional occupations who are able to pay for such services. In comparison, working parents living in Crossland may have to make use of childcare outside the immediate area, especially if their children are too young to be placed in the facilities offered by the schools. Parents living in Tinbury who need childcare in order to work face significant difficulties and may need to be willing and able to travel some distance for a place in a day nursery or with a registered childminder. However, the community crèche is providing a useful service for parents who are able to confine their working hours and travel time within the limits of a six-hour session. Three of the mothers in this position (Gillian, Sally and Bronwen) were interviewed. A childcare service based on market demand clearly leaves gaps for working parents living in areas where, for cultural or economic reasons, the majority of parents with young children do not work. In areas such as Shaw, where there is high demand, there are still significant gaps in certain kinds of childcare and for particular age groups.

Turning to *childcare for education and child development*, there are school nurseries and pre-school playgroups operating in all three areas. However, the costs of these groups were variable, generally costing significantly more in Shaw than in Crossland and Tinbury. Whilst there was a long waiting list for the pre-school playgroup in Shaw, the playgroups in Tinbury and Crossland were struggling to attract parents and children. Similarly, the after-school clubs in Shaw had waiting lists whilst the only one operating in Crossland had to close and there were none operating in Tinbury. Hence, the area-based approach to targeting funding for not-for-profit childcare leaves parents on low incomes in Shaw not catered for whilst resources were underused in Tinbury and Crossland, eventually resulting in the closure of services. These are problems of market demand and sustainability that policy-makers are well aware of and will be discussed further in Chapter 5.

With regard to *childcare to provide respite for parents*, there are significant gaps. Access will depend on having the material resources to buy time for respite, being identified as in need of support by a health visitor or social worker, or living in an area that is designated for receipt of targeted funding through programmes such as Sure Start, Flying Start or Communities First. Even for those parents residing in areas that receive targeted funding, respite care cannot be assured. Generally it comes with strings attached such as willingness to participate in further education or training or improving one's parenting skills as opposed to simply having a rest. The notion that all parents need some respite and recognition that opportunities for this might prevent families from reaching the point of crisis does not fit easily within funding regimes and discursive frames that link work, education, childcare and parental responsibility in the ways reported in earlier chapters.

Having provided a picture of main features and range of services in each neighbourhood and identified certain gaps and inequalities, the chapter will now turn to the views of the parents on their childcare arrangements.

PARENTS' CHILDCARE STRATEGIES: VALUES, CHALLENGES AND INFORMAL CARE

How did parents select an appropriate childcare facility? Did they perceive that they had a choice? Were their concerns mainly in the realm of affordability, accessibility and quality as presented in policy? Their accounts revealed some recurrent themes. First, patterns of choice were framed in terms of key values relating to the child and family's well-being. Second, issues of (in)flexibility in childcare services created challenges for many parents. Third, access to informal care from family, friends and neighbours interacted with the use of formal childcare. These themes illustrate different parental perceptions regarding the benefits and drawbacks of using formal childcare and parental capacity to exercise a choice in childcare strategies. Let us explore these themes in relation to the parents' narratives.

Childcare values and well-being

Mothers living in the three areas and in different socio-economic circum-stances agreed that if formal childcare was used it should be limited and that they should devise ways to maximize the time they could spend with their children. Danielle, a lone parent with one child and working part-time, offered comments that echoed the feelings of many of the mothers:

> I didn't want her to go to after-school club five days per week as I think that is still a bit too much. So I try to think about how much work I accepted as well. I try to keep her with me as much as possible.

Yet the research also points to some possible *differences* in patterns of use between the three areas that could reflect different local cultural practices and values. These may be connected with gendered moral codes even though they were actually expressed in terms of not gender but rather what was 'best' for children. More specifically, some mothers in Crossland and Tinbury expressed concerns regarding whether formal childcare was safe for children. This theme concerning child safety has been uncovered in other studies that explore parental perspectives on childcare (Skinner and Finch, 2006).

Whilst some parents in the Shaw sample wanted to limit their use of formal childcare and some mothers stated a preference to be home with their children, none of them expressed anxiety about using childcare in terms of safety, risk or the well-being of their children. Indeed, they justified their use of childcare in order to work on the grounds that their children were also benefiting educationally or enjoyed their time in childcare. In contrast, some of the parents in Crossland and Tinbury held strong views that it was not appropriate to send children to a formal childcare facility. This was not expressed as a general unwillingness to let their children leave their care, as all parents were supportive of pre-school education, especially where this was delivered in a school setting. For some parents, teachers are seen as trusted professionals whereas childcare workers are not. Sending children to a facility for educational and developmental reasons sits easily with these parents' sense of moral obligation and concerns over keeping children safe. These views could be a reflection of differences between those living in Shaw, Crossland and Tinbury in social class position and in their perceptions of community safety in their neighbourhood.

In the group interviews, the four mothers living in Tinbury with children attending the local nursery school articulated firm views against mothers working while their children were of pre-school age, in relation to issues of trust and safety. Whilst they were willing to trust teachers, they felt that they could not be sure of people working as childminders or in crèches. One mother commented that she trusted the teachers only because her children were attending the same school that she had attended, a view that had also been expressed by some of the Bangladeshi mothers in Crossland. Zeena, for example, who had said that she worked only because she could rely totally on her extended family to care for her child, said:

> You hear all these things in the media, as well, don't you? About children being shaken to death and things like that. I get petrified. For a while I was paranoid about leaving [son] in school as well. He is my only child and I love him to bits and I wouldn't part with him for the world. That is why this school is really good because I came here and I brought my sisters to school and everything and I got to know the teachers as well.

Those mothers and fathers who were living in difficult material circumstances seemed to have a heightened awareness of issues relating to child safety and a distrust of formal childcare. Bostock argues that we need to understand child protection 'in terms of structural rather than individual issues' (Bostock, 2002: 281) as families in poor material circumstances can face greater problems in keeping their children safe and in maintaining their well-being. In this context, the views offered by the parents are not surprising and have a material basis. Concerns about safety and being certain their child's general well-being is guaranteed may take priority over factors such as affordability and convenience in the organization of childcare.

Parents who did use formal childcare were asked to reflect on what they liked about the facilities that they had used. Their responses reflected two broad themes that each connected again with the concern to secure the well-being of their child. First, parents valued the opportunities for education and play offered to their children:

> She has a great time and she doesn't miss me. I am quite happy that she is learning lots and she gets lots of social interaction, which is really important, especially pre-school. (Diane, Crossland)

> We were clear that we wanted to use a day nursery because of the greater number of interactions that occur and the belief that kids get more rounded personalities if they socialize. (Kenneth, Shaw)

Second, there were some mothers who were not fully confident about their own role in fostering child development and felt that they could draw on the professional expertise of staff. Gillian, for example, said that she felt that she had received more advice from staff at her daughter's crèche than she had been able to get from her overworked health visitor. She continued:

> Yes, they have been marvellous. A lot of her developments, because I was working, such as potty training, a lot of that went on at the crèche. They have more knowledge than I have.

Joy, who used crèche facilities at the family centre, valued the centre's role in running parenting classes. She argued that these classes needed to be made more widely available across local community centres:

> We have discussed health, you know, healthy eating and behavioural problems. It has only been going since September and we try to cover different things each week. It is informal and nice to chat about one thing that you have found you have a problem with and come up with solutions between you.

Joy, along with other mothers involved in this research, appreciated parenting support initiatives, as did the fathers involved with a Sure Start project in Tinbury. This was a support group for fathers facing specific challenges, such as securing contact with their children or having to care for children alone. The fathers had been interviewed as a group during the research and three (Patrick, Michael and Leo) had subsequently offered individual interviews. The fathers involved with this Sure Start initiative all spoke of the valuable role that the project played in supporting them:

> It gets you out of the house and you get to meet people. Otherwise my life would just be working and looking after the children. Coming here takes me away from that routine. (Leo)

> It is not to isolate yourself from society but to come and talk and play football and pool, open yourself up a bit more than you would if you were just indoors isolated from society and you don't know where to turn. You have a target to go to and then you feel better at the end of the day. (Patrick)

The fathers also shared their thoughts on some of the problems that fathers may face in terms of wider questions of social prejudice, professional attitudes to fathers and the need for help in coping with care. This is a model that could be expanded beyond those fathers who are identified as being 'at risk'. *All* fathers could benefit from these issues being aired and addressed in family and childcare policy. The book will return to this point in the concluding chapter.

How do we make sense of these positive reports from mothers and fathers regarding their experience of family support and Sure Start projects in the city in relation to criticism that these parenting programmes are based on notions of family pathology (Gillies, 2005)? First, the expression of appreciation for parenting support reveals how local social practices (such as participation in parenting education classes) are tied into wider systems of regulation through discursive frames that remind parents of their responsibilities. These parents are engaging in processes of 'self-surveillance' that may have been reinforced through their participation in these programmes. Those parents, such as Joy, who have been identified as being in need of support and have participated in parent education programmes thus become competent in using the discourses to represent their care practices to others. The Sure Start fathers seemed to do this by referring to themselves as 'hands-on dads'. The project worker, who was also a single father, stressed the project was to provide support rather than to campaign:

> We don't want to be seen to be waving banners and all that but there is an organization called Fathers for Justice who are very active. We are doing our bit by being hands-on fathers and showing an interest in our children.

Even though the argument offered by Gillies (2005) that there is a moralizing discourse surrounding parenting initiatives is convincing, the research revealed that some of the workers in the city's Sure Start projects had a more progressive understanding of their role in working with parents and in community development. This suggests there is scope for professionals to maintain alternative understandings of how parental support should be delivered that avoid moralizing or stigmatizing. These different understandings may emerge from professional discourse and from practice. Both parenting practices and professional understandings of how parental support should be offered are thus tied into powerful discursive frames but are not entirely contained by them.

(In)flexibility in childcare provision

Parents were highly critical of the high costs of childcare revealing that the goal of policy to address affordability issues is to be welcomed. Other studies have also identified the continuing problem of affordability for families on low and modest incomes (Ben-Galim, 2011b). However, concerns over the high cost of formal childcare interacted with a more complex set of considerations over the lack of flexibility in what local services could offer. Many parents felt that formal childcare was not adaptable enough to cater for diverse needs, shifting work patterns, emergencies and sick children.

Here too, these findings echo other studies in relation to the childcare barriers that parents may face (Bryson et al., 2006).

Malcolm, who was married with a five-year-old daughter, argued that parents lacking any informal support faced particular difficulties. It was hard for working parents to manage occasional and unpredictable gaps in childcare created when schools closed on account of bad weather or occasional staff development days, or when children fell ill. Whilst it is sometimes believed that childminders offer the flexibility to cover these gaps, he had found that childminders were interested only in work from parents needing regular childcare rather than on ad hoc occasions. Similarly, Danielle, who had spoken of her disadvantage in lack of access to informal family care, said that she would like the provision of flexible paid-for care to help parents cope with emergencies. Kelly had found that there were no childminders in Shaw willing to do a pick-up from school as it paid more to give priority to pre-school children requiring a full-time place. Hence, even in an area such as Shaw that was better served by childminders than Tinbury or Crossland, it was not necessarily true that childminders offered the flexibility required by parents to cover these gaps.

Other parents commented that childcare was inflexible in that most providers wanted a regular commitment. Providers required parents to give several weeks' notice if they no longer needed a place, would operate a policy of taking children only for a minimum number of sessions per week and generally required that sessions should be on the same day each week. Whereas parents would have valued support for a short period of time to get some respite, it seemed impossible to find a provider willing to do this. Farah had been exasperated that she could not find a childcare facility willing to take a child for just one or two hours per day. Similarly, Sally, a young lone parent with no informal support, felt that there should be a facility for parents who simply wanted some respite for an hour or two:

> There is not that much choice for those on a low budget. There is not that much choice for them. There is a lot of choice for professionals with families and stuff but not much choice for women who just need a break because they have no mothers and just need one morning a week or something.

Some mothers did report that the Tinbury community crèche offered a more flexible service in this regard than other childcare providers. Gillian had found that the crèche was willing to take her daughter for ad hoc sessions and this was important because her husband worked rotating shifts, meaning their childcare needs varied each week. Bronwen had been able to use this facility for ad hoc sessions prior to using it on a more regular basis. However, this crèche is unusual in the city in offering this degree of flexibility, and the views of these parents would suggest that this is a service that should be more widely available.

Childcare providers also do not cater for the wide variety of working patterns that parents may be required to work. Bronwen, a young lone parent living in Tinbury, had to rely on informal care to cover periods when she started work early in the morning and on a Saturday. She was working shifts in a call centre that could change from week to week. She stated there should be a twenty-four-hour, seven days per week facility to cater for the needs of parents working irregular shifts. Greta, a student nurse, had also argued that there should be a twenty-four-hour nursery for hospital staff along the lines she had been used to in her home country. Joy, although deciding to stay at home while her child was young, felt that it would be difficult for her to find suitable work in the future as she lacked qualifications and most of the jobs that she would be able to do, such as shop work or elderly care, extended to weekends and hours not covered by most childcare providers.

Another theme to emerge from the interviews was of the impact of transitions in a child's life such as beginning school. The parents with older children found that managing childcare had become more difficult once their child had started school, contrary to popular perceptions. Parents who had made extensive use of formal childcare in the early years, and those with no informal support to plug gaps, faced new problems with this transition. Whereas private day nurseries, nannies and childminders may offer cover for a long day for most of the year for those able to pay, once children start school there are many gaps that not all childcare providers are willing or available to fill. Some parents found that dropping children off at school was especially difficult because schools would not accept children in the playground until there was staff supervision in the morning. This was a big source of exasperation for Kenneth:

> I start work here at half-past eight and there are times when [wife] has got a nine o'clock lecture or occasionally a nine o'clock meeting and she will be called in for that and the school starts at nine. So there is always that little quarter of an hour, twenty minutes and just to know that there was either a pre-school club, not even a breakfast club, but just pre-school supervision in the playground so that we could safely leave [child] there. (Kenneth, Shaw)

Lowri and Kelly also referred to this difficulty, as both had to start work at nine o'clock, meaning a frantic dash from school to work. Kenneth's suggestion (quoted above) was that this could be resolved through the availability of early playground supervision; other parents had made it known to the school that they would like a breakfast club. Both primary schools in the Shaw area have since opened breakfast clubs, an initiative supported by the Welsh Government. Nevertheless, one advisor to the Welsh Government who was interviewed said that the initiative had been 'sold' to schools on grounds of health rather than childcare in order to avoid objections from the teaching unions.

The parents who were using after-school clubs were highly satisfied with the service that they provided. Janet, for example, was a divorced mother living with a new partner in Shaw. She had recently taken on a full-time post in a business that required unpredictable and unsocial working hours. She had three adult children and one son aged eight years. She had been pleased that she was able to secure a place in the after-school club:

> The after-school club is brilliant. It is straight from school and it is up to six o'clock. And I find that is such good value. Because whenever I go to get him, he is always doing something – playing draughts or chess. So that is an enjoyable extension of their education as they are always doing something that is constructive. (Janet, Shaw)

Other parents had faced problems in coping with this period after school. Kelly, for example, had found that, despite Shaw being well served by registered childminders, none were available just to do a school pick-up. She was on the waiting list for the after-school club for a long time. While parents in Shaw have to wait for a place at the two after-school clubs in the area, parents using the after-school club in Crossland had been told it would close down because of insufficient numbers, leaving them with no alternative in the area. The two lone mothers living in Tinbury using after-school care, Natalie and Danielle, had moved to the area recently as a consequence of being rehoused but had continued to send their children to a school several miles away in Crossland that had an after-school club rather than move them to a local school where there was no provision. Both were extremely concerned that this after-school club was about to close down.

The remaining major gap reported by many working parents with older children concerned cover for the school holidays, a gap also revealed in other studies (Bryson et al., 2006; Smith et al., 2010). Many had no idea how they were going to manage the school holidays as it was never clear when and where holiday play schemes would run. This is one area where parents felt strongly that information and publicity could be better managed. Janet's comments were typical of other working parents with school age children:

> I don't think there is enough childcare available. I found it hard to find. I don't feel that I have got the right childcare for [child] as far as the school holidays are concerned. I know that in the long term I am going to have to look for somewhere but even the schemes that are run by the council, there are never enough places. The places are usually booked months in advance.

Many parents said that they had no idea where to go for advice on holiday cover. Some parents felt that holiday play schemes ran only in certain designated areas whilst other areas such as Shaw were left without any local provision.

Most parents valued the half-day nursery provision that is available across the city for children in the year before they start school. However, it was also acknowledged that this could be very difficult to manage where parents were working. Some parents had to change their work and childcare arrangements to accommodate this, whilst others had to forgo the free half-day place and keep a child in a private day nursery until they started school. Malcolm felt that the transition from day nursery to school was often poorly managed. Most schools in the city stagger intake to reception classes, so that parents who have been using full-time formal childcare suddenly find that their child has to start school on half-days initially, and some schools alternate between morning and afternoon sessions, so arranging childcare cover can be very difficult:

> One of my colleagues, she lived on the other side of [city] and she was having to drive out, pick the child up from nursery, take the child up to school and get back. She had an hour to do that and she had to try to get a lunch in between. The stress levels are horrendous. It was the only way that she could do it as there was no other way of getting the child from one place to the other. She also had the stress of trying to remember which way the child was going as well because the school had the [new children] mornings one week and afternoons the next week! (Malcolm, Shaw)

The inflexibility parents may encounter from certain schools was a strong concern. This suggests that some schools could manage these transitions in a way that shows more consideration to parents in paid work. Some schools are making significant effort to cater for working parents but, based on these accounts, others appear to be very unhelpful.

The interaction between informal support and use of formal childcare

The availability of social networks of support, provided by family, friends and neighbours, was important in helping many mothers and fathers manage childcare and avoid social isolation. These are predominantly gendered social networks and they do confer advantages for those mothers and fathers who have access to this form of social capital (Edwards and Gillies, 2005; Reay, 2000, 2005). Where the mothers and fathers in this research did not have any informal support available, they were acutely aware that this placed them at a disadvantage. At worst, these informal networks may actively exclude certain mothers, contributing to distress and feelings of isolation.[4] These social networks can be important for sustaining gendered moral understandings relating to the care of children: that, if it cannot be done entirely by mothers, the acceptable alternative is care by female relatives, friends or neighbours.

Parents could be divided into one of four groups to describe the inter-action of formal childcare and informal support in their management of childcare. This is an alternative way of examining childcare needs that disrupts the notion that these needs should be assessed primarily in rela-tion to whether or not parents are working. Rather, this looks at their needs in terms of their access to networks of support and moral notions sur-rounding care and children's well-being. Parents were placed in a group according to their current circumstances but it must be appreciated that their childcare histories revealed they may have moved between categories over time.

Table 4.1 locates each parent with regard to whether or not they use formal childcare and whether they have access to any informal support.

What were the characteristics of parents in each of the four childcare combinations? What did these four combinations reveal that could be

Table 4.1: Managing childcare through formal and informal support

Combination of formal and informal care	Do use formal childcare provision	Do not use formal childcare provision
No informal childcare support	A (n = 5) Kelly (S) Lowri (S) Kenneth (S) Malcolm (S) Sally (T)	B (n = 7) Becky (S) Greta (S) Gail (S) Rashida (C) Farah (C) Stella (T) Margaret (T)
Do have informal childcare support	C (n = 9) Janet (S) Emma (C) Diane (C) Tracey (C) Natalie (T) Danielle (T) Christine (T) Gillian (T) Bronwen (T)	D (n = 11) Hameeda (C) Sadiah (C) Zeena (C) Aalam (C) Sunita (C) Sheila (T)[a] Joy (T) Four nursery mothers interviewed as a group: Jane, Liz, Brenda and Yvonne (T)

Notes
The assignment of each parent to one of the four categories excluded parental use of early years education solely for the purpose of education and socialization. This was because *all* the parents expressed a willingness to enrol their child for a pre-school placement at the appropriate time. Each parent has also been identified in relation to where they live (S = Shaw; T = Tinbury; C = Crossland). The fathers from Sure Start have not been included in the analysis because their interviews focused on other issues.
a   This mother works in Tinbury but lives outside the area.

relevant for policy? These questions are addressed in relation to each of the four combinations.

Group A (no informal support/do use formal childcare) included only five parents. This group used formal childcare with no access to informal support. It might be expected that parents lacking informal support would have the greatest need to utilize formal childcare. However, as the parents' narratives revealed, formal childcare does not cater for all working patterns, is expensive, can be inflexible and does not provide cover for sickness. It can be particularly difficult to balance work and formal care in the absence of any informal support to plug gaps and to limit the costs. Parents in both two-parent and lone-parent families may find that it is easier for one parent to stay at home full-time rather than cope with trying to manage this challenge in the absence of any informal assistance. This group of five comprised mainly parents from the Shaw area who were in well-paid professional jobs. Nevertheless, Lowri and Malcolm both spoke at length about the problems created when their children were ill because they had no informal support to help manage this.

There were seven parents in *Group B (no informal support/do not use formal childcare)*. Where parents lack any informal support, this may lead to a decision for one parent to give up work or make 'shift parenting' (Lewis, 2003) arrangements rather than use formal childcare while both parents work. There were some mothers in this category who did not use formal childcare on the basis of moral values as well as practical considerations; this led them to give up work (Rashida, full-time mother), rearrange their hours of work (Stella, night nurse) or do a home-based job that enabled them to be with their children (Margaret, childminder). Other mothers, such as Gail, reluctantly gave up work, having previously used formal childcare, because it became too stressful and the demands of combining paid work and care were undermining their health. The availability of informal support might have reduced some of the strains facing Gail. Others, such as Farah, had tried to work and use formal childcare but found they could not afford the high costs.

The nine mothers in *Group C (do have informal support/do use formal childcare)* did paid work and made use of formal childcare, yet relied on informal arrangements to cover the gaps. The availability of this access to informal care made the use of formal childcare possible for these mothers. Nevertheless, for some of these mothers, there were worries that these informal arrangements may break down. Despite the availability of informal support, some mothers felt stressed out and guilty about asking for help. Danielle and Natalie, for example, had a reciprocal arrangement but felt that it was different relying on friends rather than family. This perspective is supported by other research into issues of obligation and reciprocity in informal childcare arrangements that shows grandparent care may be offered on a different basis from care by friends or neighbours (Skinner and

Finch, 2006). Both Danielle and Natalie still felt vulnerable because they had no family living in Wales. Bronwen was only able to start work at eight o'clock and use a crèche that opened at nine o'clock by relying on a friend. The friend would look after her son for an hour and take him to the crèche: 'We have sorted it, we swap children as she is on her own as well'. She had been in work for only a few weeks and had persuaded her father to babysit on those Saturdays when she was working but said she was not sure that she could keep asking him to do this. Similarly, Emma, who was a lone parent working part-time and had two children aged eight and six years, said she could ask her father to help if her children were ill. Yet she talked of feeling this should be limited:

> My dad would help then in emergencies. I don't ask him all the time to have the children. As they just run round him and he just spends silly money on them. He spoils them. I like to keep my dad for emergencies. I don't like to put on him all the time.

Janet was also able to access informal care to cover emergencies and on ad hoc occasions. This was provided by her older children, and, like Emma, Janet spoke of not wishing to take advantage of their offer of support. The management of work and childcare for parents in this category can still be a strain, informal care may not be taken for granted and it may be under-stood as a source of social capital that should not be abused. Nevertheless, it remains noteworthy that these parents' access to informal care to cover some of their childcare needs was what made it possible for them to work and make some use of formal childcare provision.

The final group of eleven mothers in *Group D (do have informal support/ do not use formal childcare)* managed childcare with informal support from family and friends entirely and did not make any use of formal childcare. Some of these parents were working and said that they were able to do so because of this informal care from family. Both Zeena and Sheila worked on the basis that they had extensive informal support. Both expressed the view that they would not continue paid work if they had to turn to formal childcare. Other mothers such as Sadiah, Sunita, Joy and the group of four mothers at the nursery did not feel it appropriate for them to work while their children were young. Hameeda and her husband were both able to work without using formal care on the basis of 'shift-parenting' and limited informal assistance if their working hours overlapped.

Each combination of managing care has its benefits and its drawbacks with implications for parental well-being. Parents' satisfaction with their arrangements can also vary significantly within each group. Parents in Group A may appear to be the most materially privileged group in that they have employment that enables them to use formal childcare, pursue a career and have respite although they have no recourse to informal care.

Four out of the five parents in this group were white, middle-class professionals living in Shaw. These are the parents for whom the private childcare market has traditionally catered and childcare policy has been seeking to extend this model to a wider group of parents through the childcare tax credit system. Nevertheless, these parents still reported stresses in plugging the gaps, such as when a child is ill. For these parents the lack of informal care to complement paid-for childcare can still be a problem despite their capacity to pay.

Parents placed in Group B varied considerably in their satisfaction with an arrangement that meant they had no relief from childcare, either formally or informally. Potentially this could be seen as the most vulnerable group, yet feelings about their position depended on how much control parents perceived they had over it. Becky and Margaret, both working as childminders, relished being home full-time with their children despite lacking informal support that would provide respite. Their current situation was expressed as a positive choice. In contrast, Rashida was resentful and depressed and felt isolated, but nevertheless felt strongly that the use of formal childcare to enable her to work was not appropriate. Both Gail and Farah had reluctantly stopped using formal childcare. These mothers all seem to conform in varying ways to the model of the 'sensitive mother' (Walkerdine and Lucey, 1989), making accommodations for their children, but their respective feelings about doing so could not be more different.

Parents of Group C seemed fortunate in that they were able to organize a combination of formal and informal care enabling them to work or study as well as to get some respite. Nevertheless, they were vulnerable in that they were aware that these informal arrangements could break down or change in the future. The need to rely on informal support also caused feelings of guilt for some. Finally, those parents in Group D seemed to have the least anxiety about their arrangements. They had access to sufficient informal support to be able to work without using formal childcare (e.g. Zeena, Sheila) and to avoid social isolation if they were not in paid work or education (e.g. Sunita, Joy, nursery mothers). Nevertheless, even in these apparently favourable circumstances, mothers' moral codes could influence how they felt about their arrangements. Hameeda enjoyed her work and was highly satisfied sharing care mainly with her husband, whilst Sheila, who had considerable family support, was unhappy about working full-time because she felt that she was missing out on precious time with her child.

These four broad patterns of managing childcare indicate that factors such as the means to pay for formal childcare (whether through well-paid work or access to tax credits) and flexible working conditions may help those parents who are in paid work, but complex moral and emotional factors will impact on the degree to which childcare will be extended beyond the family. The availability of emotional and social capital in the form of informal support for managing childcare plays a significant role in enabling some mothers to do paid work with childcare arrangements that remain in tune with their moral codes and concerns over child safety. This was especially true for mothers living in Crossland and Tinbury, supporting claims that there are geographies of childcare in which access to gendered social capital is one key distinguishing factor (Duncan, 2005).

PARENTS' USE OF OTHER SERVICES FOR FAMILIES AND CHILDREN

In placing use of childcare in the context of family well-being, it was important to find out how parents spent their time with their children, what they enjoyed most about family life, what they found difficult and which local services were used in this context. In the next sub-section, what parents liked doing with their children in their neighbourhood or beyond will be explored. After that, the chapter will return to the theme of gaps in policy and services with regard to what else parents felt could be offered to support their role.

Enjoying time with children

When asked to talk about how they spent leisure time with their children, many parents observed that the city was a good place for families with young children because of the wide range of outdoor attractions including the parks, cycle paths and the beaches:

> There are lots of parks, so there is no shortage of those. Just being near the sea, the countryside and the sea is much better than when I was in [English city]. (Kelly, Shaw)

Parents also made positive comments about the availability of parent and toddler groups in their local area, suggesting these can be a vital source of socializing opportunities for many. One mother who had been active in running a local parent and toddler group said:

> As soon as I started going to those groups I started making local friends, other mothers in a similar situation. I think there should be one for every day of the week. (Bronwen, Tinbury)

Bronwen further commented that one of the drawbacks of her return to paid work was that she was no longer able to attend these groups, cutting her off from this valued contact with other local mothers with pre-school children. Other studies of mothering have pointed to the creation of friendship groups among mothers accessing playgroups and other activities for their children. These groups can be an important source of support and access to other opportunities, but can also play a role in the reproduction of existing class and ethnic inequalities (Byrne, 2006).

Local groups can make a major difference to the well-being of parents and their children. Joy's position, referred to earlier, illustrated this point. She had been depressed until her health visitor recommended that she get in touch with her local family centre:

> I go along Monday morning to a parenting class and [son] stays down in the crèche facilities for the morning and they have lunch. Then Tuesday morning we have drop-in session, which is mums and babies and we stay for dinner. We talk about childcare or whatever. It is just nice for the mums to sit and chat and the children can play together.

Some parents acknowledged that these parent and toddler groups could exclude certain parents and this could reinforce social inequalities. Diane attended a number of parent and toddler groups in Crossland but felt that these were still run as a 'female space':

> I know some of them are changing and are called parent and toddler but it still seems to be very one-sided. I don't know if that is because women are generally the main carers. I think these places could do something to actually make men feel more comfortable about going to these groups. I think some things are still behind the times a bit, definitely.

This was also an issue for Hameeda, given that her husband was the main carer for their son during the day:

> I think [city] needs a place for babies and their fathers rather than mothers. Why can't he be paternal? That is my point really. I think they need something for single fathers, fathers who are looking after children in the daytime.

Where parents did attend local groups, they tended to hear about them through word of mouth as often they were not well advertised. More could be done in this regard to reach parents who are not part of existing social networks. Christine (Tinbury) said that she would like somewhere to go locally to meet other mothers:

> Just getting the community together. Rather than being stuck in the house, get them out and get the children playing. If you can't afford childcare, somewhere to go for the morning.

Christine was unaware that her local family centre provided this service only five minutes' walk from her home. Similarly, Sally expressed an interest in attending local parent and toddler groups but had moved into the area a few months before and did not know where to look. Local churches run the vast majority of groups, suggesting that the voluntary sector plays a valuable role in providing this service for parents. However, it may be that some help is needed in coordinating information so parents can easily find out what is available in their area. The Children's Information Service in this city was only at an early stage in development at the time of the fieldwork.[5]

Parents also appreciated evening groups for older children such as kids' clubs, Cubs and Brownies, and sporting activities, and, once again, churches play a significant role. Parents from the Bangladeshi community mentioned the role of the mosques, the local Islamic bookshop, MEWN and the Bangladeshi Welfare Association as places that offered activities for children. Zeena, for example, mentioned the valuable role played by MEWN in reaching out to women and children:

> Well, there is MEWN. They organize activities and things like that so we usually go with them to places . . . They usually try to organize it so that there is a fun day to help people get out and about a bit more. Because some people cannot afford things. So that is really helpful what they do. And they organize exercise classes for women and things like that.

These groups played a valued role in promoting the well-being of parents and in providing play and educational opportunities for children. They also have the potential to help in the creation of networks of social support that can be crucial, especially for those lacking family-based social capital. A coordinated strategy for publicizing this provision would help ensure more parents and children benefit from local facilities.

Supporting parents

Parents identified some concerns that related to environmental factors that varied between the three neighbourhoods and the parents' particular material circumstances. The key concerns included children's safety, access to transport and affordable leisure facilities for families. Parents' consideration of safety issues was identified earlier in the chapter with regard to patterns of use of formal childcare facilities. Parental concerns about safety were also articulated in relation to the need for safe play areas for children, protection from traffic and concerns over drug dealing. Mothers and fathers living in the less affluent areas of Tinbury and Crossland were especially likely to raise these concerns. Aalam (Crossland), for example, felt that he could not allow his older children to walk home from school alone:

> It is becoming a very unpredictable place, [city]. Especially with central [city], so it is quite risky leaving them on their own. It is because there are a lot of drugs about, it is because the streets are not properly maintained. People are driving fast where there are no cameras. It is getting a busier place every day. Before it used to be more like a residential area with a family atmosphere.

One of the fathers who had joined a Sure Start group for single fathers, Michael, lived in Crossland and expressed similar concerns about drugs. He felt that he could not take his daughters to the local park because he believed drug addicts and alcoholics frequented it. Emma lived opposite a children's play area in Crossland and had contacted her local councillor because the area was being used in an inappropriate way:

> And all the drunks were coming down the lane and laying on the green by the park and I just had enough one day. The kids were playing in the park and there were all these drunken men hanging around.

Some of the parents in Tinbury were frustrated that where efforts were made to provide safe play areas for children these were quickly vandalised. The mothers from the nursery regretted that there were not enough outdoor play areas for children. The mothers pointed out that there needed to be firmer efforts to tackle crime in the area. One mother said:

> My oldest boy had his bike pinched off him by an older boy and when I went to the station, they said they hadn't got enough police in the community to go around the parks. The children have bikes because it is safer for them to come home, because it is quicker for them, but nobody is around to do anything about it. (Group interview, Tinbury)

Joy (Tinbury) also spoke about the lack of outdoor play areas in the neighbourhood, which meant that she needed transport to get to a park in a safer area:

> And the parks, there aren't really many parks. They started doing a park up by the centre but the kids have started wrecking it already and there aren't swings and things for younger ones. And the nearest one, I think, there is one little one down the hill halfway between here and town but it is in the back of nowhere and it is a bit, you know, I feel a bit dubious about going down there on my own so it tends to be when I have got someone with me who can take me in the car to a park.

Joy's comments illustrate how concerns over safety in the local area may interact with access to transport. Parents in Tinbury were particularly likely to refer to problems of using public transport with their children. Joy, who was unable to drive, continued to talk about this issue:

> It is just that most things tend to be so spread out that if you haven't got a car like a lot of people up here, and before [husband] started working we didn't have a car and you have got to plan ahead. You may have to catch two buses to get to the park in [Shaw]. Or you have to wait for a day that someone can give you a lift or wait till it was a fine day and walk down. There isn't in the locality, places for you to go just on the spur of the moment, you have always got to think how am I going to get there and is it suitable to go today?

Christine (Tinbury) was also unable to drive and was reliant on her husband for her transport needs. Christine found that it was too stressful trying to use public transport with young children:

> Oh, if you take a bus to town and the bus doesn't take a buggy, you have to put the buggy down and you are trying to watch the baby. I have done it once and I am not doing it again. So if I need town I will wait until my husband can take me.

Maternal depression was linked with social isolation and lack of access to private transport, as identified in Chapter 3. Bronwen (Tinbury) felt that her life had improved since she got her own car and said: 'Especially where Tinbury is, before I had the car, I was either walking or waiting an age for buses. Basically everything was just hard work. Going shopping, that was impossible'. These responses reveal that improved public transport and the expansion of more local services for parents and children could enhance family well-being. This material supports the findings of other studies on the relationship between gender and transport (Hamilton et al., 2005; Winckler, 2009), including evidence that women are less likely than men to have access to private transport (Welsh Consumer Council/Equal Opportunities Commission, 2005).

The third common area of concern related to the availability of indoor leisure and play facilities:

> There are lots of things if the weather is good – we have the beach, the cycle paths . . . A few parks. When it comes to a pouring, rainy, wet day, then there is nothing. Excel Wales has closed down, the leisure centre has closed. (Diane, Crossland)

Many parents felt that the city was lacking in a choice of affordable and accessible indoor leisure activities. When asked about where they would go with their children when the weather was poor, some parents mentioned going to the cinema, ten-pin bowling and the soft play areas. However, parents on low and modest incomes commented on how expensive this could be:

> The covered-in play places up in the leisure centre or in [local area], it is a couple of pounds to get in, in the first place and it is a good distance to get to as well. (Joy, Tinbury)

> If you have got more than one child, two or three children, then going to places with them is expensive. If you go swimming, and you pay for each child and for yourself, it is expensive. There should be more cheaper stuff to do. (Margaret, Tinbury)

The interviews took place in the period following the closure of a local leisure centre. Many parents had made considerable use of this facility and were disappointed that it had closed. They missed the wide range of activities that they had been able to do with their children and they felt they had lost much more than another swimming pool:

> Well, being a single mum or single parent, there was a lot for single parents. If I want to keep fit, there is no way that I can do it, so I did use the leisure [sic] for the crèche. And I would go to the gym for an hour, and [daughter] would play with the other children and then we would go swimming. So we used the crèche, the gym, swimming. (Diane, Crossland)

> You know if you go somewhere, wanted to go to the gym for an hour, if he [son] could go to a crèche? They used to do that in the leisure centre but it is closed down now and there is nowhere else for him to go like that . . . they should do other things, somewhere else. I used to like going to the gym. It made me feel like I was doing something for myself. I don't get a chance now. (Sally, Tinbury)

In the cases quoted above, the mothers used the leisure centre for respite and time for themselves. This was an issue that interacted with issues of religious, cultural and linguistic needs. With regard to the use of leisure facilities, several of the mothers mentioned that they would like the wider availability of single-sex swimming, something that would be important to enable them to ensure their children learned to swim:

> There is only one place where they have women swimming facilities and that is at [local] school. On Sundays they have the swimming pool open for an hour for women and children. There are no men there at all and there is a woman lifeguard as well. It is really difficult because it is only on a Sunday and it is only for an hour. (Zeena)

I would love to use swimming pools. There is one big swimming pool available in [local] school that they do after school. But for a Muslim mother, there is not much available. (Farah)

Sunita talked about access to leisure in relation to her experience of racism and her feeling that she wanted to protect her children from this:

It is either the scarf or the skin or whatever. Like when we go to the beach you can see the stares. I still take them but, as Muslims, we have to be covered. They don't understand. They do hear but nothing violent or whatever. It does upset me sometimes but I try not to show it as I want them to grow up thinking my way of life can be compatible. (Sunita)

These experiences point to the imperative for service providers to consult with parents over the kinds of services that they value and to ensure their responses are based on principles of equality and diversity; this issue has been recognized by the Welsh Government (WAG, 2006).

'Somewhere for just an hour': needing a break from care?

Childcare policy is not geared towards the provision of respite from the parenting role for all mothers or fathers. Parents are generally left to arrange this for themselves, either through paying for a service or through informal support. Those parents who are on a low income and lack informal support may find it especially hard to get some time alone. This gap appears to contradict claims that childcare policy seeks to meet the interests and well-being of children and parents as well as to address the needs of the labour market.

Some parents raised the issue of needing a flexible, short-term care facility. Others suggested that they missed having any leisure time apart from their children but felt morally obliged to look after them. Bronwen, for example, a young lone mother living in Tinbury, was currently using formal childcare and informal support from a friend and her father in order to work and attend evening classes but did not feel that she had a right to ask for support in order to socialize. She said that she never went out with friends in the evening:

Perhaps I don't ask for as much help as I could do, as I have got good friends who are always saying, oh, perhaps you should go out . . . but I feel that unless it is something really important, it is my duty to look after him . . . When I go to college, that is something important in a way that enjoying myself isn't.

Moral discourses surrounding the duties involved in motherhood appeared to shape Bronwen's narrative: her claims reflected welfare-to-work policy discourses relating to young, single parents that time spent away from children is to improve one's prospects through hard work and study. Childcare and parenting services based on an ethic of care for both children and parents would help disrupt these ways of thinking.

Other parents did reflect that parenting was stressful and that they would value an opportunity for a break from it. Rashida (Crossland), for example, was at home full-time and expressed this need for respite:

> Activities like where you can leave your child for one or two hours. I know it is just one hour but at least you can come home and for that hour have time for myself.

Farah (Crossland) worked part-time and made a similar point:

> It is always rush, rush, rush. Now I have to go and cook and clean, the house is a tip. It is just one thing after another. There is no time to relax . . . Because if I go out, I have to take my kids, so I can't really enjoy myself . . . I would love to have more time for myself, go out and stuff.

Later, Farah went on to suggest her needs could be met through more flexible childcare services:

> They are not flexible at all. Maybe some more mother and toddler groups like the one [local school] are doing, where for a few hours you can leave the child and do things. Rather than the formal thing like [private day nursery].

A number of parents pointed out that they had used the crèche provided by the leisure centre in order to 'do something for themselves' or to go shopping:

> Just a play place for mothers who want to go to the gym and leave them there. It would be good as well to have somewhere for just an hour. You know what I mean? Like a drop-in place where they can be looked after or you can play with them. It would be good if they combined a number of things for mothers, all within one central place. It is awkward taking them here and going there. (Sally)

Sally went on to observe that, where this kind of facility was offered, it tended to be in return for parents signing up to study or training: 'Some mothers don't want to go into full-time education but would like somewhere to go and then if they could have an hour that was flexible . . . it would be much better for them'. A system of support that respects the principle of parental well-being could ensure that all parents have access to 'somewhere just for an hour'. At present, as Sally has observed, access to respite from childcare for those with limited financial resources comes, if at all, in exchange for parents being willing to improve their prospects of paid employment or their parenting skills.

CONCLUSION: RESPECTING DIVERSITY, PROVIDING UNIVERSAL SERVICES

The chapter has examined the parents' relationship to the formal childcare system in relation to the criteria of support, choice and need, rather than solely in terms of labour market position. Parents' decisions to use formal childcare or to decide not to do so are shaped by a wide range of factors. There are complex moral discourses surrounding motherhood, engagement in paid work and use of childcare (Duncan and Edwards, 1999) and these may vary geographically (Duncan and Smith, 2002). However, this research suggests that geographical variation may be less important in this Welsh city than the overwhelming evidence that all mothers seek childcare arrangements that are in tune with their understanding of being a 'good' mother. This is influenced by the ideologies of 'sensitive mothering' and 'intensive mothering' but may be interpreted in different ways by each mother. *All* mothers described their particular arrangements with regard to concerns for their child's well-being, and the similarities in the accounts of mothers across the three neighbourhoods were more striking than the differences. The most significant factor that interacts with these moral positions, and with more pragmatic decisions about whether it will be possible to maintain paid work, concerns access to informal care. Availability of informal care can be seen as a form of gendered social capital and this does seem to vary geographically. It is a form of social capital that enables many mothers who cannot, or will not, use formal care to do paid work. It also influences the decisions of those mothers who are willing to make some use of formal care but who wish to limit it or who still need informal help to cover gaps left by formal provision. Those mothers and fathers who are in paid work without any informal support at all constitute a very small group distinguished largely by being in well-paid professional occupations with flexible working conditions.

The extent to which parents reflected satisfaction with their arrangements varied considerably in relation to how far they felt they were exercising a choice over the balance between work and care in their lives, and how far they received relief and time away from childcare. Those parents lacking the financial resources to pay for respite and time for leisure and those without access to informal networks of support were particularly vulnerable to stress.

While the childcare market is developed largely to meet the demand created by working parents, the well-being of many parents, whether working or not, may be eroded. Those parents such as Joy and the fathers in the Sure Start project were very positive about the help and advice for parenting that this programme had offered them. In both Crossland and Tinbury, mothers and fathers referred to the playgroups and holiday play schemes provided through Sure Start. There was general agreement that these services were important for the well-being of both children and parents. However, this is targeted area-based provision, not a universal service, leaving other parents whose stories have been told in this book struggling to cope. It is a sad indictment of service provision in the city that so many parents referred to their regret at losing the leisure centre because it allowed them an hour off from caring for children. The evidence that parent support projects are highly valued by those mothers and fathers able to access them must be set against current public concern that Sure Start and other services for families and children are under threat in a climate of cutbacks (Ben-Galim, 2011b).

The approaches to managing childcare revealed in this study lend support to claims that policy should respect diversity in childcare choices and childcare practices (Bevan Foundation, 2005; Rahilly and Johnston, 2002). This evidence reinforces arguments that policy needs to shift from being prescriptive to being more supportive of parental preferences (Barlow et al., 2002; Duncan and Smith, 2002). The inequities in different kinds of provision between the three areas of the city are going to continue unless the funding of childcare and the reliance on the market in response to demand are reviewed. There are strong arguments in favour of a universal childcare service (Daycare Trust, 2003; Land, 2002a). At present the childcare market is supported and complemented by the gendered networks of informal care that have been described. This access to social capital enables individual mothers and fathers to fill gaps left by formal care, assuage their anxieties over child safety and continue to perform the role of the 'sensitive' or 'intensive' mother or 'hands-on dad' alongside their paid work.

Whilst these networks of social support may be claimed to offer a valued mode of complementary care, they may also service to reinforce inequalities. The example of Tracey's exclusion from the social arrangements of other local mothers on account of her disability was offered in Chapter 3. How does social support as a form of social capital fit into a wider analytic framework? Setting the themes of the chapter in a broader context, the inequalities arising between the three neighbourhoods confirm claims that childcare can be explored in relation to geographies of place that situate social networks as an element of social capital alongside formal local services for families. The considerable interest in the concept of social capital in sociological work (Franklin, 2003; Portes, 1998; Putnam, 2000) and theories of social capital have been used to examine family relationships within the context of wider social processes and contemporary social change (Charles et al., 2008; Gillies, 2003; Holland et al., 2003). As Rosalind Edwards claims, 'Families are often seen as a wellspring of social capital in the theorisation of its generation, accumulation and transmission' (2003: 305). However, there are different approaches to understanding social capital (Franklin, 2003), and the concept may be seen as a new way of describing social institutions and social processes that have long captured the imagination of social scientists (Bruegel and Warren, 2003). In the field of family lives, for example, the community studies of the 1950s and 1960s conducted by social scientists such as Rosser and Harris (1965) and Young and Willmott (1957) explored kin relations and social networks. It is claimed these studies 'have recently been revived by social capital theorists attempting to measure the value of social connectedness' (Gillies, 2003: 4).

Work on children, young people and well-being (Morrow, 1999), mothers' involvement in their children's education (Reay, 2000, 2005) and resources in parenting (Edwards and Gillies, 2004, 2005) has illustrated the value of a focus on the reproduction of inequalities through different forms of capital: social, cultural, economic and symbolic (Bourdieu, 1986, 1990). Each form of capital is understood in relation to the other forms in understanding how privilege and disadvantage may be reproduced. One form of capital may be converted to another form of capital. However, economic capital in terms of wealth, income and financial resources is viewed as 'at the root of all other types of capital' (Bourdieu, 1986: 252). As Virginia Morrow puts it, the advantage of this framework in comparison with that proposed by social capital theorists such as Coleman and Putnam is 'it is essentially a theory of privilege rather than a theory of inadequacy' (1999: 760). This is distinct from the work of Coleman (1988) and Putnam (2000), which explores social capital in relation to a moralistic and normative view of changes within families and communities (Cheong et al., 2007). Social capital thus invites attention towards the role of social connections and social networks in providing certain benefits and privileges:

> Social capital is the sum of the resources, actual or virtual, that accrue to an individual or a group by virtue of possessing a durable network of more or less institutionalized relationships of mutual acquaintance and recognition.
> (Bourdieu and Wacquant, 1992: 119)

Family resources and family practices may be significant in the reproduction of these different forms of capital and in the translation of one form of capital into another. This process may also be gendered, for, as Virginia Morrow observes, the position of women in the private sphere could mean 'there may be different rules for the conversion of capital for men and women' (1999: 755). The diversity of childcare arrangements presented in this chapter in relation to the four combinations of formal and informal childcare can illustrate this claim. It seems that, for some parents, access to gendered social capital for the provision of childcare is preferred to paid-for childcare, challenging notions that economic capital may be valued more highly than other forms of capital. The analysis presented in this chapter reveals that, in relation to the moral economy of childcare, the picture is more complex.

5

Listening to Mothers and Fathers, Disrupting Policy?

INTRODUCTION

The material from the mothers' and fathers' personal accounts and the neighbourhood case studies will now be reviewed. The key gaps and disconnections that were revealed in this research are considered as a basis for moving towards a more sensitive and reflexive childcare policy agenda. The main points of difference between mothers' and fathers' needs and experiences as expressed in their narratives and the emphases of current UK and Welsh childcare policy will be highlighted. This evidence was presented in the interviews with policy officers, and their responses reveal how they interpreted parental perspectives. The chapter will show that, although policy officers may be 'captured by the discourse' (Bowe et al., 1994) in their understanding of childcare policy, they too are aware of tensions and gaps. At the same time, some policy officers proved to be in disagreement with the themes emerging from the parents' accounts or wished to dispute certain interpretations where they claimed superiority of understanding. One of the central messages to emerge from the research was that policy officers' capacity to listen to mothers and fathers may be limited despite the rhetoric of parental choice.

This research has explored the relations between childcare, gender and social policy in Wales following the election of the New Labour government in 1997 and the establishment of the National Assembly for Wales in 1999. The policy analysis and research material has also been considered in the light of the establishment of a UK Coalition government in May 2010. In the next section there will be a review of the key findings, relating them to conceptual debates on gender, family lives and care. Following this, the chapter will draw on the personal accounts of mothers and fathers in order to highlight policy gaps. This analysis will be supported with reference to the interviews with policy officers when they were presented with material from the discussions with parents. Finally, the chapter will consider how childcare policy could be developed so that it is 'gender-sensitive' and suggest ways in which an 'ethics of care' (F. Williams, 2001) could be advanced further in this arena.

REVIEW AND REFLECTIONS

What were the main aims of this research and what were the key insights? The research set out initially to explore how mothers felt about and went about 'doing childcare' and how this connected with gender relations. As the research unfolded, opportunities to gain further insights into the links between gender and childcare were pursued with a small sample of fathers. The research also aimed to explore childcare and parenting policies in the UK and Wales in relation to questions about their implications for social justice, family well-being and gender equality. Taken together, the parents' narratives and the policy analysis illuminated gaps in current childcare policy agendas. Finally, and this is a source of new material presented later in this chapter, these gaps were debated directly with policy officers closely involved in childcare policymaking and policy delivery in Wales.

Childcare relations lie at the heart of both political economy and the moral economy of care. Returning to Dorothy Smith's (1988) claims that ruling relations embedded in work, government and economy have side-lined family and childcare issues, has her argument been supported in the present study? Whilst the focus by New Labour on family and childcare policy (DfEE, 1998; HM Treasury, 2004) might lead some to challenge the veracity of Smith's viewpoint in this context, her claims hold true in that unpaid care and domestic labour have continued to be invisible. The emergence of new forms of family, parenting and childcare policy support an economic logic that still sidelines the value of care whilst simultaneously placing further pressures on carers to 'parent well'. As the framing analysis revealed in Chapters 1 and 2, policy mainly seeks to fill gaps in the economy, not to relieve mothers or fathers of the stresses that they face, to redistribute domestic labour or to offer universal access to support. The mothers' accounts presented in Chapter 3 and the use of childcare described by mothers and fathers in Chapter 4 has demonstrated forcefully the gaps between policies, local services and what families would welcome.

The promise of 'choice' for parents contained within childcare policies is, therefore, out of tune with the 'taken for granted' nature of different family childcare arrangements. The gender-neutral language of these policies (Featherstone, 2006) also obscures the fact that mothers remain the family members most intensively involved in childcare. In their research into the impact of the National Childcare Strategy in Liverpool, Simon Rahilly and Elaine Johnston found that 'most mothers (both in and out of waged work) did not feel that they had any choice as to their childcare arrangements' (2002: 493). Similarly, in her assessment of childcare policy, Jane Lewis observes that the 'complex pattern of finance and provision presents parents – usually mothers – with choices, but not always pleasant ones' (2003:

235). This claim that mothers and fathers perceive they have very limited choices is supported by this study.

What the findings also reveal is that there is a tension between meeting mothers' and fathers' preferences, as they are currently expressed, and the advancement of childcare and parenting policy in relation to claims for gender equality. This is partially because, with regard to unpaid family care, claims for recognition or redistribution (Fraser, 1997, 2001) have not been fully integrated by stakeholders pressing for a gender mainstreaming agenda within government institutions. The narratives suggest that childcare policy is not meeting all parents' needs and preferences or advancing the cause of gender equality. These findings are reviewed next, drawing on the conceptual framework proposed in the earlier chapters to link personal standpoints on the relations between gender and childcare with public policies.

The mothers' accounts

I used institutional ethnography (Smith, 1988) to begin with the mothers' accounts and link their childcare practices to broader ideologies, discourses and institutional structures. This illuminated the resilience of gendered cultural practices, that is the 'gender culture' evident in this area of Wales. These cultural practices are shaped by societal relations and the gender regime (Connell, 1990), comprising divisions of labour, bureaucratic power and emotional attachments. The gender culture is also mediated by local social networks. The ideologies of 'sensitive' and 'intensive' mothering place women as the primary carers and represent this as 'natural' and 'moral' so that the contribution of care to society is undervalued and unrewarded. Like the mothers in Hays's (1996) study, all the mothers in my research tried to meet the expectations of the intensive mother, devoting considerable time and effort to ensuring their child's well-being. They were also actively engaged in 'self-surveillance' (Lawler, 2000) in the conduct of mothering. However, because of differences in their material circumstances and access to networks of social support, some were more easily able to meet these expectations than others. Both economic capital and social capital are thus important in enabling mothers to meet their ideal of good mothering. The mothers who lack these resources may be especially vulnerable to stress and feelings of guilt as well as to welfare intervention if they are perceived as failing to cope.

The sample was drawn from three contrasting areas of a city in Wales in order to explore claims made in other studies of childcare that mothers' value systems or gendered moral codes may vary geographically (Duncan and Edwards, 1999). Their narratives showed that *all* mothers make choices in relation to moral codes and that these choices reproduced (more or less) gendered divisions of labour. Similarities between mothers from differ-ent social class and ethnic backgrounds in wanting to 'be there' for their children were striking. Hence this common ground between mothers demonstrates that wider ideologies and discourses may be more significant in understanding the conduct of mothering than local cultural practices. Nevertheless, mothers in the three areas did differ broadly in their access to material wealth (economic capital) and social support from family, friends and neighbours (social capital). These resources do make a considerable difference to mothers' childcare strategies, their use of informal and formal childcare and thus their capacity to mother in a way that resonates with their moral codes. These moral codes are expressed not only in relation to gendered norms but also in relation to apprehension for children's safety. This is a concern expressed by fathers as well as mothers and varies by area because there *are* differences between neighbourhoods in levels of crime and access to transport and safe amenities. It seems that the worry about keeping children safe that was expressed more forcefully by parents in the more materially deprived areas, Crossland and Tinbury, may then connect to a distrust of letting children go into formal childcare. Whilst this distrust of formal childcare seemed to be treated as a cultural peculiarity by some policy officers, it seems to me on the basis of my research that it is based on rational criteria.

Childcare and parenting policy

In order to explore state agendas in relation to childcare and parenting, policy texts were analysed using the concepts of framing and the discur-sive opportunity structure. With the focus on the implications of policy for gender relations, policy texts both at the UK level and in post-devolution Wales were examined. The Wales case study enabled an assessment of the prospects created by devolution for doing things differently in policy terms. Finally, the study was able to explore some of the issues raised by the fram-ing analysis in interviews with policy officers.

The analysis revealed that the framing of policy in relation to economic interests is paramount at the UK level and this also severely limits the scope for the alternative framing of policy in Wales. Policy reveals further ways of packaging childcare needs in relation to promoting gender equality (expressed in restricted terms as work–life balance), supporting parents and meeting children's needs/rights. At the UK level, gender equality, expressed mainly as work–life balance, and children's needs have each been harnessed to the *economic* frame in terms of social investment for the future. There is also an interest in promoting social inclusion expressed in relation to social integration rather than redistribution of resources and tackling inequalities. The *supporting parents* frame is also couched in moral terms with regard to ensuring parents meet their responsibilities in raising children to be 'good citizens'. These are discursive frames that may represent a perversion or narrow understanding of the issues that policy claims to address.

In Wales, childcare policy is also framed in these ways but some differences were revealed both through policy analysis and in discussion with policy officers. The emphasis on framing childcare in relation to *children's needs/rights* is more pronounced. The commitment to children having rights of citizenship is stronger in Wales than at the UK level and the early creation of the Office of the Commissioner for Children for Wales is of huge symbolic importance in this regard. This framing has provided a space in the discursive opportunity structure through which children's organizations in Wales have been able to press for childcare as a *universal right* for all children rather than merely a means to support the 'welfare to work' agenda. The analysis shows that there is some sympathy for these claims within the Welsh Government; but there are constraints in meeting them in practice given the nature of the devolution settlement and the availability of resources. Issues of tackling poverty, promoting social inclusion and advancing social justice are understood in different ways in Wales. The *master* narratives, for example, social inclusion or tackling child poverty, have remained the same but the discursive framing has been more tied in with concerns over inequality and the need to redistribute resources. This alternative framing is significant because it leaves open a door within the discursive opportunity structure as social movement organizations continue to press their demands. With the transition from a Labour UK Government to a UK Coalition government led by the Conservative Party, this 'open door' in Wales seems likely to become more significant.

Whilst this greater awareness in Wales of the need to tackle social class inequalities is to be welcomed, there is the danger that gender has fallen out of the picture. Despite the statutory duty, support for gender mainstreaming and the entry of femocrats (feminist campaigners) into the Welsh Government and partner organisations, the research found little evidence that the connections between childcare and gender relations had been addressed. Childcare policy has been *assumed* to improve gender equality because it enables women to do paid work. At best this ties with a liberal feminist agenda for equal rights in the public realm. This ignores the connections between women's place in the private realm and their capacity to enjoy the achievements of liberal feminism in the public realm. The *differences* between women in relation to this capacity are sidelined, leaving middle-class, professional women as the main winners in this game. The femocrats who have entered the Welsh Government and regional policy bodies are those able to play according to liberal feminist rules and they have made advances in the public realm. It has been possible for some women to gain from gender equality legislation and policy whilst leaving the gender order and local gender cultures intact. It is thus possible to see how feminism may have failed in its capacity to speak for 'ordinary women'. I have moved from a position, as a single woman with no children, in which I was able to benefit from the achievements of liberal feminism in the (professional) workplace to finding that the professional workplace does not engage with the position of mothers in progressive ways. This was certainly true for some of the mothers in this study. In addition, mothers have other institutions (schools, health services) with which they have to engage on behalf of children and these continue to encourage women to be true to the ideologies of 'sensitive' and 'intensive' mothering. The femocrats' agenda to achieve independence for women through paid work is of huge importance but leaves many women feeling sidelined by this narrow interpretation of equality. It does not fully address the needs of most of the mothers who participated in this research. The statutory duty and gender mainstreaming in Wales are not being pushed to their full potential so that cultural and economic recognition for unpaid care is secured. Unless this recognition is forthcoming then a real redistribution of resources between women and men across different socio-economic groups will remain a dream.

Claims that childcare can advance gender equality sit alongside the discursive framing of childcare in relation to supporting (regulating) parents in which the parents' role in playing with their children, spending time with them and supporting their education is paramount. This is a discursive frame that is in tune with the ideology of 'sensitive' mothering and yet may be in tension with the economic goal of encouraging women to do paid work and to do it for longer hours. In this sense different discursive frames may be in tension. The mothers' accounts revealed that they were far more influenced by this agenda for effective/involved parenting than they were by the agenda to seek equality through paid work. The way that the mothers seek to resolve the conflict between the demands of 'sensitive' or 'intensive' mothering and the economic need, for most of them, to do some paid work is through accessing informal social support. Those mothers who do paid work entirely on the basis of using formal childcare are a very small group indeed and face strain in doing so. The findings thus reveal that unpaid care done mainly by women supports the institutions of the state, the economy and the education system twice over: first, through the unpaid care conducted in the home by mothers; second, where those mothers also do paid work, through the use of the unpaid childcare offered by their own mothers and other female relations, friends and neighbours to cover the gaps while they are away from the home.

This analysis thus revealed that the availability of informal care is often crucial for enabling the commodified childcare market to work at all. These findings support Hilary Land's claim that the 'sharp distinction made by policy makers between formal and informal care' (2002b: 15) is misguided. Gendered networks of social support enable mothers to plug gaps in childcare and engage in building social and emotional capital (Edwards and Gillies, 2005). These are networks that are built around educational, parent support and childcare facilities, which helps to explain the prominence of education in the accounts mothers gave of their role in childcare. The mothers' experiences are 'socially organized' (Smith, 1997: 393) through these networks. These are networks that *exclude* as well as include (Byrne, 2006), leaving some mothers isolated and vulnerable. Access to these networks may help women participate in paid work and yet may lead others to choose to *limit* work in favour of care. Sheila provided the most striking example of this in wishing to limit her professional, paid work in education in order to be able to volunteer at her child's school. She wanted to be able to engage in this form of social capital building and to provide emotional capital by 'being there' for her child.

Tensions between mothers' preferences and childcare policy frames

Mothers do show that they are engaging with the ideologies of 'sensitive' or 'intensive' mothering whilst shaping how they do this according to their circumstances. Whilst most mothers still take main responsibility for domestic labour, there are some who are seeking to share this with partners. Yet mothers may operate a division between domestic labour and the practical, educational and emotional labour involved with childcare. They are less likely to share this with partners, although they may seek support from other women if they need to do so. There is a sense then that many women still retain the role of the primary carers in relation to their children and this often remains a 'female-only' space. Yet, at the same time, mothers' wishes are expressed in a way in which this is so 'taken for granted' that it goes unrecognized. These preferences may create tensions in relation to the framing of childcare policy in terms of enabling women to do paid work and to achieve equality in the public realm. Yet these preferences do resonate with those discursive frames relating to supporting 'good' parenting and to meeting children's needs. These are discursive frames that can be read through the lens of 'sensitive' or 'intensive' mothering. Hence these frames may be doing more to *reinforce* mothers' sense of responsibility for putting children first and being there for them. Where mothers live in areas with community and child safety issues, a sense of risk may reinforce the view that childcare must come before paid work. Hence, the study reveals a more complex picture than first expected. It is more than a problem of policy seeking to achieve a goal (more mothers in paid work) that conflicts with traditional cultural practices or gendered moral values. Certain discursive frames *promoted by the state* also tie in with those cultural practices. Hence these are cultural practices that are being *recreated* in relation to new discursive frames; they are not simply entrenched attitudes based in the past. These issues were presented for discussion with policy officers and their responses are presented in the next section.

HEARING PARENTS? PERSPECTIVES FROM POLICY OFFICERS

The intention underlying the method of institutional ethnography was to use the mothers' and fathers' accounts as a basis for exposing both common ground and gaps between their preferences and needs and what was being offered through childcare policy. This potential for disrupting policy is explored next through the interviews with policy officers. These were conducted after fieldwork had been completed with parents. The policy interviews provided an opportunity to discuss some of the themes from the parent interviews that pointed to issues with which policy could or should engage. The study sought to explore how far policy officers were aware of these issues and how far they were capable of responding to parental concerns. Policy officers occupy an interesting position in that they have some power to reshape policy and yet they may also be tied into wider relations of ruling through their location within the state, political parties and professional organizations. This may limit their capacity to listen or to reframe agendas on the basis of messages from parents.

It has been argued in earlier chapters that policy discourses frame the childcare agenda in particular ways, and policy officers appeared to be operating within dominant frames whilst drawing from them in ways that resonated with their role and professional or political values. By using ma-terial from the parent interviews, it was possible to reveal gaps between particular ways of framing policy and what is happening in practice. In this way the study used the method of institutional ethnography to grasp parents' daily experiences and to use this to disrupt childcare policy frames. Some policy officers responded with enthusiasm to this approach whilst others became defensive.

What happens when we assess policy through a focus on its capacity to meet parental needs and enhance their well being? We find this throws new light on the framing of childcare in relation to the economy, children's needs, social justice and gender equality. These frames are all drawn on in policy texts, yet they may be in tension with each other and may not always chime with what parents would like. Following Marshall's call for feminist critical policy analysis to consider 'marginalized populations' (1997: 19) it can be argued that parents represent a largely silent interest group in the making of childcare policy in Wales. Despite partnership arrangements and duties to consult parents (WAG, 2006) and localized efforts to secure user involvement, the parents in this study did not feel there were any avenues to make their voice heard.[1] This was a methodology through which it was intended that the voices of some mothers and fathers could be communicated to policy officers.

There were three themes from the parent interviews that were discussed with the policy officers. The evidence that many mothers wanted to either stay at home or reduce their hours of paid employment in order to spend time with their children was one area for debate. Next, examples were presented that revealed that all parents could benefit from respite and would value support in parenting. Finally, the material that revealed strong distrust of formal childcare provision among some parents was provided for discussion. These three themes will be discussed next.

Being a 'good mother'

Mothers' values and cultural practices are shaped by a model of sensitive/intensive mothering that can best be thought of as a continuum ranging from traditional, 'old-fashioned' understandings of stay-at-home mothercare through to the image of the 'have it all' mother who can 'juggle' multiple roles at home and work efficiently. This model of sensitive/intensive mothering has to interact with the economic framing of childcare and government encouragement for women to enter the labour market. Even where mothers are in full-time paid work, they will still make accommodations in order to remain true to their understanding of the duties of the maternal role. It has been argued that policy texts approach gender roles only in relation to role equity and work–life balance considerations; the moral economy of care and the contribution of unpaid caring labour to the political economy are not addressed. The interviews provided an ideal opportunity to ask policy officers directly for their views on this matter.

The two officers from regional gender equality bodies appeared to be uneasy in talking about the issue of mothers' own preferences. Alison Connor (regional equality body one) did not accept a preference to be home as a credible position for mothers to adopt. Whilst explaining that her organization was 'centring the agenda round choice', her personal view was that there should not be a choice because:

> While there is a choice and men earn more than women, it will always be a choice that the women stay at home . . . and you are never going to break the cycle . . . when you compare with international experience, it is a cultural thing, where it has become the norm that all children go into some kind of formal childcare . . . there is much wider acceptance that is how children grow up.

This is a perspective that is, perhaps, to be expected from a policy officer campaigning for improved formal childcare provision. Simon Duncan and his colleagues comment on the validity of arguments from reformers 'that child care preference is a circular process where, if mothers had more experience of formal provision, they would rate it more highly' (2004: 263). They argue that their interviews with mothers about childcare revealed that these claims oversimplify how choices are reached. Rather 'Child care evaluations are one part of mothers' value systems, and in turn these emerge in specific social and geographical contexts' (2004: 263). My study lends support to these claims and the policy officers were presented with some cases. Examples were provided of mothers, such as Sheila and Becky, who had been in professional jobs and yet stated a preference to stay home for a time with their children either because they felt morally obliged to do so or because they had found this to be more enjoyable than work. Alison Connor responded in denial of the evidence: 'Saying that, it is needs driven, isn't it?' She cited the lack of access to well-paid employment and affordable childcare as the reason why these preferences were expressed. However, this conflicted with the evidence that some women in well-paid professional jobs living in areas that were adequately provided for in terms of formal childcare (such as Becky) or with access to generous informal care (such as Sheila) *still* stated a preference to be at home. This policy officer held strong views that paid work was good for women and would not accept that this research evidence was valid. Her response did not engage with the gendered moral codes revealed in the research, seeing them as merely outmoded attitudes:

> Because the government has said you will go out to work and here is the provision and actually we are still caught in this trap of it is best for children to be home with mummy.

Alison Connor was also in disagreement with work–life balance initiatives that enabled some mothers to choose part-time work on the grounds that this was in conflict with advancing gender equality:

> A lot of that is arguments around the business case . . . my personal view is actually that part-time working is a big contributor to the pay gap and actually providing choice has not solved the problem.

The extension of 'choice' for parents is seen as a barrier by this policy officer to achieving gender equality and redistribution of care between women and men. Yet an alternative view is that there is a need for more vigorous policies to ensure that part-time working does not lead to disadvantage in pay and conditions and opportunities for the future, rather than to suggest that the choice to work part-time should be limited. This policy officer's view is that, if women are to achieve claims that connect with a politics of redistribution of resources, this will mean sacrificing claims based on a politics of recognition for cultural and personal preferences (Fraser, 1997). The problem is that claims for recognition are treated as mutually exclusive from claims for redistribution.

Liz Spencer (regional equality body two) believed policy should provide choice for parents and stressed that the role of her organization was around ensuring a genuine choice was available for women:

> because we are not an agency that says all women must work full-time and they must all become managing directors, of course we are not saying that. Just talking about the opportunity and the information and the choice.
>
> So anybody who wants to stay at home with one child, or however many children, for whatever period of time, fantastic. If there is an opportunity to keep in touch with the world of study, the world of work, the wider community, then those are the sorts of things that [my agency] would be interested in making sure to offer as much choice and as many options as possible to women.

The organization that Liz Spencer represents is geared towards achieving role equity for women and men and enabling women to return to the labour market, fulfilling a very valuable role in this regard. Yet this does mean that the main focus is on those women who do paid work outside the home, but it does not engage with those mothers who may value recognition for work done at home in terms of financial support, respite and advice.

Other policy officers believed that there should be choice and respect for cultural preferences. Some were in favour of providing support through a redistribution of resources for those wishing to extend the time they stayed home with their children:

> it is more of a [UK government] issue than our issue, but I do agree with you that there is a substantial minority of women that, and it is women predominantly, that feel bad about going to work, certainly for the first twelve or eighteen months and that an awful lot of women are going to work earlier and that is simply because of pure economic pressure. You know it isn't their preferred choice but they just have to do it because of the reality of their economic circumstances.
>
> So, I do think ideally, and whether there is an issue of affordability . . . there is a need for more extended maternity leave that would take some pressure off parents. I think there is a political argument and there is an evidence-based argument for children. (Keith Hall, Assembly Member)
>
> I firmly believe that if parents want to stay at home and look after their children then there should be an incentive. (Rita Daniels, senior officer/EYDCP)

Policy officers thus held a variety of personal perspectives. Some wanted cultural recognition and resources such as extended maternity or parental leave for parents caring for their children at home. They wanted parents to be enabled to stay home with their children during the early years if this was their preference. Others believed that cultural preferences that leave the gendered division of labour intact needed to be challenged and that this might mean limiting choice. Yet all perspectives operate by favouring either claims for cultural recognition or claims for a redistribution of resources. What is needed is a way of integrating these claims.

Stress and respite: struggling to cope

This research revealed that there was little childcare available for the purpose of providing respite other than for parents identified by professionals as failing to cope. The notion that parents should be entitled to support for childcare for a wider variety of reasons than work or training and that caring at home is demanding and stressful work is overlooked. Policy officers were asked to comment on the availability of childcare to offer respite to parents. Some agreed that there was a gap in provision here:

> It is very difficult, not just in this, but in child protection and in health, transport, everything really, that by the time that you tackle the front line, there is not an awful lot left for upstream activities . . . we have got to deliver public services and in terms of affordability, people won't pay enough taxes to allow that sort of activity to take place. (Keith Hall, Assembly Member)

Policy officers may thus be acutely aware of particular gaps that are obscured in policy texts, and their responses reveal that these gaps are of concern to them. Debra Mason, for example, commented on the fact that people had to be seen to be in desperate circumstances before they could get help:

> In terms of respite, social services has an initiative called community childcare, but that can only be supported if health visitors are involved or social workers are involved and the parents are on income support. If there are issues of depression or parents have their child on the child protection register, then there is an initiative, but it is not self-referral, it has to be with professional help. (Debra Mason, officer/EYDCP)

Erica Bell, a Sure Start officer, also noted that it would be difficult for parents on low incomes to get respite without professional support:

> I know the [local community crèche] has got a childcare presence but again it

is cost and sometimes we would sponsor places there through the community childminders scheme for parents to get respite . . . although the [local crèche] is great in terms of its childcare, I don't know what its daily costs are for parents who just feel they need a break or whatever.

Some policy officers did acknowledge the stresses facing all parents and did not necessarily agree with the narrow emphasis on childcare to stimulate greater participation in paid work:

We haven't got childcare right and I think it has been badly influenced . . . by the work ethic, just getting more and more people into employment. And that is going to be the women, which has all kinds of other implications about longer-term career prospects for women but childcare . . . and we have got it quite wrong, actually. I have always been uneasy about, I mean, just the pure time . . . my son hardly ever slept, my daughter, she was fine, she slept a lot, but the sheer tiredness and there were two of us. (Chris Coleman, senior officer)

If childcare policy is to be directed towards the needs of children and parents, there should be an extension of childcare to support all parents in gaining some respite. This would provide help before people reach the point of crisis and in turn would help to move away from notions that those who find themselves in crisis are 'bad parents' who are thus stigmatized. As other studies have revealed, this can involve a labelling process that pathologizes certain families and is heavily gendered (Nixon, 2007). At present the childcare market leaves a substantial proportion of parents without any support whatsoever. This is a fragmented and divisive approach to offering childcare provision. Policy officers at the regional and local levels in Wales are aware that this leaves gaps yet they have to largely work within the framework devised at the national level. This reveals that policy officers may also question certain policy frames on the basis of their own experience of parenting or their professional practice.

Misgivings about formal childcare

Some mothers held strong views that being placed in formal childcare would not be in their child's best interests. Evidence was presented to policy officers that some mothers felt they would not trust a formal childcare facility and valued the availability of informal care. This was an issue that had been considered in the childcare policy arenas in Wales (Bevan Foundation, 2005; WAG, 2005b). This preference for family care has been revealed in other research studies conducted elsewhere in the UK. Dalia Ben-Galim's (2011b) research into why some parents do not use early years and childcare provision also found this could be due to a questioning of the suitability of formal care for young children, a belief that family care was more appropriate for the child's well-being.

The views of parents on this matter were well known to policy officers in this study and they had been seeking ways to take parental misgivings into account. In the Interim Report of the Welsh Government Childcare Working Group it was stated:

> Due to lack of accessible, affordable childcare provision in Wales, informal childcare – provided by family and friends – is often the only childcare option available to parents. But for many parents, informal care is a positive and preferred choice, often being cheaper, more flexible and trustworthy. (WAG, CWG, 2004: 5, para. 3.2)

Several policy officers identified this distrust of formal care as an issue:

> People who are economically inactive are in the more socially excluded communities and are suspicious of formal childcare, apart from problems of access and so forth. So if part of this is that childcare is one of the barriers that some people have to overcome to get into work but if the childcare that we are offering them is formal childcare isn't what they want or don't trust or don't believe in, then how do we develop policies in line with their aspirations and what is acceptable to them? (Keith Hall, Assembly Member)

> This group of parents or grandparents would not consider a paid for childcare facility, either because they could not afford to or would not choose to spend what money they had that way. They would consider community-based childcare that was either free or very low cost but only if they knew the person who was running it and only if they 'liked/trusted them', wouldn't necessarily worry whether that person was registered. (Liz Spencer, regional equality body two)

> Cultural differences in Wales mean that they have less trust in formal childcare and more reliance on the extended family and the grandparents. (Alison Connor, regional equality body one)

Other studies, which reveal that this distrust of formal care is not confined to Wales (Ben-Galim, 2011b; Skinner and Finch, 2006), indicate a need to take care in assuming that cultural differences and family formations in Wales can be used to explain preference for informal care. Whilst some policy officers referred to this issue as another example of cultural preferences that might need to be shifted, there were others who also questioned whether a transition to leaving children in formal childcare was desirable:

Well, I feel there should be equal opportunity. On the one hand, I am all for it. But these are my reservations. It could create a scenario where children are pushed from pillar to post and I am not happy with that. You know it can be a very long day for some children which I don't think is quality and I am concerned about that. (Rita Daniels, senior officer/EYDCP)

So perhaps two days with one grandparent, another day with another grand-parent and the last part of the week in a nursery or with a childminder. The poor child is overwhelmed by all these carers, that is the other thing that we need to be aware of. (Debra Mason, officer/EYDCP)

Discursive frames that celebrate the interests of children may be articulated by parents, policy officers and professionals who work with children to suggest that formal childcare, or at least 'too much' formal childcare, may not always be desirable for children. The study has revealed that some policy officers and professionals would also articulate the unease over the use of formal childcare expressed by some parents. It seems that the 'children's needs' frame has the capacity to be in tension with the economic and gender equality frames. Policy officers are located in different positions within the institutional relations of ruling and will utilize those discursive frames that resonate most closely with their values and professional practices. By starting from the accounts of parents about how they manage childcare, how they feel about it and what their preferences are, it is possible to *disrupt* the discourses and encourage policy officers to reveal their personal understandings of the limits of policy. Despite the emphases of policy texts, policy officers had their own reservations about certain aspects of policy, were aware of some of the significant gaps in what was on offer for parents and knew that the frames they were adopting could be contested.

CONCLUSION: MAKING CHILDCARE POLICY WORK IN WALES

After exploring the policy officers' perspectives on the themes raised by mothers and fathers, the interview addressed other issues relating to policy delivery. Their responses focused on two areas: first, the limits imposed by the nature of devolution in Wales; second, some of the specific features of the social and economic landscape in Wales. Each of these areas is relevant to an assessment of potential barriers to the successful impact of policy.

Officers inside the Welsh Government suggested that there was a difference of interpretation between the regional (Wales) and national (UK) levels of governance over the meaning of social inclusion and how the anti-poverty agenda could be progressed. This in turn had implications for childcare policy:

> one of the problems is that we haven't got much say over childcare tax credits, working tax credits because that is a UK matter anyway . . . we can say what we think in terms of how well it is working in a Welsh context. (Keith Hall, Assembly Member)

Similarly, Mike Davies (Welsh Government Advisor) observed that the use of tax credits as the main mechanism for enabling parents to access childcare did not address all the needs expressed by parents, but he pointed out that this was beyond the control of the Welsh Government:

> The [Welsh Government's] ability to do things directly there is limited. We do not handle tax and social security and all those sorts of things so it hasn't been possible to influence, we don't have the responsibility, the power to make a difference there.

These limits pertaining to the devolution settlement are highly significant with regard to childcare especially as far as meeting the needs and preferences of mothers and fathers are concerned. Direct public support to parents on low and modest incomes for the costs of childcare comes through the tax credit system and this is not a devolved area. In turn, this has implications for the availability of childcare in different neighbourhoods because UK strategy has been to let the childcare market respond to local demand from parents (Lewis, 2003). This was an issue that Keith Hall (Assembly Member) suggested was a possible area for contention:

> [The UK government] is of the view that we stimulate the market by providing tax credits and that will bring people in to the market to meet the needs. Whereas I suppose the more traditional command and control, Old Labour socialist view would be that we build something . . . So the balance between the supply side and the demand side is a bit of an issue.

The difference of vision between 'Old' Labour and 'New' Labour is thus expressed here. This is currently moving in new directions in the context of the change to a UK Coalition government as well as the movement towards greater powers for Wales as a devolved region. However, even with enhanced powers, the Welsh Government does not have control of the taxation and welfare benefits systems, so limits to how childcare policy can be progressed in Wales will continue.

Policy officers also noted that the ability of the Welsh Government to tailor childcare policy to the needs of Welsh communities is heavily circumscribed given high poverty levels, low-paid work and poor transport in rural areas. All of these factors will set limits to childcare provision that develops through market demand. As Keith Hall acknowledged:

> The level of low income, social and economic deprivation. We don't have the extremes of London, and a few other places but I think per head of population we have got a much greater and I think as well, probably geographical spread, in terms of people living in valley communities and so forth, does present a set of challenges that don't exist in England.

Those aspects of the social and geographical landscape that distinguish Wales which will benefit from 'made in Wales' policy solutions are not fully within the powers of the Welsh Government to redress. Whilst this may be a layer of government committed to a discourse of redistribution rather than merely social integration (Levitas, 1998), that is precisely what it cannot achieve. There may be more scope for pursuing 'made in Wales' solutions to cultural injustices than those relating to economic injustices.

Local policy officers discussed the challenges of policy delivery in relation to the theme of sustainability of provision. Many referred to the problem of sustaining childcare projects in areas of deprivation. This was seen as the major challenge in the delivery of childcare policy:

> I think our big issue has always been sustainability. You know it is terribly easy to give money to agencies and organizations to have so many extra places. But if you are getting it for one year and they can't sustain it in the future, what do you think you are doing? The gaps are associated largely around geographical distribution, I think. There are big issues in the welfare-to-work agenda of gaps that relate to wrap-around and after and pre-school facility in terms of whether there's sustainability. (Sarah Wilson, officer, voluntary sector/EYDCP)

> Some projects have an exit policy and this always boils down to sustainability. So that is the only drawback. Projects don't know from year to year whether they are still going to be there because there is no set agreement that funding will be ongoing. (Debra Mason, officer/EYDCP)

The distribution of childcare provision through the market alongside limited targeted funding leaves multiple gaps and makes the long-term planning of childcare difficult (Lewis, 2003). These insights place the claims of policy texts that promote the gender equality/children's rights/social inclusion narratives in their true context. At the local level and in relation to specific local childcare markets, the contradictions of policy will be highlighted. The problem of sustainability of projects thus symbolizes those contradictions.

Even though the National Childcare Strategy and Welsh childcare policy claim benefits will be available for *all* parents, in relation to funding and the structures for delivery this provision is targeted at communities of need, whether defined in geographical terms or according to other indicators. In this city, development work in areas of deprivation has taken up most of the time of partner services and agencies. The development of services that should be available *universally* to all parents, such as the Children Information Service/Family Information Service, has, in comparison, been slow. The local partner agencies were coping with significant workloads and high (and constantly shifting) expectations from the Welsh Government.

There is little evidence at either the regional or local level of a sophisticated understanding of how childcare connects with 'recognition' and 'redistribution' claims in relation to gender parity. Whilst regional policy officers were able to reflect on the potential role equity benefits of childcare, this was mainly expressed in relation to providing opportunities for women to engage in paid work, to have access to career opportunities and achieve financial independence. Local policy officers talked about the needs of vulnerable mothers and fathers for support. Their focus was mainly on a social justice agenda expressed in relation to poverty and disadvantage rather than gender. Gender really came into play only because many of these local professionals were working with lone mothers and their children. The allocation of Sure Start funding to work with fathers was important and did signify a commitment to providing support for fathers to maintain contact with their children and engage in care. However, work with fathers was contained in isolated and targeted initiatives rather than through a broadly developed strategy for change.

This study has been able to place gender at the centre of policy analysis and to link what mothers and fathers do, day to day, in specific material circumstances to a wider web of discursive and institutional relations. It has also been possible to place policy officers working within different parts of the regional and local state apparatus within this understanding of the 'institutional'. Smith's understanding of the power of 'textually mediated discourse' (1990a: 163) has been supported with regard to the shaping of social practices relating to parenting and to meeting children's needs. Yet there is conflict between the different ways of framing of childcare in relation to economic interests, gender equality and parents' preferences. Some policy officers and members of social movement organizations also contest these frames. This raises important questions regarding the prospects for respecting cultural preferences whilst at the same time pursuing an equality agenda for mothers and fathers in contemporary Wales.

Conclusion: Parenthood, Gender Relations and the Care Ethic in Wales

INTRODUCTION

How could future childcare policy be shaped in ways that are responsive to parental needs in their diversity? Some concluding thoughts on how childcare policy can both attend to calls for gender equity and yet chime with what mothers and fathers would like are offered now in relation to debates on developing an 'ethics of care' and the integration of feminist claims for *redistribution* of caring labour and *recognition* of its contribution to society. According to Nancy Fraser (1997, 2001) political action in relation to social justice has tended to be polarized in terms of claims for 'redistribution' and claims for 'recognition'; while redistribution will achieve 'a more just allocation of resources and goods', recognition celebrates difference so that 'assimilation to majority or dominant cultural norms is no longer the price of equal respect' (Fraser, 2001: 21).

This is the distinction between political claims for *equality* and political claims for respecting *difference*. Demands which relate to care bridge the divide between the public and the private realms, making the distinction hard to maintain. Are claims for extended maternity leave – to allow a mother time to care, time to recover and the opportunity to breastfeed – claims for a redistribution of resources (time and financial support) or claims for recognition that the needs of women will, at times, be different from those of men? The problem remains that this separation of 'recognition' claims from 'redistribution' claims obscures the fact that they are intrinsically linked and both are needed. Neither model taken independently can offer satisfactory outcomes in achieving gender equity. Recognition without redistribution could further entrench gender inequalities but redistribution cannot be achieved without recognition that women are culturally subordinate to men and that choices are framed by gendered cultural norms. As Fraser argues, 'Justice today requires *both* redistribution *and* recognition; neither alone is sufficient' (2001: 22). This chapter will utilize these themes in a concluding assessment of childcare policy and its relationship to the culturally and structurally rooted choices of mothers and fathers.

SHAPING A CHILDCARE ETHIC

In elucidating the connections between childcare policy, gender relations and parents' 'child care strategies' (Windebank, 1999), the study has sought to provide an alternative standpoint. Through a focus on the well-being of mothers, fathers and children in diverse families it is possible to consider a childcare ethic. Does feminist social science have a role to play in shaping this ethic? Fiona Williams makes a case for the 'importance of finding ways in which feminism informs a wider political agenda, while not losing touch with its own particular and changing history' (F. Williams, 2002: 505). The feminist voices influencing the making of childcare policy in Wales are limited mainly to the femocrats who are insiders within the Welsh Government or work as close partners, and they appear to favour a liberal feminist agenda. Based on evidence in this study, it has been argued that this will not meet the needs of all women and will neglect the issue of unpaid care: who does it and how it could be redistributed. Following Smith (1988), feminist knowledge must be grounded in an understanding of women's and men's daily lives under specific social conditions and in different social locations. In doing so it becomes possible to understand why the mainstreaming of feminism as another equal opportunities issue by political parties (F. Williams, 2002) fails to engage fully with what mothers and fathers in diverse situations want.

In terms of now suggesting a childcare ethic to guide policy in Wales it must be acknowledged that Wales is achieving distinctiveness in its style of governance and political values providing a 'policy window' (Marshall, 1999: 64) for social movement organizations seeking to influence change. The adoption of the statutory duty, the gender balance within the Welsh Government and the NafW and the efforts to work in partnership with the voluntary sector and local government exemplify this point. Yet there is little evidence of feminist movements pressing for change in the childcare arena; this means that femocrats within the Welsh Government and partner organizations may be the only ones considering gender at all. The interviews with regional policy officers revealed that they were mainly working within the terms defined by New Labour and were focused on role equity consideration in terms of gender. However, by pressing for role equity and independence through paid work for women, reformers do not engage with the ways in which many mothers experience the challenges of combining paid work and care. The starting point for this study was that mothers' values, preferences and experiences do need to be understood as a basis for moving policy forward. It is not acceptable, and is in fact disrespectful, merely to treat those preferences as old-fashioned cultural norms that must be eroded. In Chapter 5 some examples were provided of regional policy officers appearing to assume that their expert opinion on what was in mothers' best interests should prevail. Yet there are aspects of parenting and education policy that are reinforcing mothers' feelings that they must be there for their children and which are creating new forms of unpaid labour in supporting the work of schools and in managing after-school children's activities. Among local policy officers, on the other hand, there was little evidence that gender was a major concern, although there was awareness of the pressures facing mothers, fathers and children in poor communities and the need to be responsive to cultural diversity and its interaction with gendered norms. In this case gendered cultural preferences are taken for granted and some professionals (teachers, nursery workers, community workers, health visitors) may reinforce this through their own gendered values. This is also a problem.

Childcare policy in Wales has thus been limited by a very narrow understanding of the connections between gender and childcare, based on supporting role equity in paid work, at best, or simply assuming that improved access to childcare will automatically help mothers, by enabling them to enter paid work. The value of unpaid care has been neglected and the adoption of a gender-neutral discourse evades attention to the discourses and social conditions of motherhood and fatherhood and their implications for policy. In addition, attention to gender equality has been overshadowed because both the Welsh Government and activists in Wales have used the children's needs/children's rights discursive frame as a powerful political symbol or master narrative. This has proved far more potent than concern for gender equality. Celebration of children's rights is a discursive frame that can secure consensus in a way that feminist claims for recognition and redistribution will not. It is also a discursive frame that may prove valuable in the current political climate in which UK Coalition government cuts are posing a particular threat to the well-being and opportunities of families with children. Hence, this study does not seek to advance an argument for sidelining it. However, there is a need for the Welsh Government, partner organizations and local government to give as much attention to gender equality as they are paying to supporting children and young people. The well-being of children and young people is tied in with the opportunities and support available to their mothers and fathers. There also needs to be much deeper engagement with what needs to be done to advance gender equality. This will mean moving beyond the narrow liberal feminist agenda focused on providing routes into paid work.

The weaknesses of childcare policy with regard to gender equity can also be revealed if we turn to the question regarding who benefits from care policies and who loses out (F. Williams, 2001). The benefits offered through childcare policies associated with New Labour include childcare and working tax credits for those able to engage in paid work, the expansion of childcare places in response to parental demand, limited subsidized childcare and early years provision in particular areas and work–life balance initiatives in some areas of employment (Lewis and Campbell, 2008). Where parents have access to work–life balance employment initiatives this potentially enhances their control over their choices following parenthood. Many of the priorities of childcare policy and gender mainstreaming around employment rights are, therefore, essential and to be welcomed. The experiences of many of the parents in this study revealed there is a lot more to be done here. These benefits are important and must be safeguarded, for they are currently under threat of being curtailed (UK Women's Budget Group, 2010). Some of the mothers in this research had been able to access some of these benefits but this was dependent on a complex combination of other factors outside the realms of policy and often outside the control of the mother. Crucially, the ability of some mothers to take advantage of work–life balance packages allowing career breaks and part-time working was dependent on having a partner in well-paid full-time employment. Both Becky and Sheila, whose narratives have been presented, provide examples of this. It can be argued that their choices leave them vulnerable in future stages of the life course, should their relationship end or their partner lose his job or when their children achieve independence. These are thus work–life balance 'benefits' that may disadvantage women in the future. They also remain benefits out of reach for many women (Grant, 2009). The capacity of mothers to make use of the expansion of formal childcare interacted with geographical location, access to transport and ability to pay, alongside willingness to utilize this form of care. Some mothers had benefited from the introduction of tax credits; in Farah's case, for example, this had enabled her to move from full-time to part-time hours in her paid work and she had felt this had reduced some of the strains that she had been facing. Some of the lone mothers had also found that the introduction of tax credits had meant that engaging in paid work was possible. However, for many mothers, engagement in paid work was heavily dependent on the availability of informal care either to complement formal childcare or as the only form of childcare they would use.

There is thus a powerful case for assessing the issue of who benefits and who loses in relation to the contribution of *informal childcare*. Once again this supports Smith's (1988) claims that institutional structures such as education and employment rely on the unpaid care of women. Behind many working mothers are grandmothers and others providing unpaid labour to make this possible (Lewis and Giullari, 2005). It is necessary to explore the connections between divisions of labour in employment and divisions of labour at home and within wider networks of social support. What is needed are social policies that seek to work through the *connections* between the private and the public spheres, and between formal, paid-for childcare and informal support networks. The material presented in Chapter 4 revealed that access to informal care could be fundamental to a parent's ability to complement this with paid-for childcare. This evidence supports feminist claims that there is a need to shift the emphasis of New Labour, and now the UK Coalition government, on engagement in paid work as the route to citizenship (Lister, 1997; F. Williams, 2002). This sidelines care instead of respecting its value and stigmatizes those who are not able to do paid work. As Fiona Williams observes:

> constructing those in paid work as independent fails to recognize that a paid worker's independence is actually achieved through hidden systems of support by those who care for that worker's children, clean his/her house, buy and cook his/her food and so on. (2002: 507)

The ethic of paid work remained paramount under the New Labour administration and this continues, within a political climate of deep hostility to those who are dependent on the welfare state, with the UK Coalition government. There is an alternative argument that the principles underpinning social policy should be framed in terms of a political ethic of care (Kittay, 2001; Lister, 2002; Sevenhuijsen, 2002; F. Williams, 2001). These arguments recognize the value of childcare to society and insist that models of citizenship must incorporate caring. Feminist contributors to this literature agree that the 'fetishism of the work ethic' (Lister, 2002: 524) is problematic.

What can be learned from this study for framing social policy through an 'ethics of care'? Fiona Williams (2002) argues that a political ethics of care must be based on a respect for the principle of 'voice' in which those who use welfare services are able to express their needs because:

> people themselves can develop and share their own forms of knowledge and care. What this challenges is the power of expert knowledge to monopolize the definition of what is wrong with us and what we need to right it. (F. Williams, 2002: 516)

The principle of voice is one that fits comfortably with the method of institutional ethnography and would mean that mothers and fathers would be involved in naming what kind of policies would help them. In this context the 'expert knowledge' of policy officers would be placed alongside the lay knowledge of those best placed to speak about the social conditions in which they care. Social policy should be grounded in an appreciation of these everyday material circumstances rather than directed towards an ideal typical model. This could help policy move fully away from the dualism between 'paid work' and 'care' that is evident in current policy debates. This dualism must be eroded if the labour involved in caring is to achieve parity of recognition with the labour involved in paid work. Parity of recognition will also entail a significant redistribution of resources. A redistribution of caring labour between men and women is more likely to be achieved in this context.

Should those who do unpaid care be *recognized* in relation to their massive contribution to society and be rewarded accordingly, everything that we take for granted could begin to shift. The gendered division of labour will be encouraged to change once informal care gains proper recognition in terms of social respect and allocation of resources. These rewards would include adequate payment for the labour involved and the expansion of universal public services to enable those who care to have a choice over if and how they do so, and for whatever period of time is right for their circumstances:

> To say that the care of dependents must be recognized as work is to say that it must be included within a system of cooperation wherein it is adequately compensated and given the same status and social standing as any legitimate employment. (Kittay, 2001: 544)

In order to care in circumstances in which this did not lead to dependency, financial loss and the closing of alternatives for the future, claims for 'redistribution' must be connected with claims for 'recognition'. Fiona Williams argues in support of both recognition and redistribution claims for care:

> Although care may involve us all, it does so unequally. The care ethic argues against the gender imbalance in caring and for care as a valid activity for men and women, which requires time, financial and practical support and the recognition of choices (rather than rules, regulations and curfews). (2002: 510)

Regard for an ethics of childcare would also result in a social welfare system based on an acceptance of diversity in parenting and intimate relationships (F. Williams, 2002).

A discussion of the principles on which care work should be based is imperative, for implicit within the shift in policy from favouring the male breadwinner family towards an adult wage-earner model family (Land, 2004; Lewis, 2003; Lewis and Giullari, 2005) is a change in ideologies of 'political motherhood': a shift away from assuming 'mother-care' is best for children (Lewis, 2003). The research supports the claims of other studies that reveal that this shift may be in tension with the wishes of many mothers to give priority to the care of their children. In this sense, the success of the National Childcare Strategy in redefining 'political motherhood' (Windebank, 1999) may be limited in the face of the prevailing norms and values that make up the 'gender culture' in particular communities. There are also other discourses within family policy encouraging an intensification of the parenting role that resonate with the ideologies of 'sensitive' or 'intensive' mothering and that mothers may interpret in relation to their 'gendered moral codes'. It is mothers, in particular, who are likely to assume responsibility for supporting the education of their children and interpreting expert guidance on the parenting role. Given that parenting discourses place emphasis on giving time to children, they may conflict with any trends towards the adult worker model family. There does seem to be a pronounced tension between different strands of policy in this regard. This research has illustrated that the combined pressures to 'work more' and 'parent well' leave many mothers and fathers under considerable stress.

As care has an affective dimension, and because access to, and use of, caring services still need to be *organized*, individual carers will still face demands on their time even where formal childcare is utilized. Whilst formal childcare may provide support for children's emotional well-being, this does not replace the parent's responsibility in this regard. There is also evidence to suggest that, with regard to searching for and making arrangements to use formal childcare provision, for example, it is mainly mothers who undertake this role (Vincent et al., 2004b), and my study lends further support to this claim. It is certainly the case that, with regard to childcare, commodification has not extended so far as to fully replace the parenting role, embracing practical care, educational development and emotional support (Reay, 2005). There are many gaps left by formal childcare services and the gaps left by incomplete commodification were explored in Chapter 4 in relation to the parents' accounts of the use of formal and informal childcare services.

Whether women and men wish to care full-time, work outside the home full-time or integrate a variety of roles, the key to enjoying both equality and difference lies with appropriate support for the conduct of care in public expenditure and the redistribution of wealth. Social policy can be reshaped to support this vision provided that care work is rewarded financially and supported through public universal services within a package of citizenship rights. The deep relationship between gender, care-giving, dependence and vulnerability to poverty that is a feature of the UK persists within a climate of restructuring and savage budgetary cutbacks. The promotion of market-based solutions to care may do more to consolidate inequalities than to challenge them.

An ethic of care would respect the importance of both claims for redistribution and claims for recognition (Fraser, 2001) because 'integral to redistributive questions of who pays and who benefits from welfare programmes is the issue of how services and benefits are delivered and received' (F. Williams, 2002: 505). If care were to be culturally recognized and valued, this would involve a debate about who does it, why it is distributed unequally and why society could not function if those who care informally chose not to continue. This would also involve recognizing why many carers feel strongly that informal care is preferable to formal or commodified care. On this basis the preferences of carers could be respected and taken into account

in policies to redistribute resources accordingly. Policies must simultaneously improve support for carers whilst providing this in a variety of ways
so that there are genuine choices. Repo (2004) offers the example of Finland,
where parents are given a choice of using municipal childcare, using welfare benefits to purchase a private childcare place or using those benefits to
support informal parent care. This is a policy that provides choices, enables
parents to exercise their preferences and ensures all are supported through
a benefit that can be used in different ways. This appears to be a policy that
combines recognition for care with redistribution of resources in ways that
suit parents. It is a model that combines universalism with choice and support. This could shape an ethic of childcare policy in the UK.

DIVERSITY, MATERIAL HARDSHIP AND FAMILY LIVES

An ethic of childcare that reflects diversity and that engages with inequalities will reflect that some mothers and fathers will have less access to
the resources available to combine work and care according to choice.
Differences in social class, ethnic origin, employment opportunities and
geographical location will shape their capacity to benefit from policy. Those
women and men in low-paid, low-status employment, for example, are the
least likely to benefit from current employment policies relating to work–life
balance. In reviewing the impact of family-friendly employment policies,
Tess Kay draws a distinction between 'work-rich' and 'work-poor' families
in balancing paid work and care of children:

> While highly educated workers in professional occupations may be relatively
> well positioned to negotiate favourable work conditions, low-skilled employ-
> ees in insecure employment usually have less scope to do so. (2002: 232)

In her review of some recent studies into family friendly employment
practices, Geraldine Healy concludes 'there are pockets of the economy
where flexible working arrangements have made relatively few inroads'
(2004: 220). Those organizations that are adopting family friendly employment policies have distinctive characteristics and tend to employ women
with a high level of educational attainment (Healy, 2004). Childcare and
family-friendly policies have a differential impact on high- and low-paid
workers, leading Gill Scott to conclude:

> There is a growing polarization between the educated mother employed in
> the service-sector who can maintain her labour market position, and the less
> educated woman whose life becomes increasingly dominated by patterns of
> domesticity and part-time low paid work after becoming a mother. (1998: 526)

Recent research into the labour market experiences of women living in economically deprived neighbourhoods reveals that welfare-to-work policy may reproduce and exacerbate gender inequalities rather than challenge them: 'Women lack bespoke support and are channelled into "women's jobs", perpetuating gender inequalities in employment' (Grant, 2009: 330). With regard to equal opportunities policies, Kim Hoque and Mike Noon cite evidence that 'even in instances where EO policies are more than just paper exercises, they are often designed to have only a selective effect' (2004: 484). Moreover, polices are adopted only where there are clear benefits for the organization. Family-friendly employment policies fit uneasily alongside the government's commitment to flexible labour markets and a soft approach to the regulation of business (Driver and Martell, 2002). According to Susan Milner, initial optimism regarding Labour's efforts to promote family-friendly workplaces during the first term of office was eventually overshadowed as government 'gave way increasingly to a discourse of flexibility and the business case for work–life balance measures' (2010: 7).

The potential tension between supporting the needs of business and promoting the needs of families is the theme explored in Hartley Dean's research (Dean, 2002; Dean and Shah, 2002) into the experiences of low-income families. Dean argues that 'welfare to work' has to be assessed in relation to evidence of labour market polarization between 'core' and 'periphery' jobs and the demand for flexibility. In this sense 'welfare to work' may achieve greater labour market participation but this will often be into the 'peripheral' sector for those in low-paid and insecure employment, thus doing little to tackle social inequalities. This poses problems in relation to the policy goal of tackling family poverty and in offering work–life balance options for those working families on low incomes. In Dean's research it was found that employers supported work–life balance policies only where there was a business case meaning 'they were more inclined to offer parental leave or childcare subsidies to valuable highly skilled workers than to expendable low-skilled workers' (Dean, 2002: 8). Dean has been critical of New Labour's approach to family-friendly employment measures for failing to address the problems of ensuring 'peripheral' workers can benefit from them (2002: 8).

Research suggests that jobs in the 'peripheral' sector may demand the kind of 'flexibility' of workers that can make arranging childcare impossible. It may involve working unsociable and unpredictable hours, and formal childcare provision is not sufficiently flexible to meet these needs. These are challenges that were reported by the mothers and fathers in this research and that are echoed by other studies. Kathryn Backett-Milburn and her colleagues (2001), for example, explored the daily experiences of combining paid work with parenting for a sample of mothers with children of primary school age. Of these, fifteen mothers were living with partners and fifteen were lone parents. Many women took jobs below their abilities in order to reconcile work with the demands of childcare yet still encountered problems in balancing work and care. Few women were aware of any family-friendly policies in their workplace. On the contrary, many felt under pressure not to take time off when children were sick and risk being seen as unreliable. Participants spoke of the complexity of childcare arrangements and the fact that these would have to change around times when children were ill or out of the school term. The role of informal care in dealing with these situations was highlighted. The study concludes that childcare provision needs to be responsive to the flexible working hours expected by many employers to cover evenings, early mornings and weekend work and to cover times when schools are closed. However, at the same time, employment practices need to shift to take account of parenting roles. While parents are expected to be flexible, at present neither paid work nor formal childcare provision may meet their needs.

We are clearly a long way from securing work–life balance choices for all women and men. Claims that policy will promote gender equality need to be interrogated in relation to the evidence that women and men continue to occupy very different labour market positions. The movement of women into the labour market has not meant they have been provided with a passport into attractive employment. As Jane Lewis and Susanna Giullari (2005) argue, women have tended to move into the more 'flexible' forms of labour and are a long way from achieving gender equality 'in the sense of equally secure, equally well-paying jobs, to both men and women' (2005: 82). Moreover, there is a danger that existing inequalities between women within the labour market could be further enhanced since those with the resources and opportunities to take advantage of extensions to parental rights are those already in well-paid, secure employment. This serves as a reminder that any evaluation of childcare and work–life balance policy in supporting gender equality must start from an understanding of diversity and inequality in women's and men's experiences.

Recognition of diversity amongst parents and appreciation of the impact of material inequalities on their childcare arrangements will, therefore, alert policy-makers to the differential impact of specific agendas. The impact is shaped by existing structures of privilege and disadvantage. It has been noted that the intensification of the parenting role (Gillies, 2005) fits with how mothers interpret their moral responsibilities in relation to emotional and educational care of their children. Yet other strands of social policy are simultaneously exhorting mothers to do paid work. In turn, this links to social class inequalities amongst mothers who differ in their capacity to make choices over the balance of paid work and childcare and to meet the pedagogical ideals of 'sensitive' or 'intensive' mothering.

Current structures of inequality amongst mothers and fathers also mean some families are viewed as requiring intervention in the guise of 'parenting support' (Edwards and Gillies, 2004). In this context 'teenage mothers'

(Kidger, 2004), 'lone mothers' (Standing, 1999) and 'absent fathers' (Gillies, 2005) are all stigmatized in policy discourses. There has been an expansion of services that work with parents (Miller and Sambell, 2003) and this has been described as an 'increasing professionalization of childrearing practices' (Gillies, 2005: 70). This is part of a moral agenda, as parenting support policy 'reveals a class-specific concern with disadvantaged or "socially excluded" families' (Gillies, 2005: 71). Hence, behind the rhetoric of supporting parents is a moralizing discourse that claims some parents need to be re-educated in order to parent effectively. The problems that parents may face are personalized and thus dislocated from the structures that underpin their experience. Many early intervention programmes for families assessed by professionals as being 'troubled' or 'at risk', for example, tend to focus on the goal of achieving behaviour change in relation to either the child or the parents. This can be limiting given that many of the risks facing children and young people can be due to the impact of the wider social structure, government policies or local barriers. In addition, where programmes are presented in terms of tackling only negative aspects of behaviour, this can create a barrier whereby they are perceived by service users as a stigma (France et al., 2010). However, this study has indicated that parenting support programmes such as those offered within Sure Start can be highly valued by the mothers and fathers who use them and the mode of delivery at the local level can make a difference to how they are perceived and their impact. This theme will be developed further in the next section, where current changes relating to fatherhood will be considered with reference to the interview material with fathers.

'HANDS-ON' DADS: EMBRACING FATHERS' PERSPECTIVES ON CARE

A defining feature of contemporary fatherhood is an emphasis on fathers as an active, 'hands-on', sharer of child caring responsibilities . . . Today, fathers in Britain are expected to be accessible and nurturing as well as economically supportive to their children. (O'Brien, 2005: 3)

If childcare policy is to become 'gender-sensitive' and founded on the principles of 'recognition' of care and efforts to 'redistribute' it more equitably, the position of fathers will clearly warrant attention. Although the focus of this research has been on mothers and motherhood, a small number of interviews were conducted with fathers and some of this material was drawn on in Chapter 4. There is a need for further research into fatherhood as a basis for exploring gender relations and constructing a fuller picture of informal support in the care of young children. This book does not claim to have achieved this, because of the chosen focus and time and resource limitations. Nevertheless, this section will point to some potential themes for future work with reference to the limited interview material with fathers.

Dominant ideologies, cultural norms and social practices may construct both expectations and barriers for men wishing to engage in childcare (McKie et al., 2001). Research across the social sciences has become more 'father-sensitive' (Clarke and Roberts, 2002: 170) and the study of fatherhood has taken off over the last two decades (Burghes et al., 1997; Lewis, 2000; Morgan, 2000). Yet, as Clarke and Roberts observe, the shift towards father-sensitive research has not been entirely matched by policy and 'responses have been simplistic and the rhetoric has not recognized the complexity and diversity of family life' (2002: 178). The perspectives of fathers presented in this section support Clarke and Roberts (2001), who observe that fathering is multi-dimensional and may be practised in diverse ways. The practice of fathering has to be placed in context so that gaps between how fathers wish to conduct their role and what can be achieved in practice are revealed (Clarke and Roberts, 2002: 172–3).

The six fathers in this small sample reflected a wide range of personal and material circumstances. They held varied positions in relation to their role in paid work and childcare. However, none of them could be described as occupying a traditional position as sole breadwinner. These were fathers who were seeking to share care in an egalitarian way (Malcolm, Kenneth), were the main carer for their children living apart from the mother (Patrick, Michael), had part-time contact with their children following a relationship breakdown (Leo) or arranged childcare within an extended family (Aalam). It is significant that the men who were interested in the research and available to be interviewed were those who challenged the 'home-maker–breadwinner contract'. Further insights into fathering were gathered through a group interview with some fathers who were involved in a Sure Start project specifically intended to engage fathers.[1]

What did these interviews reveal about the social conditions of fatherhood (Hatten et al., 2002; O'Brien, 2005; O'Brien and Shemilt, 2003)? There are two issues that will be considered here. First, what the fathers have to say about balancing work and care will be reviewed to cast further light on the issues relating to family-friendly employment policies and access to informal care that have been suggested. Second, more generally how the fathers perceived their role and their understandings of what it meant to be an 'involved' father will reveal that, like the mothers, they may adopt moral positions as well as expressing delight in moving away from traditional roles.

Paid work and fatherhood

The two fathers in professional roles, Kenneth and Malcolm, both referred to the introduction of family-friendly employment policies and acknowledged that these were not always implemented effectively. Malcolm, who was married with one daughter aged five years, was in full-time employment in the further education sector and his wife was a full-time university lecturer. He perceived that the transition to fatherhood had a significant impact on his paid work. However, in contrast to some of the mothers, this did not mean that he had changed his job or reduced his hours to accommodate childcare. Nevertheless, he did feel that he now had less flexibility in relation to work. Moreover, as his duties included 'frontline' work with students, it was not possible for him to work flexibly or from home, meaning that if his child was ill it could cause real problems:

> some aspects of the work can be covered but there isn't anyone who can do my job when I am not around. There will be significant parts of my job that will pile up.

Given that there was no family support available it meant that Malcolm and his wife had to share and arrange cover between them in a crisis. Malcolm felt strongly that more should be offered to support parents who lack access to informal support as a complement to paid-for childcare.

Malcolm said that the question of paternal leave had been an issue for him:

> Parental legislation has come out and employers have not reacted terribly pro-actively to the legislation changing. Policies on paternal leave are still being sorted out and that is one of the problems for me. Because [daughter] was born before the paternal leave rights came into effect and it is a big issue for me as I lost a lot of annual leave over that period.

Malcolm felt that more needed to be done in the workplace to support parents:

> I would like to see a more structured approach and a more open approach within organizations. I think that would be a great help to working parents.

He went on to argue that, within his own institution, although formal policies were in place, it was well known that they were implemented in a variable way across departments:

> I think one of the frustrating things is that it is happening in some departments, particularly where they have got a line manager who understands

where employees are coming from on these issues and it is perhaps slower in others.

In contrast, Kenneth, who was in full-time professional work in higher education and whose partner worked full-time, expressed less concern than Malcolm about meeting the demands of paid work alongside care. He reflected on the benefits of having a child at a time when he was well established in his career in a senior management position:

> For me it has come at a time when I have reached the point in my career where I don't want to go anywhere else. I wouldn't say that I am winding down but even before the addition to the family I was at the point where I would rarely take work home anyway. So the impact has been less on me than might be expected. So there is not really a conflict between work and non-work.

With regard to the problem of a child falling ill, again, he seemed to feel less concerned than Malcolm that this would affect his work. This was made possible by the fact that both parents worked in jobs with flexible working conditions and where it was acceptable to take their child into the workplace:

> Well, one of you does have to drop something and it depends on the degree of illness. If one of the kids has got a sore throat or a headache then they may well come in and sit in one of our offices quietly and read. And that is very easy as well in both our places of work. Whereas if they have got a stomach upset or they are really quite poorly then it comes down to who has something on during the day or who has least on or boxing and coxing again.

Kenneth suggested that it was possible for him to refuse to attend an evening meeting when he had to collect a child from nursery on account of his seniority and long service in the institution. However, he felt that this would be less easy for other parents in this workplace who were at earlier stages of their career. The offer of family-friendly working practices was assessed earlier in the chapter and these narratives support claims that work–life balance policies can make a difference but both their impact and their implementation can vary. In the examples offered by Kenneth and Malcolm, it is clear that, even within a single workplace, the capacity to benefit from official policies can diverge between individuals on the basis of seniority or location in the organization. Their narratives underline the claim that work–life balance policies may connect with existing structures of privilege and disadvantage in paid employment.

The men in professional positions focused on workplace issues in their narratives, revealing how work remained central to their identity. Being able to 'father well' will be based on achieving rights at work rather than by accommodating the workplace in the way many of the mothers had done. With regard to the textual relations of ruling (Smith, 1990a), it was significant that the men in professional occupations turned to the discourse of 'family-friendly' employment rights to reflect on their role as fathers rather than, for example, beginning with a discussion of the distribution of care at home. Social policy frames its support for fathers mainly in relation to helping them balance their work and home life. Presumably a more equal distribution of care at home is assumed to follow but this cannot be taken for granted.

In comparison, Michael (club doorman) was in low-paid work with working hours that would pose difficulties in relation to childcare. Michael's employment as a club doorman meant his working hours started after his children's bedtime. He was a lone father but he did not perceive a difficulty because his mother was available to care for his children while he worked. He pointed out that work was very important to him and that he did not wish to live on benefits: 'but there are some arseholes out there who don't want to work at all. If they want to be dole bums then let them be dole bums'. Michael thus articulated the discourses related to 'welfare to work' and 'hard-working families' that have been promoted by New Labour and yet also occupied a non-traditional role as the main carer with custody of his children. Nevertheless, he relied on the support of his mother in order to be able to maintain paid work with unsocial hours and take care of his children.

This access to informal support was unavailable to Patrick, who had been in full-time work until his wife had become ill and, since her death, had taken on a full-time care role for his three young children. When asked about his feelings about paid work he said:

> It is not an issue for me. I can't say what the next six months will be like, or twelve months. I just don't know. But I want to try to get back into some kind of work.

However, he did not feel that this was possible at present given the demands of caring alone for three children: 'looking after myself and three children is a full-time job'. Patrick, as a lone father, stated he had no choice but to give priority to the care of his children and the Sure Start project was providing vital assistance to enable him to do this.

The remaining two fathers in the sample did not describe a conflict between work and care. Leo, a security guard, who worked unsocial hours, had regular contact with his non-resident children including having them to stay with him overnight. However, he stressed that their visits had to be arranged to fit in with his work: 'When I am working I haven't got the children. That is one thing that I cannot do. I have the children when I am not working.' Aalam was currently studying as well as doing voluntary work for a community organization. His wife was not working and he referred to the benefit of receiving considerable informal support from family, so he reported no conflict between childcare responsibilities and these other activities. He did, however, value the role of extended family in sharing the responsibilities involved.

It can be argued that the six fathers occupied diverse positions in relation to care, paid work and access to family support. Their accounts reveal that policies designed to support involved fatherhood would need to be capable of embracing this multiplicity of circumstances.

Sensitive fathering: care, joy and emotions

The fathers were invited to comment on what roles and responsibilities they felt were expected of fathers, whether they felt that gender roles were changing and whether they felt able to be fathers in a way that suited them. The two men in full-time professional positions, and who were living with their partner, largely approached this issue through a focus on paid work, as discussed already, and reflected on how far their paid work could be adapted to enable an involved role. Malcolm described an egalitarian distribution of domestic labour and childcare. As both he and his wife were in full-time professional posts, it was felt that this should be shared. In talking about what he most enjoyed about his fathering role he said:

> I suppose it is the reading at the end of the day, it is quality time that I ring-fence with [daughter]. It is having the opportunity to play at weekends as well. Again that time is generally ring-fenced. I think you have to be quite structured and quite disciplined in what you do to ensure [child] gets quality time.

Throughout the interview Malcolm returned to this notion of being disciplined, suggesting that being a 'hands-on' father could easily be eroded through paid work commitments. In the following extract Malcolm was talking about coping when his child was misbehaving:

> You just take the rough with the smooth. Children test the boundaries and that is just something that you have to live with. I suppose it is being disciplined and taking a deep breath and not to draw the frustration that you have got in your life, you know, if you have had a bad day in work and [daughter] goes and does something wrong.

Malcolm also spoke about how work would spill over into the weekend for both himself and his wife, leading to further negotiation over sharing the care. This raised the theme of work intensification and the blurring of the boundaries between home and work, with the potential to undermine the time for care.

The men who were contacted through the Sure Start project were managing care under difficult personal and material conditions. The project worker described how the group tried to provide support for fathers over issues of access and custody following a relationship breakdown. Many of the men perceived that fathers received unfair treatment in this regard. The following comment that was expressed by Patrick in our individual interview seemed to reflect the views of several fathers:

> when it comes to separation, it is seventy five per cent the mother's position and twenty five per cent the father's position and their rights are just thrown out of the window and it should be level all the way through.

The men also felt that social attitudes towards those fathers that were taking a primary caring role made things difficult for them. This included day-to-day activities such as doing the school pick-up:

> But after a time the teachers and parents get used to you. But for a lot of fathers it is difficult to get past that point because for the first couple of weeks people are giving you strange looks or acting strangely towards you, then you think, oh, I am not doing that again. (project worker, Sure Start interview)

> I have found that. Because I am a single father with three children, and there are a lot of single mothers with a couple of children in the school and then there might be the odd fathers who are standing on their own. (Patrick, Sure Start interview)

The fathers also mentioned that contact with a doctor or health visitor could be frustrating, as they would assume that the mother was the primary carer, as Michael illustrated:

> It does my head in now but I have just learned to live with it. I take them to the doctors now and they say 'where is the mother?' And I say that the mother has got nothing to do with it, she is not allowed to see her. It is me who has got them now, not the mother.

The Sure Start project worker stressed the value of the group in supporting each of the fathers in their desire to be a 'hands-on dad', and this seemed to capture what all the fathers were trying to achieve. In talking about their care routines and their time spent with their children, all of the fathers described a very active role. Michael, for example, emphasized that, although his mother provided support during his time in paid work, he saw care of the children as his responsibility. He talked about how becoming a father had changed his life for the better:

> Oh, it has changed one hell of a lot. I used to drink but once I had the baby then, I stopped. I don't drink, I don't go out, I don't smoke, I don't do nothing. The only thing that I do now is kick boxing and my children and my work. That is all there is. I have got more sense! I will do just anything for my [children]. They are my life. If I didn't have them I don't know what I would do.

Michael talked about his routines in a positive way. When asked if he found the routines hard being a lone father and given that his children were very young, he replied:

> Bathtime is probably the hardest. She has her bath first and my mum takes her downstairs then and I bath my little one then. That is the only part that I find hard. The rest is easy. And I have read all the books and everything.

Michael spoke of his deep involvement in the care of his children and his enjoyment of it. Like the other fathers, he spoke of the 'hands-on' nature of his role. He also talked about keeping his children safe, expressing worries about drink and drugs:

> I don't want the children to see all of that. I want them to have a good childhood. I didn't have one. I want my children to have a better childhood than I did.

Anxieties over child safety were also expressed by some of the other fathers in common with some of the mothers, a theme uncovered in other research (Mumford and Power, 2003). Michael challenged common views that the mother conducts these roles best in nurturing and protecting children. He challenged the construction of the 'sensitive mother' and, as the primary carer, there seemed to be no difference between the way he reflected on the caring role and the way the mothers did. His observation that he had 'read all the books' seems significant, for as the sole carer he was engaging with those textual discourses that were so powerful for the social practices of the mothers.

All of the fathers took an active role in the care of their children. Their accounts demonstrate that fathers want to care and would benefit from policies that will ensure they have the time and support to do so. Despite minimum rights for parents in employment, there is an absence of strong policies to enable men to take a more active caring role (Annesley et al., 2010). Research conducted for the Equal Opportunities Commission (Hatten et al., 2002) reveals that fathers still see themselves mainly in relation to a breadwinner role. Only a minority of the fathers surveyed saw themselves as having an equal role with partners in childcare and household labour. The research suggests that the recent moves towards family-friendly employment rights have done little so far to challenge traditional practices.

Some commentators have argued that the UK may need to consider some of the examples set by other European countries in terms of more vigorous attempts by the state to encourage equal parenting and to offer parents a comprehensive package of rights at work (Ben-Galim, 2011c). However, research studies in other European welfare regimes suggest change may still be slow in men's capacity to engage in 'family-work' (Kitterød and Pettersen, 2006) and in moving away from a traditional breadwinner role (Holter, 2007). Existing cultural norms relating to gender can present limits to redistribution, as Kevin Olson observes: 'Social policies designed to degender labor and redistribute caregiving are limited by their beneficiaries' culturally rooted choices' (2002: 381). This has been recognized as an issue for UK social policy, which has lacked a strong strategy to support men's role in childcare (Lister, 2006) so that culturally based and structurally limited 'choices' about who conducts childcare are degendered. Nevertheless, the material pertaining to the fathers in this study reveals that there is potential for policy to enhance men's capacity to be 'sensitive fathers'.

COALITION AND WELSH GOVERNMENT POLICIES IN AN AGE OF AUSTERITY

During Labour's period of office, tax credits were introduced to provide support for families on lower incomes and to help with the costs of childcare. Some critics argued that mothers on low incomes still faced particular problems in benefiting from the National Childcare Strategy (Lewis, 2003; Rake, 2001) because of gaps in the support available. The childcare tax credit, for example, has not covered the full costs of childcare for working parents who, because of their income level, meet eligibility criteria. Paying the balance can remain prohibitive for those on the lowest incomes. The working tax credit system encourages parents to work a minimum number of hours per week in order to reach the thresholds for payment. This is a real penalty where parents, often mothers in low-paid, part-time work, either cannot access longer hours or do not find it practical to do so because of their caring role. Whilst the ten-year strategy for childcare (HM Treasury, 2004) claimed to offer increased choice to parents, the choice to stay at home with young children or to reduce working hours for a period continued to depend on family income. Mothers and fathers in low-income households have a restricted 'choice' over the balance between paid work and childcare in the absence of adequate financial recognition by the welfare state for engagement in care.

Whilst it should be acknowledged that New Labour used the tax and benefit system to achieve some redistribution of income to families with children, this did not go far enough and rested too much on parents' capacity for work and the availability of suitable paid employment. Nevertheless, the increase in child benefit and the introduction of the child tax credit under New Labour benefited all families with children, since these are measures currently not linked to participation in paid work. This was a small step forward but much more needed to be done. As David Piachaud and Holly Sutherland concluded, in their assessment of New Labour's progress in reducing child poverty, 'How far child poverty can be ended and children's opportunities improved without confronting the broader inequalities in society is open to question' (2001: 115).

It is fair to conclude that those broader inequalities were not confronted by New Labour. Since the UK Coalition government took office, it has introduced measures to cut support to the most vulnerable, including families with young children. The Child Trust Fund and the Health in Pregnancy Grant, for example, were both discontinued in January 2011. Since April 2011 the Sure Start Maternity Grant has been limited to the first child only, child benefit has been frozen and support for childcare through tax credits has been cut from 80 per cent to 70 per cent of costs. Further regressive changes are to be rolled out that will make life harder for families on low and modest incomes. Although the UK Coalition government has continued with New Labour's mantra that the tax and benefits system should be reformed in order to make work pay, many of the changes, such as the reduction in support for childcare costs and the increase to the minimum working hours threshold for eligibility to working tax credit for couples with children, are likely to undermine this goal.[2] These are also changes with damaging consequences for gender equality (UK Women's Budget Group, 2010).

Further to the matter of family economic well-being, there is concern that cuts to public services will have other negative outcomes. The influence of caring responsibilities has not been given due consideration in UK Coalition government reforms, meaning that the gender impact of current changes has been disregarded. Women are major users of public services and this research has revealed that the informal care provided by women covers gaps in service provision. Those gaps are set to increase as valued public services close down. The UK Women's Budget Group has expressed concern that this will add to women's existing caring labour:

> It seems the Coalition is happy to restore an outdated 'male breadwinner, dependent female carer' model of family life that fits neither with women's aspirations nor today's financial necessities. These plans reveal gendered assumptions based on women being available to work unpaid for the Coalition's Big Society. (2010: 2)

In this unfavourable climate, the need to propose an alternative agenda is both pressing and yet unlikely to be heard at national UK level. The book will close with some thoughts on this matter.

TIME FOR AN ALTERNATIVE

Childcare policy in the UK and Wales is a long way from promoting gender equality, supporting parents and meeting the interests of all children. An ethical childcare policy cannot be 'top-down', imposed or assumed to be furthered simply by enabling more women to do paid work. There is a need to engage with cultural preferences and the ideologies and discursive frames that continue to inform those preferences, whilst simultaneously providing a range of policy options and benefits that mean the choice to care is a respected pathway and can be conducted in a variety of ways. That will be the most powerful way of enabling mothers and fathers to make decisions over how they conduct childcare and how they want to redistribute the labour that is involved to ensure that whoever does it enjoys financial independence.

Like Levitas (2001), this study recognizes that the alternatives the author is proposing rely on a utopian method. After thirteen years of office there was little to indicate that New Labour in London was prepared to redistribute wealth or revise the policy emphasis on paid work. In their assessment of the legacy of the UK New Labour government in relation to gender equality, Claire Annesley and colleagues (2010) also indicate a weakness in how gender has been framed in policy. This includes a failure to address the role of men in unpaid labour and in promoting an agenda to support fatherhood:

> The *policy* solutions that were possible to broker in the New Labour coalition were also predominantly directed at women, rather than at altering the distribution of paid and unpaid work between the genders, changing men's behaviour or challenging the dominant neoliberal discourse of the adult worker model. (Annesley et al., 2010: 401)

Some of the current welfare reforms and cuts to public services being pursued with ideological fervour by the UK Coalition government began with New Labour. However, the anticipated damaging impact on families with children of current welfare reform (CPAG, 2011; Daycare Trust, 2010) and the failure to consider adequately the gender impact of austerity measures (UK Women's Budget Group, 2010) suggests we are now living in particularly dangerous times. In this sense, the ethics of care proposed by Fiona Williams and others, which informs the book's proposals, may seem idealistic. In this environment, the evidence of distinctiveness in social policy and social justice arenas in Wales must be maintained and advanced. The future Welsh policy landscape may need to diverge further from wider UK political agendas. If devolution and the difference of style and vision that has emerged in Wales since 1999 mean anything, they will mean offering a space to explore alternatives to the agendas that have been led by Westminster.

Appendix 1: Socio-Economic Profile of the Three Neighbourhoods

The three localities were electoral wards in one city in Wales, and the study made reference to census data in assisting the selection. However, the ethical agreement confirmed with participants prevents the presentation of census figures that could identify the areas.

Crossland lies close to the city centre and is one of the several *Communities First* areas in the city. It has a higher proportion of people from minority ethnic groups other than white than either Tinbury or Shaw. Those who described their ethnic group as either Asian or Asian British constitute the largest minority ethnic group. Whilst the census records suggest that the largest proportion of people either stated their religion as Christian or reported no religion, there is a sizeable Muslim population. Over one third of people aged sixteen to seventy-four living in the area stated that they had no qualifications. A fairly high proportion of people are economically inactive. Of those who are economically active, there are more employed in elementary occupations than as managers or senior officials or in professional occupations. A higher proportion of people rent from private landlords than in the other two areas although owner occupation is the most common form of household tenure and there is some local authority housing.

Tinbury is also a *Communities First* area and provides a base for several Sure Start projects. With regard to the distribution of ethnic groups, the majority of the population is white and the proportion from minority ethnic groups is the lowest of the three wards. The majority reported their religion to be Christian (the largest group) or stated they had no religion (the second largest group). A very high proportion of people (over half) stated they had no qualifications. There were more people who reported that they were economically inactive than economically active. Of those who are in employment, the largest proportion is in elementary occupations; a very low proportion are managers and senior officials or in professional occupations. In relation to household tenure, the rate of owner occupation is comparatively low and over one half of the population is living in local authority rented housing. The area has a higher proportion of lone-parent households than in the other two areas.

Shaw lies to the west of Tinbury and is generally viewed as more affluent than either Crossland or Tinbury. The area has a lower proportion of people of minority ethnic origin than in Crossland but more than in Tinbury. Those who are recorded as Asian or Asian British represent the largest minority ethnic group. Most people recorded their religion as being Christian or stated no religion; of those reporting other religions, the largest group was Muslim. The proportion of the population stating they have no qualifications is much lower than in the other two areas. A higher proportion of the population reported that they were economically active than in the other two areas. Of the economically active, a high proportion are managers and senior officials or in professional occupations. There is a very high proportion of owner-occupied households and the proportion in housing rented from the local authority is similar to that in Crossland. This area had the lowest proportion of lone-parent households of the three wards and a very high proportion of married couples.

Appendix 2: The Sample of Mothers and Fathers

Each participant was asked to provide information in relation to the following:

- age
- marital status
- ethnic origin (defined by the interviewee)
- employment status: (a) self; (b) partner, if applicable
- number of children
- age of children.

Each participant was given a pseudonym.

PARENTS LIVING IN SHAW

Becky (thirty-nine, white Welsh)

Married; working part-time as a childminder and other occasional part-time work; on a career break from a professional job in the civil service; husband is an engineer; three children aged two, four and nine years.

Janet (forty-five, white Welsh)

Separated from children's father; living with new partner; recently moved from part-time, casual work to a full-time position in the same business and working towards her qualification in the trade; partner works in the same profession but for a different firm; has four children aged twenty-five, twenty-three, eighteen and eight years and a four-year-old grandchild.

Greta (thirty-nine, white European)

Married; full-time student; husband is a university researcher; three children aged sixteen, eleven and eight years.

Gail (thirty-nine years, white Welsh)

Married; part-time cashier for a supermarket; previously commuted to another city as a manager for a utility company but gave up after birth of second child; husband is a skilled manual worker for a local authority; two children aged three and eight years.

Kelly (thirty-seven, white English)

Married; part-time health worker in hospital; husband is a doctor; two children aged seven and four years.

Lowri (thirty-three, white Welsh)

Separated from husband; full-time manager in a financial company; two children aged seven and six years.

Kenneth (fifty-two, white Welsh)

Living with partner; senior manager in higher education; partner is a lecturer; four children aged thirteen, eleven, seven and fifteen months.

Malcolm (thirty-two, white English)

Married; manager in further education college; wife is a university lecturer; one child aged five years.

PARENTS LIVING IN CROSSLAND

Emma (thirty-four, white Welsh)

Lone parent; works part-time in clerical post in higher education; two children aged eight and six years.

Hameeda (twenty-eight, Bangladeshi)

Married; works full-time as a community worker; husband is a chef; one child aged fifteen months.

Diane (thirty-three, white Welsh)

Single parent with shared care arrangement with former partner; separation is recent; part-time manager of retail outlet; has a degree and wants to return to study; one child aged three years.

Sadiah (twenty-nine, Bangladeshi)

Married; described herself as a housewife and had previously been a factory worker prior to motherhood; husband is a waiter; four children aged nine, seven, five and three years.

Tracey (thirty-three, white Welsh)

Married; no longer working following disability and had previously been a nanny; husband works full-time in voluntary sector; two children aged five and three years.

Rashida (twenty-seven, Bengali)

Married; gave up work when she became pregnant; had been a customer services advisor; husband works in a local restaurant; one child aged three years, pregnant with a second child.

Zeena (twenty-eight, Welsh Bangladeshi)

Married; living with her parents and siblings; part-time community worker; one child aged six years.

Farah (thirty, British Bangladeshi)

Married; part-time learning support assistant; husband not working; two children aged three and two years.

Sunita (twenty-seven, Bangladeshi)

Married; gave up work as a learning support assistant when she found she was pregnant; husband works full-time as a chef; twins aged four years.

Aalam (thirty-three, Bangladeshi)

Married; part-time student and voluntary worker; wife is not in paid work; three children aged eleven, eight and four years.

PARENTS LIVING IN TINBURY

Natalie (forty-four, white European)

Divorced – child has occasional contact with father; part-time teacher; one child aged seven years.

Danielle (twenty-eight, white European)

Separated; part-time work with two jobs – teacher and skilled craft worker; one child aged seven years.

Christine (twenty-nine, white Welsh)

Married; working part-time as care worker and also a part-time student; husband was described as a 'housedad'; three children aged seven, five and three years.

Stella (thirty-five, white Welsh)

Married; part-time nurse working night shifts; husband is a manual worker; one child aged four.

Sheila (twenty-nine, white Welsh)

Married; teacher; husband is civil servant; one child aged three years.

Margaret (thirty-three, white Welsh)

Married; full-time childminder; husband is a long-distance driver; two children aged nine and three years.

Gillian (forty-five, white Welsh)

Married; in transition from civil service to local authority employment as administrative assistant, part-time; husband works as civil servant; one child aged four years.

Joy (twenty-two, white Welsh/Irish)

Married; not in paid work; husband is self-employed manual worker; one child aged nineteen months.

Sally (twenty-three, white Welsh)

Lone parent; not in paid work owing to poor health but works as volunteer in day centre; planning to go to college; one child aged eighteen months.

Bronwen (twenty-one, white Welsh)

Lone parent, having separated from partner very recently; part-time customer services representative and part-time degree student; one child aged eighteen months.

NURSERY MOTHERS

Four mothers were interviewed, all in the same friendship group and using the same nursery. All described their ethnic origin as 'white Welsh'. The group comprised Jane (two children, aged thirteen years and three years), Liz (two children, aged four years and eight years), Brenda (two children, aged ten years and four years) and Yvonne (one child aged three years, pregnant with second child).

SURE START DADS GROUP

Eight fathers drawn from the Sure Start Dads Group took part in a group interview held at a community centre in Tinbury. The group included two Sure Start project workers and six regular members. The group interview focused on matters regarding the Sure Start project and general themes relating to fathers' participation in childcare. The project workers requested that there should be no recording of any information relating to any individual's personal circumstances during this meeting. Subsequently, three of the eight fathers consented to participation in individual interviews. The details of the three fathers are:

Patrick (thirty-seven, white English)

Lone parent; recently widowed; not in paid work; three children aged ten, six and two years.

Michael (twenty-three, white Welsh)

Lone parent; works in a night club; lives with his own mother, who provides support; two children aged sixteen months and five months.

Leo (thirty-eight, Welsh/Argentinian)

Separated with contact order to see his children, who live with their mother; security officer; two children aged four and three years.

Appendix 3: Caring for Children Interview Themes

1   Details about you and your family.
2   Caring for your children: what does it involve and who does it?
3   Access to and use of informal support from family and friends.
4   Typical daily routines and how these have evolved over time; divisions of labour.
5   Perspectives on roles played by mothers and fathers.
6   Using and choosing early years and childcare provision.
7   Work, education and childcare: balancing commitments.
8   Perspectives on policy and services for parents and children (national and local).
9   What do you value and what would you like to change about your childcare arrangements?

Appendix 4: The Sample of Policy Officers

All policy officers were given a pseudonym and details of institutional affiliation have been generalized in order to protect anonymity.

REGIONAL LEVEL

Mike Davies, policy advisor, Welsh Government.
Keith Hall, Assembly Member, National Assembly for Wales.
Paul Waters, senior officer, children's organization.
Alison Connor, senior officer, regional equality body one.
Liz Spencer, senior officer, regional equality body two.
Lesley Thomas, officer, Welsh public services organization.

LOCAL LEVEL

Sarah Wilson, voluntary sector officer, member of local EYDCP.
Debra Mason, officer, local authority social services department, member of local EYDCP.
Rita Daniels, senior officer, local authority education department, member of local EYDCP.
Nicholas Peters, senior officer, local authority education department.
Chris Coleman, senior officer, local authority children and young people's services.
Susan Hall, officer, voluntary organization, member of local EYDCP.
Erica Bell, Sure Start senior officer, local authority.
Narinder Begum, community worker for Sure Start.

Appendix 5: Policy Officers' Interview Themes

1 Personal information, nature of professional involvement in childcare policy and provision and location in policy networks.
2 Reflections on the key drivers and themes of childcare policy at national, regional and local levels.
3 The main achievements of childcare policy and identification of key gaps in provision and barriers to policy delivery.
4 The role played by the Assembly in shaping childcare policy to meet needs of Welsh communities.
5 The delivery of policy through partnership working and perceived benefits and challenges.
6 Themes from parent interviews and from policy analysis.

Endnotes

Notes to Preface

1 The National Childcare Strategy (DfEE, 1998) was intended for implementation in England. Policy relating to the development of childcare in Wales, Scotland and Northern Ireland was devolved to their respective governments with the expectation that the Secretaries of State in those countries would publish their own strategies on childcare. The way in which childcare policy developed in Wales in the period following devolution is discussed further in Chapter 2 of this book.

Notes to Introduction

1 The Communities First programme is a Welsh Government initiative to tackle poverty and social disadvantage in designated areas (WAG, 2002a).

2 The period from birth to the end of primary schooling was the chosen age range because it is the period during which the childcare needs of parents are likely to be most pronounced.

3 Details about the characteristics of the sample of mothers and fathers are provided in Appendix 2.

4 The interview themes explored with mothers and fathers can be found in Appendix 3. Participants were asked to consent to the discussion being tape-recorded and this was granted in all cases except one. The interviews were all transcribed and analysed using a thematic approach. All participants had been guaranteed anonymity and have been given pseudonyms.

5 The websites included those relating to national, regional and local government alongside public, private and voluntary sector bodies such as Chwarae Teg (Fair Play), the Equal Opportunities Commission in Wales, Children in Wales, the Welsh Local Government Association and the Welsh Development Agency.

6 The Government of Wales Act 2006 established a formal separation of powers between the Welsh Government (the executive) and the National Assembly for Wales (the legislature). The executive was referred to as the Welsh Assembly Government (WAG) until May 2011 when it became known as the Welsh Government. The executive will be referred to as Welsh Government throughout the book and the legislature will be referred to as the National Assembly for Wales.

7 The roles of the policy officers are described in Appendix 4.

8 Interviews were tape-recorded and transcribed in full, enabling thematic analysis. A list of the interview themes explored with policy officers is provided in Appendix 5.

Notes to Chapter 1

1 The duty is introduced in Chapter 21, Paragraph 6 (England) and Paragraph 22 (Wales) of the Childcare Act 2006.
2 Information and guidance on legislation and good practice relating to pregnancy and parenthood is available from the Equality and Human Rights Commission.
3 The *Every Child Matters* Green Paper (DfES, 2003) introduced policies and proposals for England only with the exception of certain proposals relating to non-devolved responsibilities. The Welsh Government was able to determine which proposals it wished to adopt but within the legislative framework subsequently introduced by the Children Act 2004, Part Three, Children's Services in Wales.

Notes to Chapter 2

1 The National Assembly for Wales has sixty elected members and has legislative powers in devolved areas. The National Assembly has delegated its executive powers to the Welsh Government (formerly Welsh Assembly Government), which is made up of cabinet ministers and led by the First Minister. Reference will be made to the Welsh Government with regard to matters concerning the executive and to the National Assembly for Wales with regard to matters concerning the legislature. All acknowledgements of published sources use the nomenclature that applied at the time of publication.
2 This first strategic plan is now an archived document and was replaced following subsequent Assembly elections by *Wales: A Better Country. The Strategic Agenda of the Welsh Assembly Government* (WAG, 2003) and *One Wales: A Progressive Agenda for the Government of Wales* (WAG, 2007).
3 The *Every Child Matters* Green Paper (DfES, 2003) introduced policies and proposals for England only, with the exception of certain proposals relating to non-devolved responsibilities. The Welsh Government was able to determine which proposals it wished to adopt but within the legislative framework subsequently introduced by the Children Act 2004, Part Three, Children's Services in Wales.
4 Details summarized from *www.opsi.gov.uk/acts/acts2004/40031-d.htm*.

Note to Chapter 3

1 The reader should refer to the Introduction and Appendix 2 for details of the methodology and the sample of mothers and fathers.

Notes to Chapter 4

1 The three areas have been given pseudonyms in order to protect the identity of research participants.
2 Since the fieldwork was completed, the local authority has announced plans to close this facility despite public opposition.
3 The author does not intend to imply that the reliance on family-based childcare among the Bangladeshi parents in this small sample was culturally specific. However, there was a view expressed by some of the Bangladeshi parents and

by community workers in the Crossland area that this was a cultural preference within Bangladeshi families. This view deserves to be contextualized,
as the author noted exceptions to this among Bangladeshi parents as well as
similarities with some of the white Welsh mothers in stating a preference for
family-based care.

4 See Tracey's account in Chapter 3, for example.

5 The Welsh Government referred to the important public information role to
be offered by local authority children's information services in the *Childcare
Strategy for Wales* (WAG, 2005b). The Strategy also acknowledged the need for
the profile of these services to be raised. There are now family information
services in each local authority and these offer advice on finding childcare as
well as on other topics.

Note to Chapter 5

1 The local Sure Start Partnership, for example, had given a high priority to user
involvement and consultation.

Notes to Conclusion

1 Three of the Sure Start fathers subsequently volunteered to give individual
interviews and are included in the sample of six. The details of all the fathers
are provided in Appendix 2.

2 From April 2012 couples with children have been required to work at least
twenty-four hours a week between them, with one working at least sixteen
hours a week in order to meet the minimum threshold for working tax credit.
Prior to this change, couples with children were eligible to claim working tax
credit provided one parent worked for a minimum of sixteen hours per week.

Bibliography

Annesley, C., Gains, F. and Rummery, K. (2010). 'Engendering politics and policy: the legacy of New Labour', *Policy and Politics*, 38(3): 389–406.

Backett-Milburn, K., Cunningham-Burley, S. and Kemmer, D. (2001). *Caring and Providing: Lone and Partnered Working Mothers in Scotland*. FPSC/JRF Joint Series, London: Family Policy Studies Centre.

Bagley, C., Ackerley, C. L. and Rattray, J. (2004). 'Social exclusion, Sure Start and organizational social capital: evaluating inter-disciplinary multi-agency working in an education and health work programme', *Journal of Educational Policy*, 19(5): 595–607.

Ball, S. J. and Vincent, C. (2005). 'The "childcare champion"? New Labour, social justice and the childcare market', *British Educational Research Journal*, 31(5): 557–70.

Ball, W. (2010). 'Devolution, gender and childcare: a distinctive agenda for Wales?', in N. Charles and C. A. Davies (eds), *Gender and Social Justice in Wales*. Cardiff: University of Wales Press, pp. 83–104.

Ball, W. and Charles, N. (2006). 'Feminist social movements and policy change: devolution, childcare and domestic violence policies in Wales', *Women's Studies International Forum*, 29(2): 172–83.

Barlow, A., Duncan, S. and James, G. (2002). 'New Labour, the rationality mistake and family policy in Britain', in A. Carling, S. Duncan and R. Edwards (eds), *Analysing Families: Morality and Rationality in Policy and Practice*. London: Routledge, pp. 110–28.

Bassin, D., Honey, M. and Kaplan, M. M. (eds) (1994) *Representations of Motherhood*. New Haven, CT: Yale University Press.

Bell, L. (1998). 'Public and private meanings in diaries: researching family and childcare', in J. Ribbens and R. Edwards (eds), *Feminist Dilemmas in Qualitative Research: Public Knowledge and Private Lives*. London: Sage, pp. 72–86.

Bell, L. and Ribbens, J. (1994). 'Isolated housewives and complex maternal worlds: the significance of social contacts between women with young children in industrial societies', *Sociological Review*, 42(2): 227–62.

Bell, S. E. (2004). 'Intensive performances of mothering: a sociological perspective', *Qualitative Research*, 4(1): 45–75.

Benford, R. D. and Snow, D. A. (2000). 'Framing processes and social movements: an overview and assessment', *Annual Review of Sociology*, 26: 611–39.

Ben-Galim, D. (2011a). *Making the Case for Universal Childcare*. London: IPPR.

Ben-Galim, D. (2011b). *Parents at the Centre*. London: IPPR.

Ben-Galim, D. (2011c). *Family Policy: Where Next for Parental Leave and Flexible Working?* London: IPPR.

Bevan Foundation (2005). *A 'Childcare Revolution' in Wales*. Final Report, Policy Paper 6, Tredegar: The Bevan Foundation.

Beveridge, F., Nott, S. and Stephen, K. (2000). 'Mainstreaming and the engendering of policy-making: a means to an end?', *Journal of European Public Policy*, 7(3): 385–405.

Bostock, L. (2002). ' "God, she's gonna report me": the ethics of child protection in poverty research', *Children and Society*, 16(4): 273–83.

Bourdieu, P. (1986). 'The forms of capital', in J. E. Richardson (ed.), *Handbook of Theory for Research in the Sociology of Education*. Westport, CT: Greenwood Press, pp. 241–58.

Bourdieu, P. (1990). *In Other Words: Essays towards Reflexive Sociology*. Cambridge: Polity Press.

Bourdieu, P. and Wacquant, L. (1992). *An Invitation to Reflexive Sociology*. Cambridge: Polity Press.

Bowe, R., Ball, S. J. and Gewirtz, S. (1994). 'Captured by the discourse? Issues and concerns in researching "parental choice" ', *British Journal of Sociology of Education*, 15(1): 63–78.

Bransbury, L. (2004). 'Devolution in Wales and social justice', *Benefits*, 41(12): 175–81.

Brooksbank, D. (2001). 'The Welsh economy: a statistical profile', *Contemporary Wales*, 14: 164–92.

Bruegel, I. and Warren, S. (2003). 'Family resources and community social capital as routes to valued employment in the UK?', *Social Policy and Society*, 2(4): 319–28.

Brunel University (2000). *Unmet Demand for Childcare Services in the City and County of Swansea*. Uxbridge: Out of School Childcare Research Unit.

Bryson, C., Kazimirski, A. and Southwood, H. (2006). *Childcare and Early Years Provision in Wales: A Study of Parents' Use, Views and Experiences*, February, DfTE Information Document No: 006-06, Cardiff: WAG.

Burghes, L., Clarke, L. and Cronin, N. (1997). *Fathers and Fatherhood in Britain*. Occasional Paper 23. London: Family Policy Studies Centre.

Byrne, B. (2006). 'In Search of a "Good Mix": "Race", Class, Gender and Practices of Mothering', *Sociology*, 40(6): 1001–17.

Cabinet Office, Social Exclusion Unit (2001). *Preventing Social Exclusion*. London: Cabinet Office.

Caluori, J. (2009). *Children and the Recession: Summary*. Policy Insight Paper 3, June, London: Daycare Trust.

Chaney, P. (2004). 'The post-devolution equality agenda: the case of the Welsh Assembly's statutory duty to promote equality of opportunity', *Policy and Politics*, 32(1): 63–77.

Chaney, P. (2010). 'Delivery or déjà vu? Gender mainstreaming and public policy in post-devolution Wales', in N. Charles and C. A. Davies (eds), *Gender and Social Justice in Wales*. Cardiff: University of Wales Press, pp. 31–55.

Chaney, P. and Fevre, R. (2001). 'Ron Davies and the cult of "inclusiveness": devolution and participation in Wales', *Contemporary Wales*, 14: 21–49.

Chaney, P. and Fevre, R. (2002). *An Absolute Duty: Equal Opportunities and the National Assembly for Wales*. Cardiff: Institute of Welsh Affairs.

Chaney, P., Hall, T. and Dicks, B. (2000). 'Inclusive governance? The case of "minority" and voluntary sector groups and the National Assembly for Wales', *Contemporary Wales*, 13: 203–29.

Chaney, P., Hall, T. and Pithouse, A. (eds) (2001) *New Governance – New Democracy? Post- Devolution Wales*. Cardiff: University of Wales Press, pp. 31–55.

Charles, N. (2000). *Feminism, the State and Social Policy*. London: Macmillan.

Charles, N. (2004). 'Feminist politics and devolution: a preliminary analysis', *Social Politics*, 11(2): 297–311.

Charles, N. (2010). 'Setting the scene: devolution, gender politics and social just-ice', in N. Charles and C. A. Davies (eds), *Gender and Social Justice in Wales*. Cardiff: University of Wales Press, pp. 1–28.

Charles, N. and Davies, C. A. (2005). 'Studying the particular, illuminating the general: community studies and community in Wales', *Sociological Review*, 53(4): 672–90.

Charles, N. and James, E. (2003). 'Gender and work orientations in conditions of job insecurity', *British Journal of Sociology*, 54(2): 239–57.

Charles, N., Davies, C. A. and Harris, C. (2008). *Families in Transition: Social Change, Family Formation and Kin Relationships*, Bristol: Policy Press.

Cheal, D. (2002). *Sociology of Family Life*. Basingstoke: Palgrave.

Cheong, P. H., Edwards, R., Goulbourne, H. and Solomos, J. (2007). 'Immigration, social cohesion and social capital: a critical review', *Critical Social Policy*, 27(1): 24–49.

Childcare Act 2006, Elizabeth II, C. 21, Norwich: TSO.

Children Act 2004, Elizabeth II, C. 31, Norwich: TSO.

Children's Commissioner for Wales Act 2001, Elizabeth II, C. 18, Norwich: TSO.

Clarke, L. and Roberts, C. (2001). *Fatherhood in the New Millennium*. York: Joseph Rowntree Foundation.

Clarke, L. and Roberts, C. (2002). 'Policy and rhetoric: the growing interest in fathers and grandparents in Britain', in A. Carling, S. Duncan and R. Edwards (eds), *Analysing Families: Morality and Rationality in Policy and Practice*. London: Routledge, pp. 165–82.

Clarke, P. (2002). 'The Children's Commissioner for Wales', Policy Review, *Children and Society*, 16(4): 287–90.

Coleman, J. (1988). 'Social capital in the creation of human capital', *American Journal of Sociology*, 94, Supplement: S95–S120.

Connell, R. W. (1990). 'The state, gender, and sexual politics: theory and appraisal', *Theory and Society*, 19(5): 507–44.

Conservative Party (2010). *Big Society Not Big Government: Building a Big Society*. London: Conservative Party.

CPAG (Child Poverty Action Group) (2011). *Response to the 'Tackling Child Poverty and Improving Life Chances' Consultation*. February, London: CPAG.

CPTG (Child Poverty Task Group) (Wales) (2004). *Report of the Child Poverty Task Group*. Cardiff: National Assembly for Wales.

Crowley, A. and Winckler, V. (Save the Children and the Bevan Foundation with the New Policy Institute and Focus Consultancy) (2008). *Children in Severe Poverty in Wales: An Agenda for Action*. Final report of a study funded by the Welsh Assembly Government's New Ideas Fund, February, Cardiff: Wales Programme of Save the Children.

Daniel, B. M. and Taylor, J. (2006). 'Gender and child neglect: theory, research and policy', *Critical Social Policy*, 26(2): 426–39.

David, M. E. (1993). *Parents, Gender and Education Reform*. Cambridge: Polity Press.

David, M., Edwards, R., Hughes, M. and Ribbens, J. (1993). *Mothers and Education: Inside Out? Exploring Family-Education Policy and Experience*. Basingstoke: Macmillan.

David, M., Davies, J., Reay, D. and Standing, K. (1997). 'Choice within constraints: mothers and schooling', *Gender and Education*, 9(4): 397–410.

Davies, C. A. and Jones, S. (eds) (2003). *Welsh Communities: New Ethnographic Perspectives*. Cardiff: University of Wales Press.

Day, G. (2006). 'Chasing the dragon? Devolution and the ambiguities of civil society in Wales', *Critical Social Policy*, 26(3): 642–55.

Daycare Trust (2003). *Towards Universal Childcare*. London: Daycare Trust.

Daycare Trust (2010). *The Impact of the Spending Review on Childcare*. Policy Briefing, October, London: Daycare Trust.

Daycare Trust/NCSR (National Centre for Social Research) (2007). *Childcare Nation? Progress on the Childcare Strategy and Priorities for the Future*. London: Daycare Trust.

Daycare Trust and 4Children (2011). '250 Sure Start children's centres face closure within a year', press release, 28 January.

Deacon, A. (2003). ' "Levelling the playing field, activating the players": New Labour and the cycle of disadvantage', *Policy and Politics*, 31(2): 123–37.

Dean, H. (2002). 'Business *versus* families: whose side is New Labour on?', *Social Policy and Society*, 1(1): 3–10.

Dean, H. and Shah, A. (2002). 'Insecure families and low-paying labour markets: comments on the British experience', *Journal of Social Policy*, 31(1): 61–80.

Devine, F. and Heath, S. (1999). *Sociological Research Methods in Context*. London: Macmillan.

DfEE (Department for Education and Employment) (1998). *Meeting the Childcare Challenge: A Framework and Consultation Document*. Cm. 3959, London: The Stationery Office.

DfES (Department for Education and Skills) (2003). *Every Child Matters*. Cm. 5860, London: The Stationery Office.

Dickens, S., Taylor, J., and La Valle, I. (2005). *Local Childcare Markets: A Longitudinal Study*. Nottingham: DfES Publications.

Disability Discrimination Act 2005, Elizabeth II, C. 13, Norwich: TSO.

Dobrowolsky, A. (2002). 'Rhetoric versus reality: the figure of the child and New Labour's strategic "social investment state" ', *Studies in Political Economy*, 69: 43–73.

Dobrowolsky, A. and Jenson, J. (2004). 'Shifting representations of citizenship: Canadian politics of "women" and "children" ', *Social Politics*, 11(2): 154–80.

Dolphin, T. (2010a). *Cutting the Deficit: There Is an Alternative*. October, London: Institute for Public Policy Research.

Dolphin, T. (ed.) (2010b). *Reviewing the Spending Review: A Sectoral Analysis*. October, London: Institute for Public Policy Research.

Drakeford, M. (2005). 'Wales and a third term of New Labour: devolution and the development of difference', *Critical Social Policy*, 25(4): 497–506.

Driver, S. and Martell, L. (2002). 'New Labour, work and the family', *Social Policy and Administration*, 36(1): 46–61.

DSS (Department of Social Security) (1998). *New Ambitions for Our Country: A New Contract for Welfare*. Cm. 3805, London: The Stationery Office.

DTI (Department of Trade and Industry) (2000). *Work and Parents: Competitiveness and Choice*. Cm. 5005. London: The Stationery Office.

DTI (Department of Trade and Industry) (2005). *Work and Families: Choice and Flexibility. A Consultation Document*. London: DTI. Internet access only, URN 05/847, http://bis.ecgroup.net/search.aspx, last accessed 2 August 2012.

Dudley-Marling, C. (2001). 'School trouble: a mother's burden', *Gender and Education*, 13(2): 183–97.

Duncan, S. (2002). 'Policy discourses on "reconciling work and life" in the EU', *Social Policy and Society*, 1(4): 305–14.

Duncan, S. (2005). 'Mothering, class and rationality', *Sociological Review*, 53(1): 50–76.

Duncan, S. (2007). 'What's the problem with teenage parents? And what's the problem with policy?', *Critical Social Policy*, 26(2): 426–39.

Duncan, S. and Edwards, R. (1999). *Lone Mothers, Paid Work and Gendered Moral Rationalities*. London: Macmillan.

Duncan, S. and Smith, D. (2002). 'Family geographies and gender cultures', *Social Policy and Society*, 1(1): 21–34.

Duncan, S., Edwards, R., Reynolds, T. and Alldred, P. (2003). 'Motherhood, paid work and partnering: values and theories', *Work, Employment and Society*, 17(2): 309–30.

Duncan, S., Edwards, R., Reynolds, T. and Alldred, P. (2004). 'Mothers and child care: policies, values and theories', *Children and Society*, 18(4): 254–65.

Duncombe, J. and Marsden, D. (1999). 'Love and intimacy: the gender division of emotion and "emotion work"', in G. Allan (ed.), *The Sociology of the Family: A Reader*. Oxford: Blackwell, pp. 91–110.

Durham, M. (2001). 'The Conservative Party, New Labour and the politics of the family', *Parliamentary Affairs*, 54(3): 459–74.

Edwards, J. (2004). 'Mainstreaming equality in Wales: the case of the National Assembly building', *Policy and Politics*, 32(1): 33–48.

Edwards, J. and McAllister, L. (2002). 'One step forward, two steps back? Women in the two main political parties in Wales', *Parliamentary Affairs*, 55(1): 154–66.

Edwards, R. (2003). 'Introduction: themed section on social capital, families and welfare policy', *Social Policy and Society*, 2(4): 305–8.

Edwards, R. and Gillies, V. (2004). 'Support in parenting: values and consensus concerning who to turn to', *Journal of Social Policy*, 33(4): 623–43.

Edwards, R. and Gillies, V. (2005). *Resources in Parenting: Access to Capitals Project Report*. Families and Social Capital ESRC Research Group, London: London South Bank University.

England, K. (1996). *Who Will Mind the Baby? Geographies of Child Care and Working Mothers*. London: Routledge.

Equality Act 2006, Elizabeth II, C. 3, Norwich: TSO.

Featherstone, B. (2006). 'Why gender matters in child welfare and protection', *Critical Social Policy*, 26(2): 294–314.

Ferree, M. M. (2003). 'Resonance and radicalism: feminist framing in the abortion debates of the United States and Germany', *American Journal of Sociology*, 109(2): 304–44.

France, A., Freiberg, K. and Homel, R. (2010). 'Beyond risk factors: towards a holistic prevention paradigm for children and young people', *British Journal of Social Work*, 40(4): 1192–1210.

Franklin, J. (2003). 'Review article. social capital: policy and politics', *Social Policy and Society*, 2(4): 349–52.

Fraser, N. (1997). 'From redistribution to recognition? Dilemmas of justice in a "postsocialist" age', in N. Fraser, *Justice Interruptus*. New York: Routledge, pp. 11–40.

Fraser, N. (2001). 'Recognition without ethics?', *Theory, Culture and Society*, 18(2–3): 21–42.

Freud, D. (2007). *Reducing Dependency, Increasing Opportunity: Options for the Future of Welfare to Work* (The Freud Report). An Independent Report to the Department for Work and Pensions, Leeds: Corporate Document Services.

Geiger, S. N. G. (1986). 'Women's life histories: method and content', *Signs: Journal of Women, Culture and Society*, 11(2): 334–51.

Gelb, J. and Palley, M. (1982). *Women and Public Policies*. Princeton, NJ: Princeton University Press.

Gillies, V. (2003). *Family and Intimate Relationships: A Review of the Sociological Research*. Families and Social Capital ESRC Research Group, London: South Bank University.

Gillies, V. (2005). 'Meeting parents' needs? Discourses of "support" and "inclusion" in family policy', *Critical Social Policy*, 25(1): 70–90.

Glass, N. (1999). 'Sure Start: the development of an early intervention programme for young children in the United Kingdom', *Children and Society*, 13(4): 257–64.

Glenn, E. N., Chang, G. and Forcey, L. R. (eds) (1994). *Mothering: Ideology, Experience and Agency*. New York: Routledge.

Glover, J. (2002). 'The "balance model": theorising women's employment behaviour', in A. Carling, S. Duncan and R. Edwards (eds), *Analysing Families: Morality and Rationality in Policy and Practice*. London: Routledge, pp. 251–67.

Government of Wales Act 1998, Elizabeth II, C. 38, Norwich: TSO.

Government of Wales Act 2006, Elizabeth II, C. 32, Norwich: TSO.

Grant, L. (2009). 'Women's disconnection from local labour markets: real lives and policy failure', *Critical Social Policy*, 29(3): 330–50.

Gray, A. (2001). ' "Making work pay": devising the best strategy for lone parents in Britain', *Journal of Social Policy*, 30(2): 189–207.

Gray, A. (2005). 'The changing availability of grandparents as carers and its implications for childcare policy in the UK', *Journal of Social Policy*, 34(4): 557–77.

Grover, C. (2007). 'The Freud Report on the future of welfare to work: some critical reflections', *Critical Social Policy* 27(4): 534–45.

Gustafsson, U. and Driver, S. (2005). 'Parents, power and public participation: Sure Start, an experiment in New Labour governance', *Social Policy and Administration*, 39(5): 528–43.

Hamilton, K., Jenkins, L., Hodgson, F. and Turner, J. (2005). *Promoting Gender Equality in Transport*. EOC Working Paper Series no. 34, Manchester: Equal Opportunities Commission.

Harker, L. and Oppenheim, C. (2010). *Will New Labour Leave a Lasting Legacy?* July, London: Institute for Public Policy Research.

Hatten, W., Vinter, L. and Williams, R. (2002). *Dads on Dads: Needs and Expectations at Home and at Work.* EOC Research Discussion Series, Manchester: Equal Opportunities Commission.

Hays, S. (1996). *The Cultural Contradictions of Motherhood.* New Haven, CT: Yale University Press.

Healy, G. (2004). 'Work–life balance and family friendly policies: in whose interest?', *Work, Employment and Society,* 18(1): 219–23.

Himmelweit, S. and Sigala, M. (2004). 'Choice and the relationship between identities and behaviour for mothers with pre-school children: some implications for policy from a UK study', *Journal of Social Policy,* 33(3): 455–78.

HM Government (2010). *The Coalition: Our Programme for Government.* London: Cabinet Office.

HM Treasury (2004). *Choice for Parents, the Best Start for Children: A Ten Year Strategy for Childcare.* December, London: HM Treasury.

HM Treasury and DTI (Department of Trade and Industry) (2003). *Balancing Work and Family Life: Enhancing Choice and Support for Parents.* London: HM Treasury.

Holland, J., Weeks, J. and Gillies, V. (2003). 'Families, intimacy and social capital', *Social Policy and Society,* 2(4): 339–48.

Holloway, S. (1998). 'Local childcare cultures: moral geographies of mothering and the social organisation of pre-school children', *Gender, Place and Culture,* 5(1): 29–53.

Holter, O. G. (2007). 'Men's work and family reconciliation in Europe', *Men and Masculinities,* 9(4): 425–56.

Home Office (1998). *Supporting Families.* Cm. 3991, London: The Stationery Office.

Hoque, K. and Noon, M. (2004). 'Equal opportunities policy and practice in Britain: evaluating the "empty shell" hypothesis', *Work, Employment and Society,* 18(3): 481–506.

Jack, G. (2005). 'Assessing the impact of community programmes working with children and families in disadvantaged areas', *Child and Family Social Work,* 10(4): 293–304.

James, O. (2005). 'Spare the rod', *The Observer Magazine,* 1 May: 57.

Kay, T. (2002). 'The work–life balance in social practice', *Social Policy and Society,* 2(3): 231–39.

Kidger, J. (2004). 'Including young mothers: limitations to New Labour's strategy for supporting teenage parents', *Critical Social Policy,* 24(3): 291–311.

Kittay, E. F. (2001). 'A feminist public ethic of care meets the new communitarian family policy', *Ethics,* 111(3): 523–47.

Kitterød, R. H. and Pettersen, S. V. (2006) 'Making up for mothers' employed working hours? Housework and childcare among Norwegian fathers', *Work, Employment and Society,* 20(3): 473–92.

Krane, J. and Davies, L. (2000). 'Mothering and child protection practice: rethinking risk assessment', *Child and Family Social Work,* 5(1): 35–45.

Labour Party (1997). *New Labour: Because Britain Deserves Better.* London: The Labour Party.

Laffin, M. and Thomas, A. (2000). 'Designing the National Assembly for Wales', *Parliamentary Affairs,* 53(3): 557–76.

Land, H. (2002a). *Meeting the Child Poverty Challenge: Why Universal Childcare is the Key to Ending Child Poverty*. London: Daycare Trust.

Land, H. (2002b). 'Spheres of care in the UK: separate and unequal', *Critical Social Policy*, 22(1): 13–32.

Land, H. (2004). *Women, Child Poverty and Childcare: Making the Links*. Facing the Future Policy Papers, London: Daycare Trust.

Lawler, S. (2000). *Mothering the Self: Mothers, Daughters, Subjects*. London: Routledge.

Leon, M. (2005). 'Welfare State regimes and the social organization of labour: childcare arrangements and the work/family balance dilemma', *Sociological Review*, 53(S2): 204–18.

Levitas, R. (1998). *The Inclusive Society? Social Exclusion and New Labour*. Basingstoke: Macmillan.

Levitas, R. (2001). 'Against work: a utopian incursion into social policy', *Critical Social Policy*, 21(4): 449–65.

Lewis, C. (2000). *A Man's Place Is in the Home: Fathers and Families in the UK*. York: Joseph Rowntree Foundation.

Lewis, J. (2002). 'Individualisation, assumptions about the existence of an adult worker model and the shift towards contractualism', in A. Carling, S. Duncan and R. Edwards (eds), *Analysing Families: Morality and Rationality in Policy and Practice*. London: Routledge, pp. 51–6.

Lewis, J. (2003). 'Developing early years childcare in England, 1997–2002: the choices for (working) mothers', *Social Policy and Administration*, 37(3): 219–38.

Lewis, J. (2007). 'Gender, ageing and the "new social settlement": the importance of developing a holistic approach to care policies', *Current Sociology*, 55(2): 271–86.

Lewis, J. and Campbell, M. (2007). 'UK work/family balance policies and gender equality, 1997–2005', *Social Politics*, Spring: 4–30.

Lewis, J. and Campbell, M. (2008). 'What's in a name? "Work and family" or "work and life" balance policies in the UK since 1997 and the implications for the pursuit of gender equality', *Social Policy and Administration*, 42(5): 524–41.

Lewis, J. and Giullari, S. (2005). 'The adult worker model family, gender equality and care: the search for new policy principles and the possibilities and problems of a capabilities approach', *Economy and Society*, 34(1): 76–104.

Lewis, J., Cuthbert, R. and Sarre, S. (2011).'What are children's centres? The development of CC services, 2004–2008', *Social Policy and Administration*, 45(1): 35–53.

Lister, R. (1997). *Citizenship: Feminist Perspectives*. London: Macmillan.

Lister, R (1998). 'From equality to social inclusion: New Labour and the welfare state', *Critical Social Policy*, 18(2): 215–25.

Lister, R. (2000) 'Gender and the analysis of social policy', in G. Lewis, S. Gewirtz and J. Clarke (eds), *Rethinking Social Policy*. London: Sage, pp. 23–36.

Lister, R. (2001). 'New Labour: a study in ambiguity from a position of ambivalence', *Critical Social Policy*, 21(4): 425–47.

Lister, R. (2002). 'The dilemmas of pendulum politics: balancing paid work, care and citizenship', *Economy and Society*, 31(4): 520–32.

Lister, R. (2003). 'Investing in the citizen-workers of the future: transformations in citizenship and the state under New Labour', *Social Policy and Administration*, 37(5): 427–43.

Lister, R. (2006). 'Children (but not women) first: New Labour, child welfare and gender', *Critical Social Policy*, 26(2): 315–35.

Lister, R. (2009). 'Women in the recession: gender relations and the economic crisis', presentation to a Compass/Fawcett Society conference, 6 May. http://www.fawcettsociety.org.uk/documents/compassfawcett.pdf, last accessed 12 June 2012.

Lloyd, L. (2006). 'Call us carers: limitations and risks in campaigning for recognition and exclusivity', *Critical Social Policy*, 26(4): 945–60.

Local Government Act 2000, Elizabeth II, C.22, Norwich: TSO.

Lupton, D. and Schmed, V. (2002). '"The right way of doing it all": first-time Australian mothers' decisions about paid employment', *Women's Studies International Forum*, 25(1): 97–107.

Mackay, F. (2004). 'Women's representation in Wales and Scotland', *Contemporary Wales*, 17: 140–61.

Maclean, M. (2002). 'The Green Paper *Supporting Families*, 1998', in A. Carling, S. Duncan and R. Edwards (eds), *Analysing Families: Morality and Rationality in Policy and Practice*. London: Routledge, pp. 64–8.

Mahon, R. (2002). 'Child care: toward what kind of "social Europe"?', *Social Politics*, 9(3): 343–79.

Mahon, R. (2005). 'Rescaling social reproduction: childcare in Toronto/Canada and Stockholm/Sweden', *International Journal of Urban and Regional Research*, 29(2): 341–57.

Mahon, R. (2007). 'Challenging national regimes from below: Toronto child-care politics', *Politics and Gender*, 3(1): 55–78.

Marshall, C. (ed.) (1997). *Feminist Critical Policy Analysis: A Perspective from Primary and Secondary Schooling*. London: Falmer Press.

Marshall, C. (1999). 'Researching the margins: feminist critical policy analysis', *Educational Policy*, 13(1): 59–76.

McAllister, L. (2000). 'The new politics in Wales: rhetoric or reality?', *Parliamentary Affairs*, 53(3): 591–604.

McDowell, L., Ray, K., Perrons, D., Fagan, C. and Ward, K. (2005). 'Women's paid work and moral economies of care', *Social and Cultural Geography*, 6(2): 219–35.

McKie, L., Bowlby, S. and Gregory, S. (2001). 'Gender, caring and employment in Britain', *Journal of Social Policy*, 30(2): 233–58.

McRobbie, A. (2000). 'Feminism and the Third Way', *Feminist Review*, 64 (1): 97–112.

MEWN (Minority Ethnic Women's Network) Swansea (1998). *Who Will Look after the Children? A Childcare Feasibility Study*. Swansea: MEWN.

Millar, J. (2003). 'Squaring the circle? Means testing and individualisation in the UK and Australia', *Social Policy and Society*, 3(1): 67–74.

Miller, S. and Sambell, K. (2003). 'What do parents feel they need? Implications of parents' perspectives for the facilitation of parenting programmes', *Children and Society*, 17(1): 32–44.

Mills, C. W. (1959). *The Sociological Imagination*. New York: Oxford University Press.

Milner, S. (2010). '"Choice" and "flexibility" in reconciling work and family: towards a convergence in policy discourse on work and family in France and the UK?', *Policy and Politics*, 38(1): 3–21.

Mooney, G., Scott, G. and Williams, C. (2006). 'Introduction: rethinking social policy through devolution', *Critical Social Policy*, 26(3): 483–97.

Morgan, D. (2000). 'Gender practices and fathering practices', in B. Hudson (ed.), *Fathers and the State*. Cambridge: Cambridge University Press.

Morrow, V. (1999). 'Conceptualising social capital in relation to the well-being of children and young people: a critical review', *Sociological Review*, 47(4): 744–65.

Mumford, K. and Power, A. (2003). *East Enders: Family and Community in East London*. Bristol: Policy Press.

NAfW (National Assembly for Wales) (2000a). *Betterwales.com: The Strategic Plan*. Cardiff: National Assembly for Wales.

NAfW (National Assembly for Wales) (2000b). *Extending Entitlement: Supporting Young People in Wales*. Report by the Policy Unit, Cardiff: National Assembly for Wales.

NAfW (National Assembly for Wales) (2000c). *Children and Young People: A Framework for Partnership*. Cardiff: National Assembly for Wales.

NAfW (National Assembly for Wales) (2001a). *Plan for Wales 2001*. Cardiff: National Assembly for Wales.

NAfW (National Assembly for Wales) (2001b). *Moving Forward – Listening to Children and Young People: A Proposal for Consultation*. Cardiff: National Assembly for Wales.

NAfW (National Assembly for Wales) (2004). *Report on Mainstreaming Equality in the Work of the National Assembly*. July, Equality of Opportunity Committee, Cardiff: National Assembly for Wales.

Naples, N. A. (2002). 'Materialist feminist discourse analysis and social movement research: mapping the changing context for "community control"' in D. S. Meyer, N. Whittier and B. Robnett (eds) *Social Movements: Identity, Culture, and the State*. Oxford: Oxford University Press, pp. 226–46.

NCSTF (National Childcare Strategy Task Force) (Wales) (2001). *National Childcare Strategy Task Force Report*. Independent report submitted to National Assembly for Wales, Health and Social Services Committee, 21 November, Cardiff: National Assembly for Wales.

NESS (National Evaluation of Sure Start) Research Team (2004). 'The national evaluation of Sure Start local programmes in England', *Child and Adolescent Mental Health*, 9(1): 2–8.

Nixon, J. (2007). 'Deconstructing "problem" researchers and "problem" families: a rejoinder to Garrett', *Critical Social Policy*, 27(4): 546–64.

O'Brien, M. (2005). *Shared Caring: Bringing Fathers into the Frame*. EOC Working Paper Series No. 18, Manchester: Equal Opportunities Commission.

O'Brien, M. and Shemilt, I. (2003). *Working Fathers: Earning and Caring*. EOC Research Discussion Series, Manchester: Equal Opportunities Commission.

Olson, K. (2002). 'Recognizing gender, redistributing labour', *Social Politics*, 9(3): 380–410.

Osgood, J. (2005). 'Who cares? The classed nature of childcare', *Gender and Education*, 17(3): 289–303.

Parekh, A., MacInnes, T. and Kenway, P. (2010). *Monitoring Poverty and Social Exclusion 2010*, York: Joseph Rowntree Foundation.

Parry, J. (2005). 'Care in the community? Gender and the reconfiguration of community work in a post-mining neighbourhood', *Sociological Review*, 53(S2): 149–66.

Penn, H. (2000). 'Policy and practice in childcare and nursery education', *Journal of Social Policy*, 29(1): 37–54.

Penn, H. and Randall, V. (2005). 'Childcare policy and local partnerships under Labour', *Journal of Social Policy*, 34(1): 79–97.

Piachaud, D. and Sutherland, H. (2001). 'Child poverty in Britain and the New Labour government', *Journal of Social Policy*, 30(1): 95–118.

Portes, A. (1998). 'Social capital: its origins and perspectives in modern sociology', *Annual Review of Sociology*, 24: 1–24.

Putnam, R. (2000). *Bowling Alone: The Collapse and Revival of American Community*. New York: Simon and Schuster.

Race Relations (Amendment) Act 2000, Elizabeth II, C. 34, Norwich: TSO.

Rahilly, S. and Johnston, E. (2002). 'Opportunity for childcare: the impact of government initiatives in England upon childcare provision', *Social Policy and Administration*, 36(5): 482–95.

Rake, K. (2001). 'Gender and New Labour's social policies', *Journal of Social Policy*, 30(2): 209–31.

Rake, K. (2009). *Are Women Bearing the Burden of the Recession?* A Fawcett Society report, March, London: Fawcett Society.

Randall, V. (2004). 'The making of local child daycare regimes: past and future', *Policy and Politics*, 32(1): 3–20.

Reay, D. (1998). *Class Work: Mothers' Involvement in Children's Schooling*. London: University College Press.

Reay, D. (2000). 'A useful extension of Bourdieu's conceptual framework? Emotional capital as a way of understanding mothers' involvement in their children's education?', *Sociological Review*, 48(4): 568–85.

Reay, D. (2005). 'Gendering Bourdieu's concepts of capitals? Emotional capital, women and social class', *Sociological Review*, 52(S2): 57–74.

Rees, T. (1999). 'Mainstreaming equality', in S. Watson and L. Doyal (eds), *Engendering Social Policy*. Buckingham: Open University Press, pp. 165–83.

Rees, T. (2002). 'The politics of "mainstreaming" gender equality', in E. Breitenbach, A. Brown, F. Mackay and J. Webb (eds). *The Changing Politics of Gender Equality in Britain*. Basingstoke: Palgrave, pp. 84–97.

Rees, T. and Chaney, P. (2011). 'Multilevel governance, equality and human rights: evaluating the first decade of devolution in Wales', *Social Policy and Society*, 10(2): 219–28.

Renzetti, C. M. and Lee, R. M. (eds) (1993). *Researching Sensitive Topics*. London: Sage.

Repo, K. (2004). 'Combining work and family in two welfare state contexts: a discourse analytical perspective', *Social Policy and Administration*, 38(6): 622–39.

Ribbens, J. (1994). *Mothers and Their Children: A Feminist Sociology of Childrearing*. London: Sage.

Ribbens, J. (1998). 'Hearing my feeling voice? An autobiographical discussion of motherhood', in J. Ribbens and R. Edwards (eds), *Feminist Dilemmas in Qualitative Research: Public Knowledge and Private Lives*. London: Sage, pp. 24–38.

Ribbens McCarthy, J. and Edwards, R. (2002). 'The individual in public and private: the significance of mothers and children', in A. Carling, S. Duncan and R. Edwards (eds), *Analysing Families: Morality and Rationality in Policy and Practice*. London: Routledge, pp. 199–217.

Ribbens McCarthy, J., Doolittle, M. and Sclater, S. D. (2012). *Understanding Family Meanings: A Reflective Text*. Bristol: Policy Press.

Ridge, T. and Millar, J. (2011). 'Following families: working lone-mother families and their children', *Social Policy and Administration*, 45(1): 85–97.

Roberts, B. (2002). *Biographical Research*. Buckingham: Open University Press.

Rosser, C. and Harris, C. (1965). *The Family and Social Change*. London: Routledge and Kegan Paul.

Scott, G. (1998). 'Child-care: the changing boundaries of family, economy and state', *Critical Social Policy*, 18(4): 519–28.

Scott, G., Campbell, J. and Brown, U. (2002). 'Child care, social inclusion and urban regeneration', *Critical Social Policy*, 22(2): 226–46.

Scourfield, J. B. (2001). 'Constructing women in child protection work', *Child and Family Social Work*, 6(1): 77–87.

Secretary of State for Work and Pensions (2010a). *21st Century Welfare*. July, Cm. 7913, London: Department for Work and Pensions.

Secretary of State for Work and Pensions (2010b). *Universal Credit: Welfare that Works*. November, Cm. 7957, London: Department for Work and Pensions.

Secretary of State for Work and Pensions (2011). *Welfare Reform Bill*. Bill 154 of Session 2010–2011, London: The Stationery Office.

Sevenhuijsen, S. (2002). 'A third way? Moralities, ethics and families: an approach through the ethic of care', in A. Carling, S. Duncan and R. Edwards (eds), *Analysing Families: Morality and Rationality in Policy and Practice*, London: Routledge, pp. 129–44.

Shemilt, I., O'Brien, M. and Thoburn, J. (2003). 'School breakfast clubs, children and family support', *Children and Society*, 17(2): 100–12.

Skinner, C. and Finch, N. (2006). 'Lone parents and informal childcare: a tax credit childcare subsidy?', *Social Policy and Administration*, 40(7): 807–23.

Smith, D. E. (1988). *The Everyday World as Problematic: A Feminist Sociology*. Milton Keynes: Open University Press.

Smith, D. E. (1990a). *Texts, Facts and Femininity: Exploring the Relations of Ruling*. London: Routledge.

Smith, D. E. (1990b). *The Conceptual Practices of Power: A Feminist Sociology of Knowledge*. Toronto: Toronto University Press.

Smith, D. E. (1997). 'Comment on Hekman's "Truth and method: feminist stand-point theory revisited"', *Signs*, 22(2): 392–98.

Smith, R., Poole, E., Perry, J., Wollny, I., Reeves, A., Coshall, C. and d'Souza, J. (NCSR) (2010). *Childcare and Early Years Survey Wales 2009*. Main Report, Social Research Document No. 01/2011, Cardiff: WAG Social Research Division.

Sparks, R. (1992). *Television and the Drama of Crime: Moral Tales and the Place of Crime in Public Life*. Buckingham: Open University Press.

Standing, K. (1999). 'Lone mothers' involvement in their children's schooling: towards a new typology of maternal involvement', *Gender and Education*, 11(1): 57–73.

Strategy Unit (2002). *Delivering for Children and Families*. Inter-Departmental Childcare Review (DfES/DWP/HMT/WEU), November, London: Strategy Unit.

Sullivan, M. (2004). 'Wales, devolution and health policy: policy experimentation and differentiation to improve health', *Contemporary Wales*, 17: 44–65.

Tanner, E., Welsh, E. and Lewis, J. (2006). 'The quality-defining process in early years services: a case study', *Children and Society*, 20(1): 4–16.

Tisdall, E. K. M. and Davis, J. (2004). 'Making a difference? Bringing children's and young people's views into policy-making', *Children and Society*, 18(2): 131–42.

Tunstill, J., Allnock, D., Akhurst, S. and Garbers, C. (2005). 'Sure Start local programmes: implications of case study data from the national evaluation of sure start', *Children and Society*, 19(2): 158–71.

Turney, D. (2000). 'The feminizing of neglect', *Child and Family Social Work*, 5(1): 47–56.

UK Women's Budget Group (2010). *The Impact on Women of the Coalition Spending Review 2010*. November, London: Women's Budget Group c/o the Fawcett Society.

Vincent, C. and Ball, S. J. (2001). 'A market in love? Choosing pre-school childcare', *British Educational Research Journal*, 27(5): 633–51.

Vincent, C and Ball, S. J. (2006). *Childcare, Choice and Class Practices: Middle-Class Parents and Their Children*. Abingdon: Routledge.

Vincent, C and Ball, S. J. (2007). ' "Making up" the middle-class child: families, activities and class dispositions', *Sociology*, 41(6): 1061–77.

Vincent, C., Ball, S. J. and Kemp, S. (2004a). 'The social geography of childcare: making up a middle-class child', *British Journal of Sociology of Education*, 25(2): 229–44.

Vincent, C., Ball, S. J. and Pietikainan, S. (2004b). 'Metropolitan mothers: mothers, mothering and paid work', *Women's Studies International Forum*, 27(5/6): 571–87.

Vincent, C., Braun, A. and Ball, S. J. (2008). 'Childcare, choice and social class: caring for young children in the UK', *Critical Social Policy*, 28(1): 5–26.

WAG (Welsh Assembly Government) (2002a). *Communities First Guidance for Local Authorities*. Cardiff: National Assembly for Wales.

WAG (Welsh Assembly Government) (2002b). *Improving Services for Children and Young People: A Framework for Partnership*. Cardiff: National Assembly for Wales.

WAG (Welsh Assembly Government) (2002c). *Children and Young People's Framework Planning Guidance*. Cardiff: National Assembly for Wales.

WAG (Welsh Assembly Government) (2002d). *Early Entitlement: Supporting Children and Families in Wales*. Cardiff: National Assembly for Wales.

WAG (Welsh Assembly Government) (2002e). *Extending Entitlement: Support for 11 to 25 Year Olds in Wales. Direction and Guidance*. Cardiff: National Assembly for Wales.

WAG (Welsh Assembly Government) (2002f). *Cymorth: Children and Youth Support Fund Guidance*. Cardiff: National Assembly for Wales.

WAG (Welsh Assembly Government) (2002g). *Childcare Action Plan*. Cardiff: National Assembly for Wales.

WAG (Welsh Assembly Government) (2003). *Wales: A Better Country. The Strategic Agenda of the Welsh Assembly Government*. Cardiff: National Assembly for Wales

WAG (Welsh Assembly Government) (2004a). *Children and Young People: Rights to Action*. Cardiff: National Assembly for Wales.

WAG (Welsh Assembly Government) (2004b). *Cymorth: Funding for a Better Childhood, Youth and Family Life in Wales. A Review of the Inaugural Year of the Cymorth Fund 2003–04*. Cardiff: National Assembly for Wales.

WAG (Welsh Assembly Government) (2005a). *A Fair Future for Our Children. The*

Strategy of the Welsh Assembly Government for Tackling Child Poverty. Cardiff: National Assembly for Wales.

WAG (Welsh Assembly Government) (2005b). *The Childcare Strategy for Wales: Childcare Is for Children*. DfTE Information Document No. 047-05, Cardiff: National Assembly for Wales.

WAG (Welsh Assembly Government) (2005c). *Flying Start*. Consultation Document, Cardiff: National Assembly for Wales.

WAG (Welsh Assembly Government) (2005d). *Parenting Action Plan: Supporting Mothers, Fathers and Carers with Raising Children in Wales*. DfTE Information Document No. 054-05, Cardiff: National Assembly for Wales.

WAG (Welsh Assembly Government) (2006). *Practice Guide for Children and Young People's Partnerships*. DELLS Information Document No. 019-06, Cardiff, WAG.

WAG (2007). *One Wales: A Progressive Agenda for the Government of Wales*. Cardiff: WAG.

WAG (2010a). *Potential Impact in Wales of the CSR and Budgetary Measure by the UK Coalition Government*. Cardiff: WAG.

WAG (2010b). *Children and Families (Wales) Measure 2010*. Cardiff: WAG.

WAG (2011a). *Child Poverty Strategy for Wales*. February, Information Document No. 095/2011, Cardiff: WAG.

WAG (2011b). *Nurturing Children, Supporting Families: Our Policy Priorities for Childcare*. February, Guidance Document No. 046/2011, Cardiff: WAG.

WAG, CWG (Welsh Assembly Government Childcare Working Group) (2004). *Consultation on the Interim Report of Childcare Working Group*. Cardiff: National Assembly for Wales.

WAG, CWG (Welsh Assembly Government Childcare Working Group) (2005). *A Flying Start: Childcare for children, parents and Communities*. Final Report of the WAG Childcare Working Group, Cardiff: National Assembly for Wales.

Walkerdine, V. and Lucey, H. (1989). *Democracy in the Kitchen: Regulating Mothers and Socialising Daughters*. London: Virago.

Watt, N. (2003). 'Equality: women win half Welsh seats', *The Guardian*, 3 May: 19.

Welfare Reform Act 2012, Elizabeth II, C. 5, Norwich: TSO.

Welsh Affairs Select Committee (1999). *Childcare in Wales*. Third Report of the Committee, Session 1998–99, HC156, London: The Stationery Office.

Welsh Consumer Council/Equal Opportunities Commission (2005). *Gender and Bus Travel in Wales*. Cardiff: Welsh Consumer Council/EOC.

Welsh Office (1998). *The National Childcare Strategy in Wales: A Consultation Document*. Cm. 3974, London: The Stationery Office.

Wheelock, J. and Jones, K. (2002). ' "Grandparents are the next best thing": informal childcare for working parents in urban Britain', *Journal of Social Policy*, 31(3): 441–63.

Williams, Catriona (2003). 'The impact of Labour on policies for children and young people in Wales', *Children and Society*, 17(3): 247–53.

Williams, Charlotte (2001). 'Can mainstreaming deliver? The equal opportunities agenda and the National Assembly for Wales', *Contemporary Wales*, 14: 57–79.

Williams, F. (2001). 'In and beyond New Labour: towards a new political ethics of care', *Critical Social Policy*, 21(4): 467–93.

Williams, F. (2002). 'The presence of feminism in the future of welfare', *Economy and Society*, 31(4): 502–19.

Williams, F. (2004a). 'What matters is who works: why every child matters to New Labour. Commentary on the DfES Green paper *Every Child Matters*', *Critical Social Policy*, 24(3): 406–27.

Williams, F. (2004b). *Rethinking Families*. London: Calouste Gulbenkian Foundation.

Williams, J. (2005). 'Effective government structures for children? The UK's four Children's Commissioners', *Child and Family Law Quarterly*, 17(1): 37–53.

Winckler, V. (ed.) (2009). *Equality Issues in Wales: A Research Review*. Research Report 11, Manchester: Equality and Human Rights Commission.

Windebank, J. (1999). 'Political motherhood and the everyday experience of mothering: a comparison of the child care strategies of French and British working mothers', *Journal of Social Policy*, 28(1): 1–25.

Work and Families Act 2006, Elizabeth II, C. 18, Norwich: TSO.

Young, M. and Willmott, P. (1957). *Family and Kinship in East London*. London: Routledge and Kegan Paul.

Young Foundation (2010). *Investing in Social Growth. Can the Big Society Be More than a Slogan?* London: Young Foundation.

Index